The Boston Globe
COOKBOOK

Other cookbooks by Margaret Deeds Murphy

The Cook It and Freeze It Cookbook
Food Processor Cookery
Meat Makes the Meal
Fondue, Chafing Dish and Casserole Cookery
Freezer Cookery
The Farberware Turbo Oven Cookbook

Known to her friends as Maggie, **Margaret Deeds Murphy** shares here the expertise she culled from a lifetime of professional cooking. She was the former head of General Foods Corporation's recipe test kitchen and developed recipes for a number of well-known national food companies. She was a member of the American Home Economics Association, the Boston chapter of Home Economists in Business, and was a board director of the Cape Cod Seafood Council.

Gail Perrin is the food editor of *The Boston Globe* and the former editor of the Woman's Page. She has worked as the newspaper's assistant metropolitan editor and began her career in 1954 at the *Washington Daily News*.

Helen (Wilber) Richardson was born and raised in Boston. As food editor of the *Providence Journal* for eighteen years, she expanded what started as a column into a full weekly section. She retired from the newspaper after her marriage in 1982 but is still very interested in, and challenged by, cooking, entertaining, and working out new recipes.

The Boston Globe COOKBOOK

A Collection of
Classic New England Recipes

Third Edition

by Margaret Deeds Murphy

Introduction by Gail Perrin,
Food Editor, *The Boston Globe*

Edited by Helen Richardson

Photography by Georgiana Silk

The Globe Pequot Press

Chester, Connecticut

Copyright © 1981, 1990 by The Globe Pequot Press
Photography copyright © 1981 by Georgiana Silk
Copyright © 1948, 1963, 1974 by The Globe Newspaper Company

Library of Congress Cataloging-in-Publication Data

Murphy, Margaret Deeds.
    The Boston globe cookbook / by Margaret Deeds Murphy :
introduction by Gail Perrin : edited by Helen Richardson. — 3rd ed.
        p.   cm.
    Includes index.
    ISBN 0-87106-535-5
    1. Cookery, American—New England style.   I. Richardson, Helen.
II. Title.
TX715.2.N48M87   1990
641.5974—dc20   90-39525
                                                                                          CIP

Illustration on page 190 by Lauren Brown
Selected line cut illustrations on pages 37, 83, 121, 171, and 229 are used with permission from *Old American Kitchens*, by Louise K. Lantz. Everybody's Press, publisher.

Manufactured in the United States of America
Third Edition/First Printing

Contents

Introduction

Capturing the flavor of New England cooking is a little like trying to put the aroma of fresh-baked bread into a jar. It's definitely there but elusive all the time.

Yet somehow veteran cook Margaret Deeds Murphy performed the magical feat, extracting and preserving the New England essence between these covers.

True, there are a number of "general" cookbooks on the market. But none of them is geared to the cook eager to turn out some area classics that reflect a maximum of taste with a minimum of effort.

The Boston Globe Cookbook is an outgrowth of *The Boston Globe Cook Book for Brides*, first published in 1948. The original version relied almost solely on recipes that had been submitted by various readers to "Confidential Chat," a reader exchange dating back to 1884. "Chat" contributors, who use pen names such as "Suburban Secretary," have but one rule when it comes to recipes: all must be "tried and true," personal favorites that work every time.

Margaret Murphy culled the best from the Chat barrel, updated other "tried and true" classics and introduced new ideas streamlined for the busy homemaker who wants to cook well without having to use every pot and pan in the kitchen—or every minute of the day.

She is informative without being pedantic and concentrates on the most important element of any cuisine—good taste. And she shows how good taste need not be expensive taste. While there are touches of the elegant, those touches do not rely on caviar, lobster, or champagne. Also, while there are touches of convenience, she helps hamburger without resorting to a commercial mix.

Perhaps the most important thing, however, is that Margaret Murphy embodied the spirit of the *Globe*, first put forth by founder Gen. Charles H. Taylor, whose words are on the *Globe* cornerstone today. Said Taylor:

"My aim has been to make the *Globe* a cheerful, attractive and useful newspaper that would enter the homes as a kindly, helpful friend of the family. . . . My ideal for the *Globe* has always been that it should help men, women and children to get some of the sunshine of life, to be better and happier because of the *Globe*."

Gail Perrin

Note from the Editor

One's first impression of Margaret Deeds Murphy was of a quiet, capable woman. But then, there was that inescapable twinkle in the eyes, the lovely gentle humor and lightness she brought to her work. It quickly became evident to new acquaintances that here was one you wished to call "friend." And so many of us did.

In her lifetime career of professional cooking, Maggie was head of the General Foods Corporation's test kitchen, and she developed recipes for many other national food companies as well. In her retirement home on Cape Cod, her kitchen never retired, nor did Maggie. At the time of her death in the spring of 1989, Maggie had begun a new revision of this book.

The Boston Globe Cookbook has always been a truly useful aid to those who strive to fulfill the important work of placing good-tasting, nutritious, basic meals on the table. This always-demanding task is even more complicated these days because so many women are no longer simply homemakers but also hold full-time jobs outside the home.

When I was asked to take over this revision, it was with the awareness of many other changes as well. We are all learning new health rules, particularly regarding lower consumption of fats and red meats. Less sugar and fewer eggs are also on that side of the balance sheet. On the plus side, more fish and poultry, more vegetables and fruits, and more cereals and whole-grain breads are recommended. I have attempted to put all these requirements together in this book.

Born and raised in Boston, I had the good fortune of having been taught by my mother, a superb cook and homemaker, how to prepare foods—from everyday meals for eight (or more) and weekly sessions of bread making to seasonal canning and holiday cooking and baking. Then, as food editor at the *Providence Journal* for many years, while raising two sons, I learned firsthand how to juggle career and home.

For me cooking has always been, and remains now, a living art to share and enjoy. If you enjoy the new Chat recipes as well as many of my tried-and-true favorites contained in this revision, I'll know the art is indeed alive. And well.

Helen (Wilber) Richardson

First Things

First Things

Discovering new ways to prepare familiar foods can make cooking an interesting venture rather than a chore. With increased awareness of the effects of eating on health, the responsible cook will turn to modern versions of recipes to help reduce the use of fats, sugar, and salt.

Substitute recommended vegetable oils (soy, safflower, olive, corn) for animal fats and coconut and palm oils. The resulting dishes will taste just as good and will be more healthful. Use fresh fruits often for dessert, and when a baked dessert is to be a treat, search out recipes that call for less sugar and fewer eggs.

To lower consumption of salt, turn to fresh or dried herbs. You will find that they heighten flavors and add a new spark to favorite recipes. A wide variety of fresh herbs are showing up more and more on produce stands in markets all year round. A bunch will last a week to ten days in the refrigerator, or you can chop and freeze your favorites. Freshly ground pepper in many dishes makes reduced salt use less noticeable.

And do taste, taste, taste as you prepare a dish. A judiciously added dash of seasoning or lemon juice or a pinch of an herb can turn a so-so dish into a flavorful treat.

Tips on Food Preparation

The preparation of food begins before cooking ever starts. In fine professional kitchens, there are two principles leading the way—first, "prep" work; second, "CAYG" (clean as you go).

One leads directly to the other; both make meal preparation so much easier.

So, you've decided on a menu. Does the chicken (or fish or meat) need trimming or cleaning? Do that, cut it into portion sizes if desired, then wrap and refrigerate. Wash, trim, and cut up vegetables and put them into proper cooking pans, ready to have small amounts of water added just before cooking. Scrub or peel potatoes—if the latter, cover them with cold water until cooking.

Wash and dry salad greens, and break them into small pieces. Then put them into a plastic bag or salad bowl. Add celery slices, radishes, and shredded carrot, cover, and refrigerate. Quartered tomatoes and dressing should be added just before serving.

Peel and cut fruit for dessert, put it into a serving bowl, cover, and refrigerate. If dessert is a bit more special, get it made and baking; then immediately wash, dry, and put away all utensils.

The second step follows completely naturally: cleaning up scraps and rinsing off knives, cutting boards, and the like, so the kitchen and the food are completely ready for the actual cooking of the meal.

An important health note: If you have trimmed or cut up poultry, it is extremely important not only to thoroughly wash, but also to sterilize, cutting board and knife. After washing with hot water and detergent, pour either boiling water on both, or chlorine bleach, which should then be thoroughly rinsed off. By doing this, you prevent the spread of any bacteria to foods that are not then cooked. When you cook the poultry, bacteria is destroyed, but if you used the same board without sterilizing for cutting bread or salad makings, for instance, that food could be contaminated.

Once you have gotten into the habit of getting the "prep" work done, and CAYG, it will almost seem as if there is a wonderful genie hiding somewhere who has made cooking much easier.

Kitchen Equipment

Kitchen shops today are wonderfully exciting places to browse through. Who could ever imagine the variety and styles of all that great stuff!

Restraint is in order here, however. Cooking utensils and equipment are, to my mind, extremely individualistic and personal articles. A strange thing to say about such mundane items as spatulas, wooden spoons, and such? Not really. For those of us who must prepare meals each day, the tools at hand are of the utmost importance. Anyone who has tried to make do with cheap, dull knives, for instance, knows that buying three sizes of the very best knives one can afford is vital.

And that principle—buying the very best affordable—holds true for all kitchen equipment. Cheap sets of pans are never a bargain. Pans designed to spread heat evenly and hold heat well will conserve energy and make cooking easier and results better.

Nor are complete sets of pans generally needed, either. For most home kitchens, two small saucepans, one medium-sized (2½-quart) saucepan, and a large Dutch-oven type pan are sufficient. All should have tight-fitting covers. Three graduated sizes of skillets—the best nonstick style—should be on hand, though on that subject, never will I part with my large, heavy, old-fashioned iron skillet—the only way to get fine crusty hash, properly browned chicken, and such.

Depending on the kind of cooking you do, you will amend this list to include other sizes or styles of pots and pans, adding perhaps an electric skillet, a slow-cooker, or a wok.

As far as kitchen tools are concerned, again, keep on hand those you use with regularity. That will certainly include a couple of sizes of metal and nonmetal (or heavy plastic) spatulas for turning foods while cooking. You should also have rubber spatulas in two, or even three, sizes. In addition, a couple of sizes of stainless-steel whisks, so important for smooth sauces and gravies, should be on hand.

You'll probably have a half dozen wooden spoons, with one or two evolving as "pets" that see constant use. A wide metal scraper is a must in my kitchen for cleaning a floury counter or picking up all the bits and pieces of chopped vegetables.

Be sure to choose a very good peeler. These come in many styles, but the important point is to select stainless steel for best service. Do invest in a pastry blender if you make biscuits or pie crust. Trying to cut in shortening properly by using two knives is almost impossible. A pastry blender does this job efficiently and quickly.

As far as measuring cups are concerned, two sets are better than one, as inevitably, when in the midst of a recipe, you'll find that you have already used the half-cup measure for something liquid and now need it for a dry ingredient. These are not expensive, so buying a couple of sets is not an extravagance. (This is also true of measuring spoons.) A couple of glass measuring cups are needed—a 1-cup size and a 2-cup or quart size, depending on the use you put these to. The larger sizes are handy for mixing up small amounts of ingredients, as well.

A good colander; strainers in a couple of sizes; muffin tins; baking and roasting pans (one 7×11×2-inch—and one 9×13×2-inch); a rolling pin; a ladle; two casserole dishes (1-quart and 2-quart); mixing bowls in various sizes; and a flour sifter—all are prerequisites in a well-equipped kitchen.

It is worth purchasing expensive electrical equipment—heavy-duty mixers, food processors, and blenders—*if* you regularly do the kind of food preparation that requires such equipment. I have and use all. Bread making becomes far easier on the arm muscles when the mixer does several minutes of kneading, for instance.

Keep in mind the virtues of regular cleaning out of kitchen drawers. Get rid of seldom used, nonfunctioning, obsolete things. Your kitchen space is valuable and should not be cluttered.

Keep what you use; use what you keep.

Liquid and Dry Measure Equivalents

g = grams (dry measure)   *kg = kilograms*   *dL = deciliters*   *L = liters*

The metric amounts represented here are the nearest equivalents.

a pinch = slightly less than ¼ teaspoon

a dash = a few drops

3 teaspoons = 1 tablespoon

2 tablespoons = 1 ounce = ¼ dL (liquid), 30 g (dry)

4 tablespoons = ¼ cup = 2 ounces = ½ dL (liquid), 60 g (dry)

1 jigger = 3 tablespoons = 1½ ounces

8 tablespoons = ½ cup = 4 ounces = 1 dL

2 cups = 1 pint = ½ quart = 1 pound* = ½ L (liquid), 450 g (dry)*

4 cups = 32 ounces = 2 pints = 1 quart = 1 L

4 quarts = 1 gallon = 3¾ L

8 quarts (dry) = 1 peck = 7¼ kg

4 pecks (dry) = 1 bushel

*Dry ingredients measured in cups will vary in weight

Appetizers
— and —
Beverages

*indicates a recipe variation

Blueberry Cheese Cake with Fresh Blueberry Topping (recipes on page 261)

Appetizers

This course is the most flexible in all your meal planning. What is served depends completely on the kind of party you are giving; indeed, the word appetizer may not even be an appropriate one to describe this course.

If you are giving a dinner party for four, six, or eight—or whatever number of guests you are able to serve at table—then this course, offered with alcoholic or nonalcoholic drinks, is indeed an appetizer. As such, it should be very simple: crisp vegetables with a simple dip, assorted nuts, perhaps one hot nibbler. Keep in mind that you are merely whetting the appetite and not trying to ruin it for the meal you have prepared to serve at table.

A buffet party for a larger number of guests is quite another matter. Then you will have small plates at hand for the several foods offered. Two or three kinds of cheese with crackers or thin-sliced dark bread, chicken wings or small drumsticks, seviche or marinated mussels, a pâté, thin slices of quiche, plus a platter of vegetable nibblers with a dip or two will provide fine fare.

To assure your own enjoyment of the party, do have everything ready to place on the table just before your guests arrive. Unless you have serving help, avoid foods that must be baked or broiled just before serving. Hectic dashes between kitchen and guests will definitely not make for relaxed hosts.

The sharing of food with friends continues to be pleasurable to all concerned, no matter how simple the meal may be. Simply being invited to another's home is a welcoming gesture. Early planning and preparations by the hosts assure a cheerful occasion for all.

Cranberry Meat Balls

The combination of flavors and colors makes this a particularly pretty, as well as a very good, hot hors d'oeuvre.

½ cup uncooked oatmeal	1 pound ground beef
1 egg	2 tablespoons butter or margarine
2 tablespoons water	¼ cup (about) flour
1 tablespoon grated onion	1 can (8 ounces) jellied cranberry sauce
1 teaspoon salt	1 can (8 ounces) tomato sauce
1 teaspoon Worcestershire sauce	½ cup dry white wine

Mix oatmeal, egg, water, onion, salt, and Worcestershire sauce and let stand about 5 minutes. Mix lightly with beef and shape into 40 small meat balls.

Heat butter in large skillet. Roll meat balls in flour and brown quickly in butter, removing as browned. When all are browned, return to skillet. Mash cranberry sauce and blend with tomato sauce and wine. Pour over meat balls. Cover and simmer about 30 minutes. Serve in a chafing dish or keep hot over a candle warmer. These meat balls may be prepared in advance and reheated. Makes 40 meat balls.

Spinach Cheese Squares

A close relative of a quiche, but easier to make and very tasty for a party. The squares are better warm and can be reheated in the oven or in a covered skillet over low heat.

4 eggs
¼ cup cooking oil
½ teaspoon salt
½ teaspoon freshly grated nutmeg
1 cup buttermilk biscuit mix

1 package (10 ounces) frozen chopped spinach, thawed, well drained
2 cups firmly packed grated Swiss cheese (about 8 ounces)

Beat together eggs, oil, salt, nutmeg, and biscuit mix. Stir in spinach and cheese. Spoon into a well-greased and floured 9×9×2-inch pan and bake at 400°F for 30 to 35 minutes. Cut while still warm into 1½-inch or slightly smaller squares. Makes 36 squares if cut 1½ inches.

Barbecue Spare Ribs

(pictured between pages 232 and 233)

These tiny ribs make hearty cocktail fare and are particularly popular for informal outdoor gatherings. Serve with plenty of napkins.

5 pounds pork spare riblets*

Salt and freshly ground pepper

Barbecue Sauce

½ cup chopped Spanish onion
2 tablespoons butter or margarine
1 tablespoon Dijon mustard
1 chicken bouillon cube
½ cup water

½ cup dry white wine
2 tablespoons Worcestershire sauce
2 tablespoons lemon juice
1 teaspoon sugar

Cut the ribs into individual fingers. Arrange on rack in pan. Sprinkle with salt and pepper and bake at 425°F for 30 minutes.

Meanwhile combine ingredients for sauce, bring to boil, then simmer, covered, for 10 minutes.

Reduce oven temperature to 375°F and bake and baste ribs frequently with sauce for another 30 minutes. Serve hot or cold. Makes enough for about 15 people.

If riblets are not available, use regular spare ribs; have butcher cut rack in two crosswise and then cut between ribs.

Hot Cheese

Sometimes simple recipes are too good to believe. This one, from a neighbor, is one of those. The cheese mixture could be prepared several days in advance and refrigerated until party time, then heated.

1 package (10 ounces) sharp white cheese
1 cup mayonnaise (not salad dressing)

1 tablespoon minced onion
Crackers and crisp vegetables

Grate cheese and mix with mayonnaise and onion; put into a small ovenproof dish that can be used for serving. Bake at 350°F for about 20 minutes or until mixture bubbles. Serve hot with crackers and crisp vegetables. Makes about 2 cups.

Stuffed Baked Mushrooms

Mushrooms should never be washed. Simply brush them gently with paper towels or use a soft mushroom brush to clean as necessary.

24 medium (about 2-inch) mushrooms
¼ cup cooking oil
1 cup fresh bread crumbs
1 garlic clove, pressed
¼ cup chopped fresh parsley
½ teaspoon dried oregano or
    1 teaspoon minced fresh oregano

½ teaspoon salt
Freshly ground pepper to taste
¼ cup melted butter
1 tablespoon lemon juice

Remove stems from mushrooms and reserve the caps. Chop the stems fine; sauté them in oil until lightly browned, about 10 minutes. Mix lightly with bread crumbs, herbs, seasonings, melted butter, and lemon juice. Spoon mixture into mushroom caps and place in buttered flat pan. Bake at 350°F for 20 minutes. Serve hot. Makes 24.

Mushroom "Liver" Canapes

The "liver" in the name probably alludes to the many well-loved pâtés that, unlike this one, are actually made from liver.

¼ pound fresh mushrooms,
    finely minced
2 tablespoons butter
1 package (3 ounces) cream cheese,
    softened

⅓ cup mayonnaise
½ teaspoon salt
⅛ teaspoon garlic powder
⅛ teaspoon pepper
Assorted crackers

Sauté mushrooms in butter until brown. Mix with cream cheese, mayonnaise, and seasonings. Chill well. Serve with assorted crackers. Makes about 1 cup.

from Suburban Secretary, *Confidential Chat*

Cheese Crock

This cheese crock is nice to have on hand to serve when unexpected guests arrive. It is also very popular at parties. Serve with a variety of crisp crackers.

¾ pound sharp cheddar cheese
¼ pound Danish blue cheese,
    crumbled
2 tablespoons butter or margarine,
    softened

1 teaspoon dry mustard
1 teaspoon Worcestershire sauce
Dash Tabasco sauce
Onion salt or garlic salt to taste
¾ cup (about) beer

Grate cheddar cheese and mix with blue cheese, butter, and seasonings. Gradually beat in beer until mixture is smooth and spreadable.

Store in refrigerator in covered crocks or jars. Keeps several weeks. Makes 2½ to 3 cups.

Clam Dip

This is the traditional clam dip, which first came on the scene in the 1940s. It is still popular and disappears fast.

1 package (8 ounces) cream cheese
1 can (6½ ounces) minced clams
1 teaspoon lemon juice
1 teaspoon Worcestershire sauce

Dash Tabasco sauce
Salt and pepper to taste
Crackers or chips

Let cream cheese stand at room temperature to soften. Drain clams, saving liquid. Combine cream cheese with clams, lemon juice, and seasonings, stirring to blend. If necessary to get a dipping consistency, add a teaspoon or so of clam juice. Serve with potato or corn chips and crackers. Makes about 2 cups.

Apple Cottage Cheese Dip

A simple mixture, particularly popular with people who want neither fish nor meat. Nice with sesame crackers.

1 cup finely chopped apples
    some with peel
1 tablespoon lemon juice
1 cup creamed cottage cheese

½ teaspoon celery salt
½ teaspoon onion salt
½ teaspoon curry powder
Assorted crackers

Mix apples and lemon juice. (Leaving some red skin on part of the apples gives a little color.) Add all remaining ingredients and mix lightly. Serve with assorted crackers. Makes 1½ cups.

Savory Vegetable Dip

A good dip that keeps under refrigeration. If you have any left over, add a bit more yogurt and use as a dressing for a green salad.

1 package (10 ounces) frozen chopped
    spinach, thawed
½ cup sour cream
½ cup plain yogurt
1 cup mayonnaise

1 package (2 ounces) country vegetable
    soup mix
3 green onions, finely chopped
1 can (8 ounces) sliced water chestnuts,
    drained and chopped

Squeeze all liquid out of spinach. Combine spinach with all remaining ingredients. Chill at least 3 hours or overnight. Serve as a dip with crisp vegetables and/or crackers. Makes 3 cups.

Pickled Green Beans

Serve pickled green beans, drained, as a finger food.

1½ pounds green beans
1½ cups cider vinegar
¼ cup firmly packed brown sugar

¼ teaspoon salt
1 garlic clove, cut in half
1 tablespoon pickling spice

Choose fresh young beans and snip off stem end. Steam or cook in a small amount of water for about 8 to 10 minutes or until tender-crisp. Cool and pack into a large jar.

Combine all remaining ingredients in a saucepan and bring to a boil. Pour hot over beans in jar. Cover and let stand in refrigerator for several days before using. Makes about 1 quart.

Marinated Mushrooms

For the quickest cocktail finger food, simply slice fresh white mushrooms, put them into a colorful bowl, then sprinkle liberally with fresh lemon juice and ground pepper. This light and tasty nibbler has almost no calories, which will be appreciated by those watching the scales. The following version may be prepared ahead of serving time and refrigerated until needed.

2 cups small whole mushrooms
    (about ¾ pound)
1 cup water
½ cup cooking oil
2 tablespoons lemon juice
1 stalk celery
1 clove garlic

¼ teaspoon dried rosemary
¼ teaspoon dried thyme
½ bay leaf
½ teaspoon chili powder
½ teaspoon salt
6 peppercorns

Cut a slice off stem end of mushrooms and rinse under running water. Combine with all remaining ingredients. Simmer 15 minutes. Marinate, covered, in the refrigerator. Will keep several weeks. To serve, drain and serve with toothpicks. Makes 2 cups.

Maine Stuffed Eggs

If 24 halves of eggs is more than you want, halve the recipe. In that case the leftover sardines can be doused liberally with lemon juice and served on oblong pieces of buttered toast.

12 eggs, hard cooked	½ teaspoon salt
1 can (3¾ ounces) sardines, drained	Freshly ground pepper to taste
4 teaspoons lemon juice	6 tablespoons mayonnaise
2 teaspoons horseradish	8 to 10 stuffed olives, sliced

Remove shells from hard-cooked eggs and cut in half lengthwise. Carefully remove yolks and put into a bowl with drained sardines. Mash together with a fork or spoon until well blended. Add lemon juice, horseradish, salt, pepper, and mayonnaise and mix well. Pile lightly into egg whites. The sardines add enough bulk so that the filling in each half egg will be generous. Decorate each egg with a slice of stuffed olive. Keep chilled in refrigerator until ready to use. Makes 24 halves.

Quick Pâté

A lot of the flavor of this pate will depend on the flavor of the liverwurst. Buy a good, spicy one to be enhanced with the seasonings in the recipe.

1 tablespoon butter or margarine	2 tablespoons sherry
½ teaspoon chopped garlic	1 pound liverwurst
2 tablespoons chopped onion	Softened butter
1 tablespoon cognac	Crackers or melba toast

Heat butter in a small saucepan and cook garlic and onion over low heat until transparent. Stir in cognac and sherry. Remove from heat. Peel rind from liverwurst, cut into pieces, and blend well with garlic and onion. Spread softened butter on inside of a 2-cup mold and pack pâté into mold. Chill for several hours. To serve, unmold on plate and serve with crackers or melba toast. Makes 2 cups.

Anchovy Garlic Dip

A long-popular accompaniment for any and all fresh vegetables.

2 cans (2 ounces each) anchovy fillets
½ cup margarine, softened

2 cloves garlic, halved
Minced fresh parsley

Drain all but about a tablespoon of the oil from the fillets. Put fillets into blender with margarine and garlic; blend until smooth. Put into small bowl, garnish with parsley, and serve with carrot, celery, and zucchini sticks, whole scallions, red and green pepper strips, and whole small mushrooms. Makes about ¾ cup.

Blue Cheese Mold

Prepare this tasty combination a day ahead of serving. Cover with plastic wrap before placing in the refrigerator.

1 tablespoon unflavored gelatin
¼ cup cold water
¼ cup milk
¼ cup blue cheese
1 package (8 ounces) low-calorie cream cheese, softened

¼ teaspoon grated onion
½ cup plain yogurt
2 teaspoons Worcestershire sauce
Sliced stuffed olives
Celery or crackers

Sprinkle gelatin over water in small saucepan. Add milk and stir over low heat until gelatin is dissolved. In a bowl, combine thoroughly the gelatin mixture with cheeses, grated onion, yogurt, and Worcestershire. Pour into a 2-cup mold; chill until firm. To serve, unmold onto serving plate and garnish with the sliced olives. Surround with celery cut into 2-inch pieces and crackers. Makes about 1½ cups.

Marinated Mussels

Few can resist these delectable morsels.

5 pounds mussels, well scrubbed
½ cup dry white wine
1 bay leaf
1 cup vegetable oil

⅓ cup wine vinegar
1 tablespoon Dijon-style mustard
Pepper to taste
Finely chopped fresh parsley

Put cleaned mussels in large pan; add wine and bay leaf. Cover pan and bring to boil. Lower heat and simmer until all shells are open, about 5 to 10 minutes. Allow to cool briefly, then remove cooked mussels from shells, discarding any that do not open. Place mussels in bowl. In a small bowl, combine oil, vinegar, mustard, and pepper. Whisk thoroughly to blend. Pour over mussels. Cover with plastic wrap and chill until serving time. Top with chopped parsley; serve with picks. Makes 8 to 10 servings. (Broth left from cooking mussels can be saved to add lovely flavor to a fish or clam chowder. Refrigerate or freeze.)

Seviche

A low-calorie and delicious addition to the appetizer table. The citrus juices "cook" the fish as it marinates. If lemons and limes are expensive, halve the number and add 1 cup white vinegar to marinade.

4 pounds skinless cod fillets
Juice of 10 limes
Juice of 6 lemons
1 teaspoon chili powder
1 red onion, thinly sliced

3 cloves garlic, chopped
½ teaspoon salt
¼ teaspoon pepper
½ cup chopped fresh parsley

Cut fish into bite-size squares. Put into bowl. Mix remaining ingredients, except parsley. Pour over fish. If fish is not completely covered, add more lemon or lime juice. Cover and marinate in refrigerator several hours or overnight, until fish is white and opaque. Just before serving, drain well. Place in glass serving bowl, top with parsley, and serve with picks. Makes 10 to 12 servings.

Marinated Broccoli

Bright fresh vegetables add great eye appeal to a selection of hors d'oeuvres and are appreciated by calorie watchers.

1 bunch fresh broccoli	1 large garlic clove, chopped
1/4 cup white vinegar	1 teaspoon sugar
3/4 cup vegetable oil	1/3 teaspoon dried dillweed

Trim broccoli into flowerets with about an inch of stalk on each. Large pieces should be split to make them bite-size. Combine remaining ingredients in a bowl and whisk well. Put broccoli in sealable plastic bag; pour marinade into bag, mix gently, then seal bag and refrigerate several hours. Drain broccoli before serving. The following dip may be added on the side and is also fine with other *crudités*. Makes about 1 quart of broccoli flowerets.

1 cup mayonnaise	1 tablespoon ketchup
2 teaspoons curry powder (or to taste)	1/2 teaspoon white-wine Worcestershire

Mix all ingredients thoroughly in small bowl. Makes about 1 cup.

Zucchini Appetizers

A different way to use up a bountiful supply of zucchini from the summer garden.

3 cups thin-sliced zucchini (unpeeled)	1/2 cup grated Parmesan cheese
1 cup biscuit mix	1/2 teaspoon dried oregano
1/2 cup finely chopped onion	1/2 cup vegetable oil
1 clove garlic, finely minced	4 eggs, beaten
2 tablespoons chopped fresh parsley	

Heat oven to 350°F. Grease 13×9-inch baking pan. In large bowl, mix all ingredients thoroughly. Spread evenly in prepared pan; bake 25 to 30 minutes. Cool 15 minutes before cutting into small squares. Makes about 4 dozen pieces.

Deviled Shrimp

For a special party, a special nibbler—low-calorie and tasty.

1 cup vegetable oil	1 teaspoon paprika
½ cup dry white wine	½ teaspoon coarsely ground pepper
½ cup wine vinegar	1 clove garlic, finely minced
2 tablespoons Dijon-style mustard	2 pounds medium or large shrimp,
2 tablespoons prepared horseradish	cooked, shelled, and deveined

Put all ingredients, except shrimp, into blender; process until well mixed. (May be done in a bowl, whisking thoroughly until completely blended.) Pour marinade over shrimp in a bowl; refrigerate several hours. To serve, drain shrimp and arrange on serving plate with picks nearby. Makes 12 to 14 appetizer servings.

Pecan-Honey-Mustard Chicken Wings

This recipe is used often in the small catering business of a Chat *contributor.*

1 stick butter	1½ cups pecans, finely chopped
½ cup honey	2 cups fresh fine bread crumbs
4 tablespoons Dijon-style mustard	4 pounds chicken wings

In a small saucepan, melt butter. Whisk in honey and mustard; simmer, stirring occasionally, for about 5 minutes. Set aside to cool slightly.

Combine pecans and bread crumbs. (A food processor makes quick work of this step.) Set aside. Remove and discard (or save for soup pot) tips from wings. Cut wings into two pieces and place in a large shallow dish. Pour butter mixture over wings and stir to coat completely. Roll wings in crumb mixture and place in single layer in a large foil-lined baking dish. Bake at 350°F for 50 minutes.

If necessary to reheat, bake at 400°F for 15 minutes. Or, wings may be frozen after baking, then reheated, still frozen, at 350°F for 30 minutes. Makes 4 dozen.

from Beautiful Babies, *Confidential Chat*

Vegetables for Parties

The French call them *crudités*, we call them crisp fresh vegetables, but by any name they have become part of the appetizer scene whether eaten as is or served with a spread or dip. The choice of vegetables is endless. I'll list them alphabetically, with suggestions for preparation.

ANISE can be cut in sticks and eaten as is or used to dunk.

ARTICHOKES appear at parties mostly as artichoke hearts, though the leaves of cooked artichokes can be dunked. Never used raw.

ASPARAGUS: Raw asparagus is delightful when dipped in a cold mixture. Choose thin asparagus for serving raw and cut tip end about 3 inches long.

BEANS: Crisp, young green beans are excellent raw. Cut off both ends. Pieces should be about 2 inches long.

BROCCOLI: Trim heads from stalk and cut heads in 2 or 3 pieces lengthwise, depending on size. Pretty and good raw.

BRUSSELS SPROUTS: Cut fresh Brussels sprouts in 2 or 3 pieces (depending on size) and use as a dipper.

CARROTS can be peeled and julienned or made into carrot curls. For julienne strips, cut tiny sticks about 3 inches long and very thin. For curls, use larger carrots and cut length of carrot with potato peeler to make thin strips; curl, fasten with toothpick, and store in ice water for several hours. Remove toothpick to serve.

CAULIFLOWER: Use raw flowerets as is or cut in pieces, depending on size.

CELERY: Use from second layer of stalks into center to make julienne strips. Hearts can be quartered lengthwise with leaves left on.

CUCUMBERS: If waxed, peel; otherwise use with peel on. Cut into slices crosswise, or in lengthwise strips about 2 to 3 inches long.

ENDIVE, Belgian: Endive leaves are excellent as a dipper, larger ones can be cut in half lengthwise.

GREEN ONIONS add variety to vegetables. Cut green tops off so only a inch or so remains and choose small onions.

JERUSALEM ARTICHOKES are a tuber—no relation to either Jerusalem or artichokes, but the root of a variety of the sunflower plant. Peeled and thin sliced, they make a good addition to the dunkers.

JICAMA is a root tuber that, when peeled and thin-sliced, makes a very good crisp, water chestnut-like vegetable to use for dipping. Choose smaller size, as the larger may be woody.

MUSHROOMS: There are so many other uses for mushrooms as appetizers that I seldom use them for dunking. But there is no reason why one cannot. Use small mushrooms whole, cut larger ones in quarters.

PEAS: Snow peas or young, tender, undeveloped pea pods can add interest to the crisp vegetables.

PEPPERS: Green or red peppers can be seeded and cut into strips. They are flavorful and add color.

RADISHES are always welcome. If you buy (or grow) radishes with leaves, strip off all but the tiniest leaves. Radish "roses" may be made by slicing into the red peel with a small, sharp knife, top to bottom, leaving bottom of cut attached to radish. Soak in ice water.

RUTABAGAS, peeled and sliced thin, add a nice flair.

SUMMER SQUASH (zucchini or yellow) need not be peeled. Scrub well and cut in medium-thin slices.

TOMATOES: Cherry tomatoes are a popular item.

All of these vegetables, except mushrooms, can be prepared ready to serve the day before the party. Store in plastic bags with ice cubes and securely fastened with tie or rubber band. Refrigerate each separately, then when ready to serve, arrange vegetables to look like bouquets in bowls with cracked ice.

Beverages

Beverages are an essential part of our daily diet, as we should drink at least eight glasses of liquid a day in the form of water, milk, fruit juice, and similar beverages.

This short section on beverages will not attempt to give directions for making tea or coffee as there are many fine methods for both, each of which has its advocate.

Instead, here are a few party recipes together with some family ideas to induce both children and adults to drink more milk. Cutting down on calories? Remember to buy nonfat milk either in dry form to be reconstituted or in liquid form. Ice milk and sherbets can be substituted for the richer ice creams. You will also be getting less of the saturated fats.

Fruit Milk Shakes

These good beverages can be varied to suit tastes and seasons. They are perfect for the blender but can be whipped up with a fork and a whisk.

To 1 cup nonfat or regular milk, add one of the ingredient combinations.

1 banana, peeled and cut up	2 tablespoons honey

or

1 ripe pear, peeled and core removed 2 tablespoons sugar	¼ teaspoon cinnamon

or

½ cup crushed strawberries	3 tablespoons sugar

or

½ cup applesauce	¼ teaspoon nutmeg

Blend in blender until smooth, or mash fruit with fork and beat in milk and seasonings until blended. These amounts make 1 serving. They can be varied by adding a small scoop of ice cream.

Spiced Mocha Frosted

A pleasant drink for a refreshment, served with cookies or sandwiches.

2 squares unsweetened chocolate, grated
2 tablespoons instant coffee
½ teaspoon cinnamon

1 quart nonfat milk
½ cup (about) sugar
1 pint vanilla ice milk or ice cream

Mix chocolate, coffee, and cinnamon and add about 1 cup of the milk. Cook and stir until chocolate is melted and mixture blended. Slowly add remaining milk and sugar to taste, stirring. Divide between 6 tall glasses and add a scoop of ice milk to each. Makes 6 servings.

Chocolate Milk Shake

A chocolate milk shake is popular with all ages. If you prepare your own cocoa syrup, it is less expensive than commercial chocolate syrup.

2 tablespoons Cocoa Syrup (recipe below)

1 cup cold nonfat or regular milk

Cocoa Syrup

1 cup cocoa
1½ cups sugar
⅛ teaspoon salt

1¼ cups hot water
1 teaspoon vanilla extract

Blend well and serve. Makes 1 serving.

Cocoa Syrup: Combine cocoa, sugar, salt, and hot water. Cook and stir over moderate heat for 5 minutes. Cool and add vanilla extract. Store, covered, in the refrigerator. Makes 2¼ cups.

Variations

Chocolate Frosted: Add one scoop chocolate ice cream.

Chocolate Banana Milk Shake: Add one-half sliced banana and blend in blender.

Chocolate Banana Frosted: Add one-half sliced banana and one scoop chocolate ice cream and blend in blender.

Orange Nog

Orange nog can substitute for breakfast when one is in a rush. In any event it's a nourishing beverage and flavorful.

1 egg	1 cup milk
¼ cup frozen orange juice concentrate	2 teaspoons honey
	Crushed ice

Combine egg, juice concentrate, milk, and honey in blender and blend on high for about 10 seconds. Serve over crushed ice. Makes 1 serving.

Variation

Add one-half banana, sliced.

Banana Frappe

A pleasant afternoon treat for youngsters, but also substantial enough to substitute for a quick breakfast.

1 ripe banana	1 tablespoon wheat germ
1 cup plain yogurt	½ cup orange juice
1 tablespoon honey	

Peel banana and cut into chunks. Put with all remaining ingredients into blender; process until smooth. Makes 1 serving.

Spiced Tea

The tea can be prepared in advance and poured over the crushed ice when ready to serve. An especially pleasant beverage for a hot summer day.

2½ cups water	½ cup orange juice
1 stick cinnamon (about 2 inches)	¼ cup lemon juice
6 whole cloves	¼ cup cranberry juice
6 individual tea bags	Crushed ice
½ cup sugar	

Heat water with cinnamon and cloves until boiling. Remove tags from the tea bags and add to boiling water. Remove from heat, cover, and steep 5 minutes. Strain and add sugar and fruit juices. Chill. Serve over crushed ice. Makes 4 servings.

Pink Punch

A refreshing combination of juices that would go well with both sandwiches and cookies.

1½ quarts cranberry juice
    cocktail
¼ cup lime juice
1 quart apple juice

2 cans (6 ounces each) frozen
    limeade concentrate
4½ cups water
Fresh mint

Combine juices and water and chill well. Serve over ice and garnish with fresh mint. Makes 4 quarts or about 26 5-ounce servings.

Easy Fruit Punch

A pretty punch and a good combination of fruit flavors. An ice ring can be made of any fruit juice with a flavor compatible with the punch in which it is to be used, or of plain water.

2 cups sugar
2 cups water
¾ cup lemon juice

1 can (46 ounces) pineapple juice
1 quart bottle sparkling water, chilled
Orange ice ring (recipe below)

Orange Ice Ring

Orange juice

Fruit in season

Combine sugar and water and boil for 5 minutes. Cool and mix with lemon and pineapple juices. Chill well. When ready to serve, pour into a 6- to 8-quart punch bowl; add sparkling water and ice ring. Makes about 20 5-ounce servings.

Orange Ice Ring: To make an ice ring, start a day in advance. Use a 6-inch or 8-inch ring mold (depending on the size of the punch bowl). A 6-inch ring mold takes 3 cups of juice; an 8-inch mold, 5 cups. Pour juice into mold and allow to freeze partially. This takes several hours (cover the juice with a piece of aluminum foil so it will not frost the freezer). When partially frozen, take off the foil and with a sharp knife or skewer, poke fruit in season into the partially frozen juice. Use fresh strawberries, or quarters of thin orange slices with the peel left on, or pineapple chunks. The mold should be frozen overnight.

Wine Punch

An easy punch to prepare and special to serve for a special occasion. If you don't want to prepare the whole recipe at once, buy two splits of champagne and make half at a time.

⅔ cup sugar
2 cups orange juice
4 bottles (25.4 ounces each)
   Sauterne, chilled
1 bottle (25.4 ounces) burgundy,
   chilled

Ice block to fit bowl
1 bottle (25.4 ounces) dry champagne,
   chilled
Thin orange slices
Fresh mint sprigs

Combine sugar and orange juice and stir until sugar is dissolved. Chill. In an 8-quart punch bowl mix Sauternes and burgundy wines with orange juice. Add ice block. When ready to serve, pour in champagne. Garnish with thin orange slices and fresh mint sprigs. Makes about 35 5-ounce servings.

Party Punch

Small cookies would go nicely with this party punch. As Precious Gifts says, the recipe can be doubled with no problems.

1 quart chilled orange juice
1 quart chilled cranberry juice

1 quart chilled ginger ale
1 pint vanilla ice cream

Combine orange and cranberry juices in a 4-quart punch bowl. Add ginger ale and ice cream divided into 8 pieces. Stir. Makes about 20 5-ounce servings.

from Precious Gifts, *Confidential Chat*

Apple Cranberry Punch

Festive to look at with its rosy cranberry blush and just the right tart flavor for a good punch.

1 quart cranberry juice cocktail
3 cups apple juice
½ cup fresh lemon juice
   (2 to 3 lemons depending on size)

1 can (8½ ounces) pineapple tidbits
1 tray ice cubes
1 quart ginger ale

Combine juices and pineapple tidbits (including juice) and chill well. When ready to serve, pour into punch bowl and add ice cubes and ginger ale. Makes about 20 5-ounce servings.

Hot Cocoa

Hot cocoa and cookies will always be a favorite snack. If there is any left over, chill it and serve as "chocolate milk."

5 tablespoons cocoa
4 tablespoons sugar
½ cup water

1 quart nonfat milk
½ teaspoon vanilla extract
Tiny marshmallows (optional)

Mix cocoa and sugar with water and bring to a boil; cook, stirring, 3 minutes. Add milk and heat just to the boiling point (but do not boil). Beat with a rotary beater or whisk until frothy. Add vanilla. If desired, top each serving with a few marshmallows. Makes 5 5-ounce servings.

Hot Spiced Wine

A very easily made hot wine that hits the spot on a cold winter day.

2 bottles (25.4 ounces each)
   dry red wine
¾ cup sugar
1 stick cinnamon (about 2 inches)

4 whole cloves
3 or 4 lemon slices
10 thin orange slices

Combine wine and sugar and heat slowly, stirring to dissolve sugar. Add cinnamon; stick cloves into lemon slices and add them to wine also. Heat below boiling point for 10 minutes. Strain and serve hot in cups with an orange slice in each serving. Makes 10 5-ounce servings.

Hot Cranberry Juice Combo

Serve up with plenty of doughnuts for a refreshment for a cold evening.

1 quart cranberry juice cocktail
1 can (18 ounces) pineapple juice

1 teaspoon whole cloves
1 stick cinnamon (about 3 inches)

Combine all ingredients and bring slowly to a boil. Cover and simmer 15 minutes. Strain to remove spices. Serve hot. Makes about 10 5-ounce servings.

Breads

Breads

Yeast and Baking Powder

Bread making is such a joy. It can never be a bore because even the most routine recipes can be varied to produce new and interesting results. The care and baking of bread, whether it is a yeast or a baking powder product, is a labor of love.

In order to make that labor of love as easy and perfect as possible, here is a short course in baking.

Ingredients

Flour

Wheat flour is the ingredient used in the largest quantity in bread recipes. Its purpose is to provide gluten, which gives bread its texture and, of course, bulk. White flour has the highest content of gluten-forming properties. For this reason it is usually used as at least part of the flour in recipes where other flours are incorporated. Without white flour, the bread has a heavy texture.

All-purpose white can be purchased as a bleached or unbleached flour. Either is satisfactory for baking, though unbleached is preferred by some because it has gone through less milling.

Bread flour is also available. It has a higher gluten content, which is good for baking bread. While all-purpose flour can be used for other products (such as pastry, baking-powder breads, or cakes) where gluten is not a factor, bread flour should be saved for yeast breads.

Whole wheat flour is wheat flour that has bran left in the flour. Do not sift whole wheat flour.

Other specialty flours such as soy, rye, buckwheat, corn, millet, and oat are available, some only in specialty stores. As a rule they are used in small quantities to enhance the flavor. Cake flour can be purchased also. It is very low in gluten and designed to give lightness of texture to cake products.

Yeast

Yeast is used in recipes to make the products rise. It is temperamental in that it requires moderate temperature, 105°–115°F, to become active and create a good result. Liquids too cold or too hot are enemies of yeast. In some specialized recipes temperatures of 120°–130°F are suggested. With these recipes the higher temperature is satisfactory as it is still in the high warm range.

Yeast can be purchased in individual airtight packages as active dry yeast. This same dry yeast also comes in bulk, in jars. One scant tablespoon is equivalent to one package. After bulk yeast is opened, store tightly in the refrigerator. Yeast packages are dated and should be used before that date or fairly close to its expiration. Also available are moist yeast cakes; a 0.6-ounce cake is interchangeable with one package or one tablespoon of active dry yeast. It is not wise to purchase bulk yeast unless one does a great deal of baking, as it deteriorates faster than the hermetically sealed packages.

Other Leavening Agents

Baking powder, baking soda, and cream of tartar are the leavening agents for quick breads, so named because they do not require the long rising period of those made with yeast. Modern recipes and those in this book can be made with any brand of baking powder. It is usually mixed with flour and/or other dry ingredients. Cream of tartar is occasionally found in recipes.

In preparing quick breads, do not overbeat. Plan to bake immediately after mixing, as once the baking powder, soda, or cream of tartar is mixed with liquid, it begins to act.

Sweetening

In yeast products, something sweet such as sugar, honey, or molasses is needed to cause the yeast to form gas and the bread to rise. Sweetening is also used to give flavor and improve texture, the latter particularly in quick breads.

Liquids

Liquids used in baking vary from water to wine and run the gamut in between. Liquid is necessary to dissolve the yeast or baking powder, bind the ingredients, and give flavor and consistency to the product. Liquids used in yeast breads should be warmed. Those in quick breads are used cold.

Other Ingredients

Shortening and eggs improve texture and add flavor. The shortening can vary from solid white shortening to butter, margarine, or cooking oil. Use shortening specified in recipe. Sometimes spices, nuts, or fruits are used for flavor and texture.

Techniques

Making yeast products teaches one patience, if nothing else. They should not be hurried, although they can be slowed down to a degree. Once you get your hand into bread making, mixing, kneading, and watching for the proper rising all become second nature.

Mixing

Use a bowl that is large enough so that the ingredients can be easily handled. An electric mixer or vigorous hand beating at the first stage can begin the formation of the gluten. After enough flour has been worked into the liquid so that the dough may be handled, it is then kneaded.

Kneading

Use a clean flat surface sprinkled with a little flour. Flour your hands and take the dough from the mixing bowl. Shape it into a ball and begin to knead.

Fold the dough toward you and, with the heels of your palms, push the dough ball away from you; then turn it one-quarter of the way around; repeat the folding, pushing, and turning motions. Knead the dough until it is smooth and elastic, about 10 minutes. Add more flour to board and hands as needed, but try not to add more than necessary. Toward the end of the kneading time, beginners will be surprised at the very small amount of flour needed.

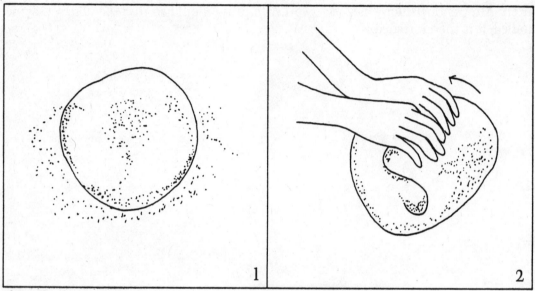

1
Shape dough into a ball.

2
Fold dough toward you.

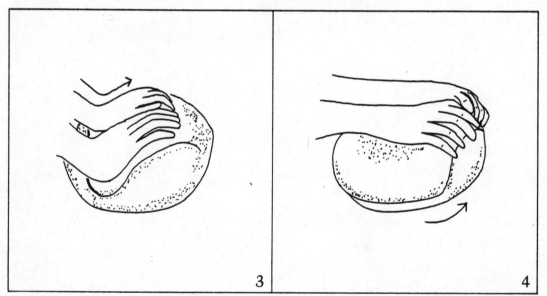

3
Push away with the heels of your palms.

4
Turn it one-quarter of the way around.

Rising

A place that is free from drafts and with a temperature of about 85°F makes the best nest in which to raise the bread. This can be achieved in several ways. In the unlit oven place a large bowl of boiling water and set the bread in another bowl beside it or over it. If your oven has a pilot light or an electric bulb, that alone may be sufficient heat. Cover the bread with plastic wrap and a clean towel during this period. Check after one hour. The dough, when sufficiently risen, should double in size. If you press the tips of two fingers lightly into the dough and the dent stays, the dough is doubled. Since many factors can govern the temperature surrounding the dough, check rising whenever you make bread; do not count on time only.

If recipe calls for two risings (this helps make a finer-textured bread), punch dough down in center and turn over in bowl. Re-cover and let rise again until doubled in bulk, about 30 minutes.

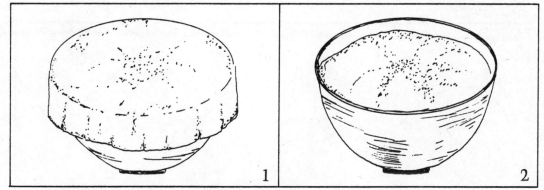

Cover bowl with plastic wrap and a clean towel.

Check after one hour.

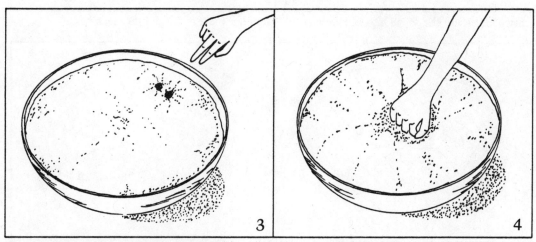

Test to see if dough has risen sufficiently by pressing the tips of two fingers into the dough. If the dents stay, the dough has doubled.

Punch dough down with your fist.

Shaping

For making bread into loaves, cut the dough into the number of pieces the recipe says (two pieces for two loaves, three for three, etc.). Directions vary for shaping. Here are two methods; I suggest you try both, and follow the one that gives you the most satisfactory loaf.

One suggestion: Roll each piece into a rectangle, using a rolling pin, gently but firmly, to remove gas bubbles. Then begin with upper short side and roll toward you. Seal with thumbs. Seal ends also and fold ends under. Carefully transfer to a greased bread pan, putting sealed side on bottom.

Another suggestion: Cut bread mass into required-size pieces. Knead each piece two or three minutes and with hands shape into loaf. Put into greased bread pan.

Bread then must be allowed to rise again in the pan. Place in the 85°F space, cover, and let rise until double in bulk, one to two hours. Use the two-finger test, pushing gently into one end of the loaf. If dent stays, bread is ready to bake.

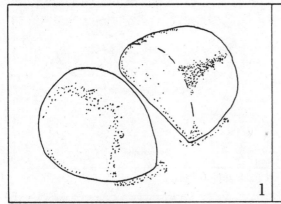

1

For two loaves, cut the dough into two pieces.

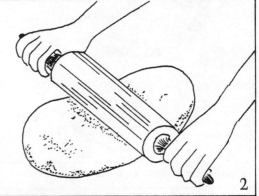

2

Roll one piece of dough into a rectangle.

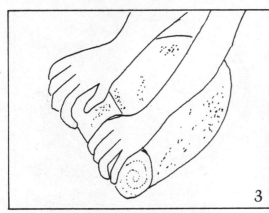

3

Begin with short side and roll toward you.

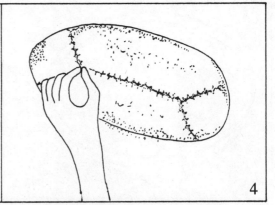

4

Fold ends under and seal ends and edge by pinching seams together.

Baking

Follow temperature given and put bread in a preheated oven. Place bread so heat can go around the pans. At end of time suggested, remove a loaf from pan and tap on bottom or side. If bread sounds hollow and is nicely browned, it is done.

Remove loaves from pans and cool on a rack. I like to rub tops of the hot bread with butter or margarine and save the wrappers from the quarters for this purpose. This makes a soft crust. If you like a crisp crust, do not butter the top.

When making quick breads and muffins, fill well-greased loaf or muffin tins two-thirds full to allow for rising. Paper liners may be used for muffins, if preferred. Follow recipe directions for oven temperature and cooking time.

When baked in loaf pans, quick breads usually have a split in the top when done. To test for doneness, this split should look dry, and when a cake tester is inserted in the center, it should come out clean. The loaf also will be pulled away slightly from the sides of the pan.

Muffins should be tested for doneness in the same way. Tops should be nicely browned and dry, and when a cake tester is inserted in the center of one or two of the muffins, it should come out dry. If not, return pan to oven for another 3 or 4 minutes of baking, until they test done.

Storing Bread

Cooled bread can be frozen. Wrap in freezer wrap, seal, label, and date. You can freeze for two to three months.

Bread left unfrozen for immediate use should be kept in a cool place (not in refrigerator) in a plastic bag kept closed with a closure.

Final Note

If you are going to bake a lot of loaf bread, get a good bread knife for cutting. That is a necessity for nice, neat slices.

Old-fashioned bread makers

White Bread

This white bread is delicious when served warm. It freezes very well and is always a treat.

¼ cup sugar	1⅔ cups boiling water
1½ tablespoons salt	12 cups (about) unbleached
6 tablespoons butter or margarine	all-purpose flour
1 can (13 ounces) evaporated milk	2 packages active dry yeast

Combine sugar, salt, butter, evaporated milk, and boiling water in a very large bowl. Add 4 cups flour and yeast and beat 2 minutes with an electric mixer or by hand. Gradually add remaining flour until mixture is thick enough to knead.

Turn out on a lightly floured surface and knead for 10 minutes or until dough is smooth and elastic. Put into a greased bowl and turn to grease dough. Cover and let rise until double in bulk.

Punch down, turn dough in bowl and let rise again until double in bulk. Punch down.

Cut dough into 4 pieces and let rest 10 minutes, covered.

Shape into loaves and put into 4 greased 9×5×3-inch loaf pans. Let rise, covered, until double in bulk. Bake at 400°F for 30 to 35 minutes. Makes 4 loaves.

Oaten Wheat Bread

A slightly heavier-textured bread, but very flavorful.

1 cup uncooked quick oatmeal	2 tablespoons butter or margarine
1 cup whole wheat flour	2 cups boiling water
⅔ cup nonfat dry milk powder	1 envelope active dry yeast
or granules	½ cup warm water
½ cup firmly packed brown sugar	6 to 7 cups all-purpose flour

Mix oatmeal, whole wheat flour, dry milk, brown sugar, and butter in a large bowl. Add boiling water and stir to blend. Cool to room temperature. Soften yeast in warm water and stir into oatmeal mixture. Stir in all-purpose flour until mixture is stiff enough to knead. Turn out onto a lightly floured surface and knead for 10 minutes until smooth and elastic. Put into a greased bowl and turn to grease dough. Cover and let rise until double in bulk. Punch down.

Cut dough into 2 pieces. Shape into loaves and put into greased 9×5×3-inch loaf pans. Let rise, covered, until double in bulk. Bake at 375°F for 35 minutes. Makes 2 loaves.

Honey Wheat Bread

A few years back I bought some aluminum 1-pound meat loaf pans. They measure 7³/₄×3⁵/₈×2¹/₄ inches. Very often instead of 3 loaves of bread in 9×5×3-inch pans, I make 4 in the smaller size. Bake at the same temperature for 10 minutes less time.

1 quart milk	8 cups whole wheat flour
¹/₂ cup butter or margarine	2 packages active dry yeast
6 tablespoons honey	4 cups (about) all-purpose flour
2 tablespoons salt	

Heat together milk, butter, honey,and salt just until bubbles begin to form around edge of milk. Butter does not need to be completely melted. Remove from heat and beat in 4 cups whole wheat flour and yeast. Beat until well blended.

Stir in remaining whole wheat flour and add enough white flour to make dough stiff enough to knead.

Turn out on a lightly floured surface and knead 10 minutes or until dough is smooth and elastic. Put into a greased bowl and turn to grease dough. Cover and let rise until double in bulk.

Punch down, turn dough in bowl, and let rise again until double in bulk. Punch down.

Cut dough into 3 pieces and let rest 10 minutes, covered. Shape into loaves and put into greased 9×5×3-inch pans. Let rise, covered, until double in bulk. Bake at 375°F for 35 to 40 minutes. Makes 3 loaves.

French Bread

Commercial French bread is baked in an oven into which steam is introduced. This accounts for the crisp crust. It is difficult to achieve the commercial effect in a home oven, but this home-baked French bread is mighty good anyway.

2 packages active dry yeast
2 tablespoons sugar
2 teaspoons salt
7 to 8 cups unbleached all-purpose flour
2 cups very warm tap water

2 tablespoons butter or margarine, softened
3 tablespoons cornmeal
2 to 3 tablespoons water for brushing

Combine yeast, sugar, salt, and 2 cups flour in a large bowl. Mix well and stir in the 2 cups warm water and the butter. Beat 2 minutes. Then gradually stir in remaining flour until dough is stiff enough to knead. Knead on a lightly floured surface until dough is smooth and elastic. Place in a greased bowl and turn to grease dough. Cover and let rise until double in bulk.

Cut dough into 2 pieces and knead each piece 2 to 3 minutes. Shape each into a 15-inch roll and place on a baking sheet that has been sprinkled liberally with cornmeal. Cut 4 to 5 gashes across the top of each loaf with scissors and brush with water. Cover and let rise until double in bulk. Brush again with water and bake at 400°F for 20 minutes or until browned. Cool on rack. Makes 2 loaves.

Note: Some authorities suggest placing a pan of boiling water in the bottom of the oven while the French bread is baking. The steam supposedly makes a crustier loaf of bread. It has never seemed to make much difference in my oven, so the judgment is yours.

Variation

Whole Wheat French Bread: Substitute 4 cups whole wheat flour for 4 cups of the all-purpose flour. Directions for mixing remain the same.

Anadama Bread (recipe on page 43)
and Blueberry Muffins (recipe on page 57)

Down East Health Bread

A well-flavored bread with a lot of good ingredients. Good fresh and makes excellent toast.

½ cup enriched cornmeal
½ cup nonfat dry milk powder
   or granules
2 cups boiling water
⅓ cup molasses

1 tablespoon salt
¼ cup margarine
2 packages active dry yeast
1½ cups whole wheat flour
4 cups (about) all-purpose flour

Combine cornmeal and dry milk. Stir gradually into boiling water. Add molasses, salt, and margarine. When cool to touch, stir in yeast and whole wheat flour and beat for 2 minutes.

Stir in white flour until mixture is stiff enough to knead. Knead on a lightly floured surface until smooth and elastic, about 10 minutes, adding flour as needed.

Place dough in a greased bowl; turn to grease dough. Cover and let rise until double in bulk (about 2 hours). Punch dough down. Divide in half and knead each piece 3 minutes. Shape into loaves and place in greased 9×5×3-inch pans. Cover and let rise again until double in bulk. Bake at 375°F about 45 minutes. Makes 2 loaves.

Herbed Batter Bread

A loaf of herbed bread would accompany a salad meal well; or plan to bake it at the same time as a casserole dish for supper.

½ cup warm water (105°–115°F)
1 package active dry yeast
½ cup warm dairy sour cream
3 tablespoons butter or
   margarine, softened

3 tablespoons sugar
1 teaspoon salt
1 teaspoon Italian herb seasoning
1 egg
2 to 2½ cups all-purpose flour

Measure water into large bowl. Add yeast and stir until softened. Add sour cream, margarine, sugar, salt, herbs, and egg. Beat in 2 cups flour until well blended, about 1 minute. Stir in enough additional flour to make a soft dough (one that will hold its shape when a spoon is pulled out of it). Cover and let rise until double in bulk, about 40 minutes. Stir down. Spoon dough into a greased 1-quart casserole. Cover and let rise until double in bulk, 40 to 50 minutes. Bake at 375°F for 35 minutes or until brown. Remove from casserole and cool on rack. Makes 1 loaf.

Rye Bread with Orange and Caraway

In some circles this is called "Swedish Rye Bread." Whether that claim to national origin stands up or not, it is still a very good recipe.

1 tablespoon sugar	2 tablespoons shortening
½ cup lukewarm water	3 cups rye flour
1 package active dry yeast	1 tablespoon grated orange rind
1½ cups milk	2 teaspoons caraway seed
1 tablespoon salt	3 cups (about) all-purpose flour
¼ cup molasses	

Combine sugar, water, and yeast in a small bowl and let stand 5 minutes.

Heat milk with salt, molasses, and shortening until lukewarm. Add yeast and 1½ cups of the rye flour and beat for 2 minutes. Stir in remaining rye flour, orange rind, and caraway seed. Gradually stir in white flour until dough is stiff enough to knead. Knead on a lightly floured surface until smooth and elastic. Put dough in a greased bowl and turn to grease dough. Cover and let rise until double in bulk, about 2 hours. Punch down and divide into 2 pieces. Cover and let rest 10 minutes. Shape into loaves and put into greased 8×4×2¼-inch loaf pans. Cover and let rise until double in bulk, about 1½ hours. Bake at 375°F for 25 to 30 minutes or until nicely browned. Remove from pan and cool on rack. Cool before cutting. Makes 2 loaves.

Anadama Bread

(pictured between pages 40 and 41)

Supposedly a New England fisherman became angry with his wife because all she gave him to eat, day after day, was cornmeal and molasses. One night he tossed flour and yeast into the cornmeal and molasses, put it all into the oven, and baked it. He sat down to eat a loaf of bread for a change, mumbling "Anna, damn her!"— shortened to Anadama.

½ cup yellow cornmeal	1 package active dry yeast
3 tablespoons cooking oil	¼ cup warm water
¼ cup molasses	1 egg
2 teaspoons salt	2¾ cups all-purpose flour
¾ cup boiling water	Extra cornmeal

Stir together in a large mixing bowl the cornmeal, oil, molasses, and salt. Add the boiling water and mix well. Cool to lukewarm.

Dissolve yeast in the warm water. Add yeast, egg, and half the flour to the lukewarm cornmeal mixture. Beat 2 minutes on medium speed of mixer or by hand. Scrape sides and bottom of bowl frequently.

Add rest of flour and mix with a spoon until flour is thoroughly blended into batter. Spread batter evenly into greased loaf pan (8½×4½×2¾-inch or 9×5×3-inch). Batter will be sticky. Smooth out top of loaf by flouring hand and patting into shape.

Let rise in warm place until batter reaches top of 8½-inch pan or 1 inch from top of 9-inch pan. Sprinkle top with a little cornmeal. Bake at 375°F for 50 to 55 minutes. Crust will be dark brown. Immediately remove from pan and cool on rack. Makes 1 loaf.

from The Royal Family, *Confidential Chat*

Parker House Rolls
or Rich Yeast Dough—with variations

Parker House rolls are named after Boston's Parker House hotel, established 1855. They are more of a shape than a recipe since any rich yeast dough recipe can be formed into Parker House rolls. These rolls freeze well.

5 cups (about) all-purpose flour	¼ cup butter or margarine
½ cup sugar	2 eggs
1½ teaspoons salt	½ cup melted butter or margarine
2 packages active dry yeast	for brushing
1 cup milk	

In a large bowl, mix 2 cups flour with sugar, salt, and yeast. Heat together milk and butter until bubbles appear around the edge of the milk. Pour at once into flour mixture and beat 2 minutes. Add eggs and beat until well blended. Gradually add remaining flour until mixture is stiff enough to knead. Knead on a lightly floured surface until smooth and elastic. Place in a greased bowl; turn to grease dough. Cover and let rise until double in bulk, about 2 hours.

Turn dough out onto a lightly floured board and with a floured rolling pin, roll dough ¼ to ½ inch thick. Cut with a floured 3-inch round cutter. Brush lightly with melted butter and make a crease across the center of the cut dough with the dull edge of a knife. Fold one half over the other half. Place fairly close together on a greased pan or cookie sheet. Brush with melted butter. Cover lightly and let rise again until double in bulk, about 1 hour.

Bake at 375°F for 15 to 20 minutes or until lightly browned. Brush hot rolls with butter. Makes about 3½ dozen rolls.

Other shapes into which rich yeast dough may be formed:

Hamburger Rolls: Roll raised dough ½ inch thick. Cut with a 4-inch biscuit cutter. Brush with butter and place on a greased cookie sheet. Cover and let rise until double in bulk. Bake at 375°F for 15 to 20 minutes or until lightly browned.

Crescent Rolls: Roll raised dough in 9-inch circle about ¼ inch thick. Brush with melted butter. Cut into 8 wedges. Roll from large side. Shape into crescents and place on a greased cookie sheet. Cover and let rise until double in bulk. Bake at 375°F for 15 to 20 minutes or until nicely browned.

Cloverleaf Rolls: Shape raised dough into tiny balls. Dip in melted butter and place 3 in each section of a greased muffin tin. Let rise until double in bulk and bake at 375°F for 15 to 20 minutes or until nicely browned.

Hot Cross Buns: Make ¹/₂ recipe rich yeast dough, adding 1 teaspoon cinnamon to dry ingredients. Knead ¹/₂ cup currants or raisins into risen dough. Form into 1¹/₂-inch balls and place in a greased 8×8×2-inch pan. Brush with egg yolk diluted with 2 teaspoons water. Cover. Let rise until double in bulk, about 1 hour. Bake at 375°F for 30 minutes or until lightly browned. Remove from pan and cool on rack. When cooled, form cross on top with frosting made by mixing ³/₄ cup confectioners' sugar with a few drops of hot water.

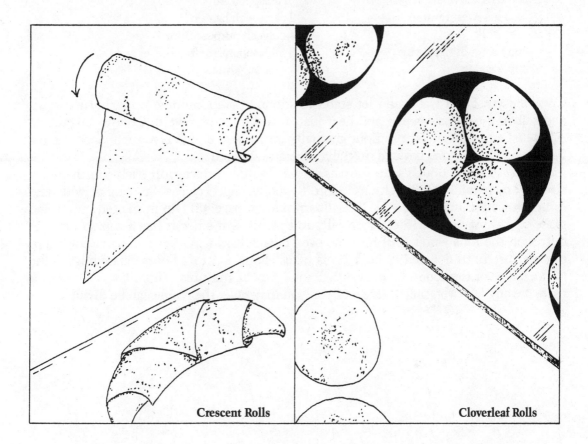

Crescent Rolls

Cloverleaf Rolls

Refrigerator Rolls

This recipe for rolls came to me many years ago from a dear family friend. They are marvelously easy to make and to eat. They show up at all my holiday meals. Some of our most circumspect friends will eat four or five at one sitting.

2 packages active dry yeast
¼ cup lukewarm water
¾ cup milk
½ cup butter or margarine
¼ cup sugar

½ teaspoon salt
2 eggs, well beaten
4 cups all-purpose flour
5 tablespoons melted butter or
    margarine

Combine yeast and water and let stand to soften yeast. Combine milk, butter, sugar, and salt in a 6-cup saucepan and heat just until butter is melted. Cool to lukewarm. Add yeast and eggs and stir in flour gradually until a soft dough is formed. Spoon into a 2-quart bowl and store, covered, in the refrigerator 24 hours.

To bake: Divide dough into fourths. On a floured surface, roll each fourth into a circle ¼ inch thick. Cut each circle into 8 wedge-shaped pieces. Starting at wide end roll each wedge into a crescent. (See illustration on page 45.) Dip in melted butter and place on baking pan. A 15×10-inch jelly roll pan is best since it has a rim so that the butter on the rolls won't spill into the oven during baking. Cover and let rise at room temperature until doubled in bulk. This takes about 1½ to 2 hours depending on the temperature of the room. Bake at 425°F for 10 to 12 minutes. This makes 32 rolls. If there are any left over, they freeze well; or, you may note, the recipe can be divided.

Potato Refrigerator Rolls

A rich roll with an extra flavor from the potatoes. You can use instant potatoes to make the mashed potatoes if you wish.

1 cup mashed potatoes
¾ cup butter or margarine,
    softened
½ cup sugar
2 teaspoons salt
2 eggs

2 packages active dry yeast
½ cup lukewarm water
1 cup milk, scalded and cooled
7 cups (about) all-purpose flour
Melted butter for brushing

Mix potatoes with butter, sugar, salt, and eggs in a large bowl. Soften yeast in water and mix with cooled milk and potato mixture. Beat for 2 minutes. Gradually stir in flour until stiff enough to knead. Knead on a lightly floured surface until smooth and elastic. Put into a greased bowl and turn to grease bread. Cover and let rise until double in bulk. Punch down. Place in a greased 2-quart casserole. Butter top of bread and cover with casserole lid. Place in refrigerator until ready to bake, at least 24 hours. About 1 hour before baking, remove desired amount of dough and shape into rolls. Place on greased baking sheet; spread rolls with melted butter. Cover and let rise until double in bulk, about 1 hour. Bake at 400°F for 15 to 20 minutes. The whole recipe makes 5 dozen medium-sized rolls. Dough will keep under refrigeration up to 1 week.

Pecan Rolls

Luscious homemade pecan rolls are welcomed by family and friends and also make a lovely gift at Christmas. An easy way to cut up pecan rolls is to take a short length of string, put under roll where you want to cut, bring up ends, and cross.

Dough

2 packages active dry yeast	1 cup milk
½ cup sugar	½ cup butter or margarine
2 teaspoons salt	2 eggs
5 cups all-purpose flour	

Dough: Combine yeast, sugar, salt, and 2 cups flour in a bowl. Heat milk and butter in saucepan just until bubbles begin to form around edge of milk. Butter does not need to be completely melted. Remove from heat and add to yeast mixture. Beat 2 minutes with an electric mixer or by hand. Add eggs and beat until blended. Slowly stir in remaining flour until a dough is formed that will not stick to the hands. Turn out on a lightly floured surface and knead until smooth and elastic, about 10 minutes. Put into a greased bowl and turn to grease dough. Cover and let rise until double in bulk, about 2 hours.

When dough has risen to double, cut into 3 pieces. Roll each into a rectangle, about ¼ inch thick, 8 inches wide, and 12 inches long.

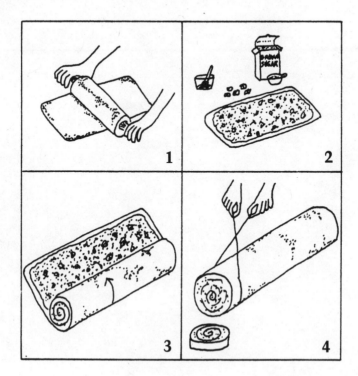

Pecan Filling

1 cup (about) butter or
    margarine, melted
2⅓ cups firmly packed brown
    sugar

1½ cups chopped pecans
¾ cup whole pecans

For filling, spread each rectangle with about 2 tablespoons melted butter, and sprinkle with about ⅓ cup brown sugar and ½ cup chopped pecans. Roll tightly from long side and seal edge. Cut each into 12 slices.

Divide remaining butter (melt more if there is not enough to cover bottom of pans) among three 8-inch round cake pans. Sprinkle with remaining sugar and place ¼ cup whole pecans in each pan. Place 12 slices, cut side down, in each pan. Cover and let rise until double in bulk, about 1 hour. Bake at 375°F for about 25 minutes or until nicely browned.

Place rack over large baking pan and turn out rolls from pans at once on rack over pan. If any syrup or nuts stay on pan, they can be retrieved and put back on rolls. Serve hot or cool, or wrap in freezer wrap and freeze. Makes 3 dozen pecan rolls.

Cranberry Bread

A basic cranberry bread that makes marvelous sandwiches when combined with softened cream cheese.

3 cups all-purpose flour
1 cup sugar
4 teaspoons baking powder
1 teaspoon salt
1 egg

1½ cups milk
2 tablespoons oil
1 cup fresh cranberries, coarsely
    chopped
½ cup chopped nuts

Mix flour, sugar, baking powder, and salt together in a bowl. Beat egg with milk and oil. Stir into dry ingredients just to blend. Fold in cranberries and nuts. Spoon into a greased 9×5×3-inch baking pan. Bake at 350°F for 60 to 70 minutes or until a cake tester inserted in center comes out clean. Cool bread in pan 10 to 15 minutes. Remove carefully from pan and cool on rack. To store, wrap in plastic wrap or aluminum foil. During hot weather, store bread in refrigerator.

Wrap in freezer wrap, seal, label, and date to freeze up to 3 months. Makes 1 loaf.

Cranberry Orange Bread

Cranberries have a unique place in New England history. They were first cultivated in Dennis on Cape Cod and from that small beginning have grown to one of our prime fruit crops. If you have a food processor, chop the cranberries and nuts in it.

2 cups all-purpose flour	1/4 cup shortening
1 cup sugar	1 teaspoon grated orange rind
1 1/2 teaspoons baking powder	3/4 cup orange juice
1/2 teaspoon baking soda	1 egg
1/2 teaspoon salt	1 cup fresh cranberries, coarsely chopped

Mix flour, sugar, baking powder, soda, and salt in a bowl. Cut in shortening with 2 knives or a pastry blender. Beat together orange rind, juice, and egg. Mix into dry ingredients just to blend. Stir in cranberries. Spoon into a greased 9×5×3-inch loaf pan. Bake at 350°F for 60 to 70 minutes or until a cake tester inserted in center comes out clean. Cool bread in pan 10 to 15 minutes. Remove carefully from pan and cool on rack. To store, wrap in plastic wrap or aluminum foil. During hot weather, store bread in refrigerator.

Wrap in freezer wrap, seal, label, and date to freeze up to 3 months. Makes 1 loaf.

Variation

Cranberry Nut Bread: Add 1/2 cup chopped nuts with cranberries.

Banana Nut Bread

Here's a quick and easy way to make this popular loaf. This freezes beautifully, so mix and bake when bananas are good and ripe. Wrap well in foil and freeze until needed.

2 cups all-purpose flour	2 eggs
1 teaspoon baking soda	3 large ripe bananas, cut in chunks
1/2 teaspoon baking powder	3/4 cup sugar
1/2 teaspoon salt	3 tablespoons milk
2/3 cup walnuts	1/2 teaspoon vanilla
1/2 cup vegetable oil	

Grease and flour a 9×5×3-inch loaf pan. Heat oven to 350°F. Into large mixing bowl, sift together flour, baking soda, baking powder, and salt. Set aside. Place all remaining ingredients in blender; process 3 to 4 minutes, until you have a thick, smooth liquid. Pour into dry ingredients and stir until thoroughly mixed, but do not beat. Pour into prepared pan; bake for 1 hour. Remove from pan to cool completely on rack before slicing. Makes 1 loaf. (*Note:* If you like a crunchy texture, stir in an additional 1/3 cup of coarsely chopped walnuts to the batter or sprinkle on top before baking.)

Banana Carrot Bread

All quick-bread loaves are better if allowed to cool and stored overnight before cutting. This is true of banana carrot bread, too.

1 cup mashed banana (about 2
    large bananas)
1 cup sugar
³/₄ cup oil
2 eggs
2 cups all-purpose flour

1 teaspoon baking soda
¹/₂ teaspoon salt
¹/₂ teaspoon cinnamon
¹/₄ teaspoon nutmeg
1 cup finely grated raw carrot
    (about 3 medium carrots)

Combine banana with sugar, oil, and eggs in a large bowl. Beat for 2 minutes at medium speed. Mix together dry ingredients and fold into banana mixture. Add carrots. Spoon into a well-greased and floured 9×5×3-inch loaf pan. Bake at 350°F for 1 hour or until cake tester inserted in center comes out clean. Cool in pan on rack 10 minutes. Remove loaf from pan and cool on rack. To store, wrap in aluminum foil or plastic wrap.

Wrap in freezer wrap, seal, label, and date to freeze up to 3 months. Makes 1 loaf.

Apple Bread

The flavor of this bread combines very well with cheese for a healthy sandwich.

1 cup all-purpose flour
2 teaspoons baking powder
¹/₂ teaspoon baking soda
1 teaspoon salt
1³/₄ cups whole wheat flour
¹/₂ cup raw unprocessed bran
5 tablespoons brown sugar

2 eggs
¹/₄ cup oil
1 teaspoon vanilla extract
1 cup peeled, cored, quartered
    apple (1 large apple)
1 cup plain yogurt
¹/₂ cup walnut meats

Mix all-purpose flour with baking powder, soda, salt, whole wheat flour, and bran.

Beat together sugar, eggs, oil, and vanilla. Chop apples very fine and mix into sugar mixture. Add yogurt alternately with dry ingredients, stirring just to blend after each addition. Fold in nuts. Spoon into a greased 9×5×3-inch loaf pan. Bake at 350°F for 1 hour or until a cake tester inserted in center of loaf comes out clean. Cool in pan on rack 10 minutes. Carefully remove loaf from pan and cool on rack. To store, wrap in aluminum foil or plastic wrap. Store unused portion of bread in refrigerator.

Wrap in freezer wrap, seal, label, and date to freeze up to 3 months. Makes 1 loaf.

Blueberry Fruit Nut Bread

A moist loaf that makes a nice tea bread. One loaf to eat, one to freeze for future use.

1 cup whole wheat flour
2 cups all-purpose flour
1 cup sugar
1 tablespoon baking powder
½ teaspoon baking soda
½ teaspoon salt
½ teaspoon nutmeg

2 eggs
1 cup commercial applesauce
¼ cup oil
2 cups fresh or dry-pack frozen
  blueberries*
½ cup chopped nuts

In a bowl mix together flours, sugar, baking powder, soda, salt, and nutmeg. Beat eggs and mix with applesauce and oil. Stir into dry ingredients just enough to blend. Fold in blueberries and nuts. Spoon into 2 greased and floured 8×4×2¼-inch loaf pans. Bake at 350°F for 50 minutes or until a cake tester inserted in center of loaves comes out clean. Cool in pans on rack for 10 minutes. Remove from pans and cool on rack. When cooled, wrap in aluminum foil or plastic wrap to store. Store unused portion in refrigerator. Wrap in freezer wrap, seal, label, and date to freeze up to 3 months. Makes 2 loaves.

If dry-pack frozen blueberries are used, rinse and drain.

Pumpkin Orange Bread

⅔ cup shortening
2 cups granulated sugar
⅔ cup firmly packed brown sugar
4 eggs
1 can (16 ounces) pumpkin
⅔ cup water
3⅓ cups all-purpose flour
½ teaspoon baking powder

½ teaspoon baking soda
1 teaspoon salt
1 teaspoon cinnamon
½ teaspoon cloves
½ teaspoon nutmeg
1 orange
⅔ cup chopped nuts
⅔ cup chopped raisins or dates

Cream shortening and sugars until light and fluffy. Beat in eggs. Stir in pumpkin and water. Mix flour with baking powder, soda, salt, and spices and fold into pumpkin mixture.

Remove seeds from orange, cut into pieces, and grind, rind and all, in a blender, grinder, or food processor. Stir into batter. Fold in nuts and raisins. Spoon batter into 2 well-greased 9×5×3-inch loaf pans. Bake at 350°F for 1 hour or until cake tester inserted in center comes out clean. Cool in pan on rack for 10 minutes. Remove loaves carefully from pans and cool on rack. To store, wrap in aluminum foil or plastic wrap.

Wrap in freezer wrap, seal, label, and date to freeze up to 3 months. Makes 2 loaves.

Wheat Date Nut Bread

Wheat date nut bread is baked in a round pan for a change. It is full of healthful ingredients.

¼ cup butter or margarine, softened
½ cup firmly packed brown sugar
2 eggs
1 cup small-curd cottage cheese
⅔ cup chopped dates
2 cups whole wheat flour

4 teaspoons baking powder
¼ teaspoon baking soda
¼ teaspoon salt
½ teaspoon cinnamon
½ cup milk

In a large mixing bowl, beat together butter and sugar. Add eggs, cottage cheese, and dates and beat to blend.

Mix flour with dry ingredients and add alternately with milk to creamed mixture, beating just to blend. Spoon batter into a greased 8-inch round cake pan. Bake at 350°F for 60 minutes or until a cake tester inserted in center comes out clean. Cool in pan on rack for 5 minutes. Then cut in wedges or slices.

The bread can be baked in disposable aluminum pans for gift giving.

from The Fiddler's Wife, *Confidential Chat*

English Scones

Wonderful for breakfast; equally good with lunch or a light supper.

2 cups all-purpose flour
3 teaspoons baking powder
½ teaspoon salt
4 teaspoons sugar

¼ cup margarine or shortening
2 eggs
⅓ cup milk
½ cup raisins or currants

Sift flour, baking powder, salt, and sugar into mixing bowl. Cut in margarine or shortening with pastry blender until mixture has the consistency of coarse cornmeal. Break eggs into a small bowl, reserving a tablespoon or so of the whites to brush tops of scones. Beat eggs until light; stir in milk. Add to dry ingredients and stir until thoroughly mixed and dough leaves side of bowl. Stir in raisins. On lightly floured board, pat out dough to about 3/4-inch thickness. Cut into 10 triangles or 12 squares. Brush tops with reserved egg white and sprinkle with a little sugar. Bake on a greased cookie sheet at 450°F for 12 to 15 minutes. Makes 10 to 12 scones.

Boston Brown Bread

Very good commercial Boston brown bread can be bought, but no New England cookbook would be complete without a recipe so you can make your own. Traditionally, brown bread is served with Boston baked beans.

2 cups buttermilk	2 teaspoons baking soda
¾ cup molasses	2 tablespoons sugar
1 cup Kellogg's All-Bran cereal	1 teaspoon salt
1 cup whole wheat flour	½ cup raisins
1 cup cornmeal	

Mix buttermilk, molasses, and bran cereal. Let stand 10 minutes or until all liquid is absorbed by bran.

Mix flour, cornmeal, soda, sugar, salt, and raisins. Fold into bran mixture, stirring just to blend. Fill into greased molds, ⅔ full; this recipe will make three 1-quart molds or two 1½-quart molds.

Cover molds tightly, with either a greased lid or greased aluminum foil. Put molds upright into a large kettle; add water halfway to top of molds. Bring to a boil, cover, then keep water simmering to steam breads for 3 hours. Uncover molds and bake in oven at 250°F for 20 to 30 minutes or until tops are dry. Remove bread from molds and serve hot. To store, cool bread and wrap in aluminum foil. Reheat in foil in top of double boiler.

To cook in a pressure cooker: Set molds on rack in pressure cooker. Add water to depth of 2 inches. Steam 15 minutes with valve open. Close and steam 60 minutes longer for large mold, 40 minutes longer for small. Reduce heat at once. If you wish a little drier bread, bake as directed in steaming directions above.

Sour Cream Coffee Cake

A few years back sour cream coffee cake hit the coffee klatch circuit. It became popular at once and is good enough to deserve a place in our baking section.

½ cup butter or margarine, softened
1 cup granulated sugar
2 eggs
1 teaspoon vanilla extract
1 cup dairy sour cream
1 teaspoon baking soda

2 cups all-purpose flour
¼ teaspoon salt
1½ teaspoons baking powder
¼ cup chopped nuts
¼ cup brown sugar
1 teaspoon cinnamon

Beat butter, granulated sugar, eggs, and vanilla together until light and fluffy. Stir in sour cream and soda, mixing well. Mix flour, salt, and baking powder and fold into sour-cream mixture. Do not beat.

Spoon half of batter into a well-greased 9-inch angel-cake pan. Mix nuts, brown sugar, and cinnamon and spoon half on batter in pan. Spoon in remaining batter and sprinkle with rest of nut mixture. Bake at 350°F for 45 minutes or until cake tester inserted in cake comes out clean. Let stand 5 minutes and then invert pan on a plate and remove cake. Serve warm. Makes 1 cake.

Breakfast Puffs

These taste like doughnuts—but look, no frying!

1½ cups all-purpose flour
1½ teaspoons baking powder
½ teaspoon salt
¼ teaspoon nutmeg
⅓ cup shortening
½ cup sugar

1 egg
½ cup milk
3 to 4 tablespoons melted margarine
½ cup sugar and 1 teaspoon cinnamon,
    mixed

Onto a sheet of waxed paper, sift together the flour, baking powder, salt, and nutmeg. Set aside. In mixing bowl, cream shortening with sugar, then beat in egg. Add flour mixture and milk alternately, beating well after each addition. Spoon batter into greased muffin tins, filling them about half full; bake at 350°F 20 to 25 minutes. Remove immediately from tins.

Have the melted margarine ready in a small bowl, and on a sheet of waxed paper, the sugar-cinnamon mixture. Dip tops of each puff first in melted margarine, then in sugar-cinnamon mixture. Makes 9 large or 12 small puffs.

Cornbread

In this area, stone-ground cornmeal is not hard to find, and many prefer it to other kinds. Cornbread is an easy hot bread to make for dinner.

1 cup all-purpose flour	1 cup yellow cornmeal
3½ teaspoons baking powder	1 egg
½ teaspoon salt	1 cup milk
2 tablespoons sugar	¼ cup oil or melted bacon fat

Mix all dry ingredients in a bowl. Combine egg, milk, and oil. Stir into dry ingredients just to blend. Spoon into a well-greased 8×8×2-inch pan. Bake at 425°F for 40 minutes or until nicely browned. Cut into squares and serve hot. Makes 16 squares.

Variations

Cornsticks: Bake cornbread batter in greased cornstick pans at 425°F for 15 minutes or until nicely browned. Makes 12.

Buttermilk Cornbread: Decrease baking powder to 1½ teaspoons and add ½ teaspoon soda. Substitute 1 cup buttermilk for 1 cup milk.

Irish Soda Bread

In Connemara we visited a farm where we had buttermilk with flecks of butter in it. There are innumerable recipes for Irish soda bread. To our own, we added the butter to make up for our anemic buttermilk.

3½ cups all-purpose flour	2 teaspoons baking soda
2 teaspoons salt	2 tablespoons butter or margarine
1 tablespoon sugar	1¾ cup buttermilk

Mix flour, salt, sugar, and soda in bowl. Blend butter into flour mixture with fork. Add buttermilk and stir with fork until all flour is dampened. Flour hands and shape dough to fit into a well-greased 8-inch round cake pan. Cut across top from side to side to make an X. Bake at 400°F for 35 minutes or until nicely browned. Remove from pan and cool on rack. Do not cut Irish Soda Bread until well cooled. Then cut into thin slices and serve with butter. Makes 1 loaf.

Variations

Raisin Soda Bread: Stir ½ to 1 cup raisins into batter with buttermilk.

Brown Soda Bread: Decrease all-purpose flour to 1 cup. Add 2¾ cups whole wheat flour.

Basic Muffins

A basic muffin recipe can have many variations. If you get the basic recipe down pat, you can add a lot of favorite flavors to it. Remember that muffin batter should never be beaten—just stirred to barely blend dry and liquid ingredients.

2 cups all-purpose flour	1 egg
1 tablespoon baking powder	1 cup milk
½ teaspoon salt	3 tablespoons oil or melted butter
2 tablespoons sugar	or margarine

Mix dry ingredients in a bowl. In another bowl, beat together egg, milk, and oil or melted butter. Add to dry mixture and stir just to blend. Fill 3-inch (top measure) muffin tins that have been greased (or lined with paper liners) about ⅔ full and bake at 400°F for 20 to 25 minutes. Makes 12 to 15 medium muffins.

Variations

Cheese Muffins: Mix ½ cup grated American cheese with dry ingredients.

Bacon Muffins: Add ½ cup crumbled crisp fried bacon to dry ingredients.

Raisin Muffins: Add ½ cup raisins to dry ingredients.

Blueberry Muffins

(pictured between pages 40 and 41)

Muffins go together in a hurry and bake quickly. They add a personal touch to a meal. During blueberry season make them often, spiked with this popular New England berry.

2 cups all-purpose flour	1 cup fresh blueberries*
1 tablespoon baking powder	1 egg
½ teaspoon salt	1 cup milk
¼ cup sugar	3 tablespoons oil
½ teaspoon cinnamon	

Mix flour with dry ingredients in a bowl. Stir in blueberries. In another bowl beat together egg, milk, and oil. Add to flour mixture and stir just to blend.

Fill 3-inch (top measure) muffin tins that have been greased (or lined with paper liners) about ⅔ full and bake at 400°F for 20 to 25 minutes. Makes 12 to 15 medium muffins.

Frozen blueberries can be used; thaw before using.

Bran Muffins

Nothing tastes as good as warm bran muffins at breakfast, lunch, or dinner.

1¼ cups milk
1½ cups Kellogg's All-Bran cereal
1½ cups all-purpose flour
3½ teaspoons baking powder

½ teaspoon salt
⅓ cup sugar
1 egg
5 tablespoons soft shortening or oil

Combine milk and bran cereal and let stand. Mix flour with dry ingredients. Add egg and shortening to bran mixture and beat well. Stir in dry ingredients just to blend. Fill 3-inch (top measure) muffin tins that have been greased (or lined with paper liners) ⅔ full. Bake at 400°F for 25 minutes. Makes 12 muffins.

Variations

Raisin Bran Muffins: Add ½ cup raisins to batter.

Honey Bran Muffins: Substitute ¼ cup honey for sugar in recipe. Add honey to bran and milk. Directions for mixing remain the same.

Refrigerator Buttermilk Bran Muffins

A handy way to have hot muffins when you want them.

4 cups Ralston Bran Chex cereal
1 cup boiling water
½ cup butter or margarine, softened
1 cup sugar
2 eggs
2½ cups all-purpose flour

2½ teaspoons baking soda
½ teaspoon salt
½ cup buttermilk powder*
2 cups water
1 cup raisins

Crush cereal to make 3 cups. Measure 1 cup and combine with boiling water. Set aside to cool.

Cream butter and sugar until light. Add eggs and beat well. Mix flour, soda, salt, and buttermilk powder. Add to creamed mixture alternately with water, stirring just to blend. Stir in moistened cereal, remaining 2 cups cereal, and raisins. Put batter into a container that can be tightly covered and store in the refrigerator. Will keep up to 5 weeks.

To bake: Fill greased or paper-lined 3-inch (top measure) muffin tins ⅔ full. Bake at 375°F for 20 to 25 minutes. Makes 28 muffins.

*2 cups fresh buttermilk can be used. Omit buttermilk powder and 2 cups water.

Yeast Raised Muffins

These yeast muffins do not need any kneading. Serve them piping hot.

3 cups all-purpose flour
1 package active dry yeast
¾ cup nonfat dry milk powder
    or granules
2 tablespoons brown sugar

2 teaspoons salt
½ cup butter or margarine, softened
2 cups hot tap water
1½ cups whole wheat flour
½ cup raw unprocessed bran

Mix well all-purpose flour, yeast, dry milk, sugar, and salt in a bowl. Cut softened butter into pieces over flour mixture. Gradually add hot water to flour mixture and beat 2 minutes. Stir in whole wheat flour and bran. Mixture should be thick enough so that when the spoon is lifted from batter, it will hold its shape. Cover with plastic wrap and a towel and let rise about 1 hour or until double in bulk. Stir down.

Grease well 2½ dozen 3-inch (top measure) muffin tins. Half fill with batter. Let rise about 45 minutes or until doubled in bulk. (Do not cover.) Bake at 425°F for 15 to 20 minutes or until nicely browned. Let stand about 3 minutes before removing from pan. If 2½ dozen is too many at one time, the muffins freeze well.

Buttermilk Biscuits

2 cups all-purpose flour
1 teaspoon baking powder
½ teaspoon baking soda
½ teaspoon salt

4 tablespoons buttermilk powder*
5 tablespoons shortening
⅔ cup (about) water

Mix together flour, baking powder, soda, salt, and buttermilk powder in a bowl. Cut in shortening with a pastry blender or 2 knives until texture of dry crumbs. With a fork, stir in water to form a soft dough. Turn out on a lightly floured surface and knead 2 or 3 times. Pat into a ½-inch-thick rectangle. Cut with a floured 2-inch biscuit cutter or use a knife and cut square biscuits. Place on a greased baking sheet and bake at 425°F for 12 to 15 minutes or until nicely browned. Makes about 14.

*⅔ cup fresh buttermilk can be used. Omit buttermilk powder and water.

Baking Powder Biscuits

It is possible to make very good biscuits from a commercial mix, but sometimes there is no mix on hand, and biscuits are easy to whip up from scratch. For a tender biscuit, use a light hand.

2 cups all-purpose flour	4 tablespoons shortening
1 tablespoon baking powder	¾ cup (about) milk
1 teaspoon salt	

Mix together flour, baking powder, and salt in a bowl. Cut in shortening with a pastry blender or 2 knives until texture of dry crumbs. With a fork, stir in milk to form a soft dough. Turn out on lightly floured surface and knead 2 or 3 times. Pat into a ½-inch-thick rectangle. Cut with a floured 2-inch biscuit cutter or use a knife and cut square biscuits. Place on a greased baking sheet. For crusty biscuits, place 2 inches apart; for softer biscuits, place close together. Bake at 425°F for 12 to 15 minutes or until nicely browned. Makes about 14.

Variations

Sweet Biscuit Shortcake: Increase shortening to 6 tablespoons, add 3 tablespoons sugar to dry ingredients, and decrease milk to ⅔ cup. Roll or pat dough to ¼ inch thick. Spread with softened butter. Cut with 3-inch round cutter and place one biscuit on top of other on baking sheet to bake until nicely browned. To serve, separate biscuits, cover bottom half with fruit, place top on fruit, and add more fruit to top. Serve with plain or whipped cream. Makes 5 or 6 shortcakes.

Cheese Biscuits: Add ⅔ cup grated cheese to flour mixture with shortening.

Herb Biscuits: Add 4 tablespoons finely chopped fresh parsley and 2 tablespoons of your favorite herb, chopped, such as rosemary or tarragon or thyme, with the milk. Or mix 1 teaspoon powdered sage or poultry seasoning with the dry ingredients.

Drop Biscuits: Increase milk in biscuit recipe to 1 cup. Drop biscuit dough by tablespoonfuls onto a greased baking sheet. Bake as directed.

Wheat Germ Biscuits: Substitute 1 cup of whole wheat flour for 1 cup all-purpose flour and add ¼ cup wheat germ to dry ingredients.

Jonnycake

Neither yeast nor baking powder leavened, Jonnycake from Rhode Island is something else again. These recipes are courtesy of the Society for the Propagation of the Jonnycake Tradition in Rhode Island.

The Jonnycake should be made only from white stone-ground meal ground in Rhode Island from flint corn. If you can't get flint cornmeal, use stone-ground white cornmeal and don't tell anyone. Store unused cornmeal in the refrigerator to keep its fresh flavor.

The name Jonny with no "h" probably evolved from the original "journey cake," as the first cakes were called.

Jonnycake

West of Narragansett Bay

1 cup white cornmeal
½ teaspoon salt
1 cup bubbly boiling water

3 or 4 tablespoons milk or cream
1 teaspoon sugar or molasses (optional)

Mix all ingredients to mashed-potato consistency, adding more liquid if necessary. Drop by spoonfuls onto hot greased griddle to make cakes ½ inch thick and 2½ inches across. Fry 6 to 8 minutes on each side until there is a brown crunchy crust and inside is done. Makes 12 Jonnycakes.

Jonnycake

East of Narragansett Bay

1 cup white cornmeal
½ teaspoon salt

1⅞ cups cold milk

Mix all ingredients into thin, soupy consistency. Ease large spoonfuls onto hot greased griddle to make cakes about ⅛ inch thick and 5 inches across. Fry 2 to 3 minutes on each side or until brown. Makes 8 Jonnycakes.

Whole Wheat Popovers

Popovers do not fall into either a yeast or baking powder category, but they are a bread, so we include them in this chapter. If I am baking something else at the 425°F temperature that does not need to have the oven opened, I bake the popovers at the same time.

½ cup whole wheat flour	2 eggs
½ cup all-purpose flour	1 cup milk
½ teaspoon salt	1 tablespoon oil

Combine all ingredients in a bowl and beat with rotary beater until batter is smooth, 1½ to 2 minutes. Apply a coating of nonstick spray to 3-inch (top measure) aluminum muffin tins and grease lightly with oil. Fill about half full of batter. Bake at 425°F for 45 minutes. Do not open oven during baking. Remove from pans at once and serve hot. Makes 9.

Popovers may be made with 1 cup all-purpose flour, leaving out the whole wheat called for in the recipe. The recipe may be divided in half if 9 is too many. Popovers can be baked in tin muffin pans but are more satisfactorily baked in aluminum. If you have iron popover pans, use them (and then you will not need the Pam).

Banana Yogurt Loaf

This is in answer to a request for a moist banana bread and was a first Chat *contribution by Quan Yin. This recipe makes 1 loaf.*

½ cup butter or margarine	½ teaspoon salt
¾ cup brown sugar	1¼ cups mashed very ripe banana
1 egg	¼ cup plain yogurt
1 cup unsifted whole wheat flour	¾ cup chopped walnuts
½ cup unbleached white flour	3 walnut halves
1 teaspoon baking soda	

Cream butter or margarine and sugar together until creamy using a large bowl. Beat in the egg.

Mix flours, soda, and salt on a sheet of waxed paper. In a small bowl, combine mashed bananas and yogurt, stirring just to mix. Add dry ingredients alternately with banana/yogurt mixture to creamed mixture, stirring just to mix. Add chopped walnuts. Put batter into greased 8½×4½×2½-inch loaf pan and top with walnut halves. Bake at 350°F for 55 to 60 minutes, until tester comes out clean. Cool in pan for 5 minutes, then remove and cool completely on rack.

from Quan Yin, *Confidential Chat*

Cranberry Muffins

Here is our family's favorite cranberry muffin recipe. This recipe makes 12 muffins.

³/₄ cup fresh or frozen cranberries
¹/₂ cup confectioners' sugar
2 cups all-purpose flour
3 teaspoons baking powder
¹/₂ teaspoon salt

4 tablespoons sugar
1 egg, beaten
1 cup milk
4 tablespoons melted shortening, cooled

Chop berries coarsely (no need to thaw if frozen). Mix with confectioners' sugar and let stand. Sift remaining dry ingredients together into mixing bowl. Add beaten egg, milk, and melted, cooled shortening. Mix, but do not beat. Fold in sugared berries. Divide batter into 12 paper-lined muffin tins. Bake at 350°F for 20 minutes or until they test done.

from Happy Sun Tan, *Confidential Chat*

Scottish Oat Scones

This produces a delicious, golden brown, raisin-filled scone. Use either quick-cooking or regular oats. This recipe makes 8 to 12 scones.

1¹/₂ cups all-purpose flour
1¹/₄ cups uncooked oats
¹/₄ cup sugar
1 tablespoon baking powder
1 teaspoon cream of tartar

¹/₂ teaspoon salt
²/₃ cup butter or margarine, melted
¹/₃ cup milk
1 egg
¹/₂ cup raisins or currants

Combine dry ingredients in mixing bowl. Add butter, milk, and egg. Mix just until dry ingredients are moistened. Stir in raisins or currants.

Shape dough into a ball. Pat out onto lightly floured surface, forming 8-inch circle. Cut into 8 or 12 wedges. Place on greased cookie sheet and bake at 425°F for about 15 minutes, until light golden brown. Serve warm with butter, preserves, or honey.

from Cantarps, *Confidential Chat*

Pumpkin Muffins

Baked in miniature muffin tins, these make fine treats for children. May also be baked in a loaf pan. This recipe makes 1 dozen muffins or 1 loaf.

⅓ cup water
2 eggs
½ cup vegetable oil
¾ cup canned pumpkin
½ cup honey or molasses
1¾ cups all-purpose flour

1 teaspoon baking soda
1 teaspoon salt
¾ teaspoon cinnamon
¾ teaspoon nutmeg
¼ teaspoon ginger and cloves (optional)

Mix together water, eggs, oil, pumpkin, and honey (or molasses). Add dry ingredients, mixing thoroughly. Drop batter into paper-lined miniature 1-inch muffin tins. Bake at 350°F for 18 to 20 minutes, or until they test done.

For loaf, put batter into greased 8½×4½×2½-inch loaf pan; bake for 1 hour at 350°F. Cool thoroughly before slicing.

from Blue Sky Days, *Confidential Chat*

Colonial Coffee Cake

An old-fashioned breakfast bread, delicious when warm from the oven. Reheat in either toaster oven or, very briefly, cut in squares, in microwave. This recipe makes one 9-inch cake.

2 cups all-purpose flour
1 cup sugar
3 teaspoons baking powder
1 teaspoon salt

⅓ cup butter or margarine, softened
1 cup milk
1 egg

Streusel Topping

½ cup chopped pecans or walnuts
½ cup packed brown sugar
¼ cup all-purpose flour

½ teaspoon cinnamon
3 tablespoons firm butter or margarine

Beat all ingredients for cake in large mixing bowl at low speed for 30 seconds. Beat on medium, scraping bowl occasionally, for 2 minutes. Mix until crumbly all ingredients for streusel topping. Spread half the batter in a greased 9-inch square pan. Sprinkle with half the streusel topping. Top with remaining batter; sprinkle with remaining topping. Bake at 350°F 35 to 40 minutes, until cake tester inserted in center comes out clean.

from Jessica's Polonaise, *Confidential Chat*

Pasta

Numbers refer to pages where recipes appear in this book.

Pasta

Is there any more international food than pasta? While the word itself is Italian, meaning paste or dough, many other countries have long had their own versions of this food, as well as generic recipes.

Marco Polo is said to have brought the idea to his country from China. Certainly the Italians get full credit for the wide variety of shapes—spaghetti, fettuccini, tortellini, ravioli, lasagna, to name but a few. With the equally broad and delicious range of recipes for pasta preparation, it is difficult to find anyone who does not like this fine food in one style or another.

Most packaged pastas found in our markets today are marked "enriched," meaning that B vitamins and iron have been added, boosting the already good nutritional values. Generally the plain product has no salt or cholesterol. Some varieties do have egg yolks; check labels if this is a concern.

Freshly made pastas have also become available in many specialty shops and large supermarkets. They are often of a more exotic variety, made with ingredients like tomatoes, spinach, squid, or saffron added to the basic dough.

Increasingly today there is a tendency to make more lightly sauced pasta dishes, in which fresh garden vegetables are combined with fresh herbs to sauce the pasta.

If you follow the trend, you will be using more pasta; you will sauce it with lighter combinations of vegetables and meat, fish, or cheese; and your spaghetti is more likely to be cooked al dente. You may even be making your own pasta.

In cooking with pasta, use fresh herbs whenever possible. The general rule is to use three times more fresh herbs than dried. Freshly grated Parmesan cheese is superior, and it is a breeze to make, especially if you have a food processor.

For many years I have been cooking all pastas in far less water than the directions indicate. This uses less energy (to heat the water), besides saving water. The pasta may be a bit more al dente when cooked in less water, but there is no loss of quality.

Here are some of the old pasta favorites, as well as new recipes to give you a base for doing your own thing.

Egg Noodles

(pictured between pages 72 and 73)

If you have a food processor, noodles can be made in it; the food processor recipe book will tell you how.

1 cup all-purpose flour
¼ teaspoon salt
1 egg yolk, lightly beaten
2 tablespoons water

Additional flour
2 quarts boiling water
2 teaspoons salt

Mix flour and salt in a bowl or on a board. Make an indentation in center and add egg yolk mixed with water. Work flour into egg yolk with fingers until the mixture is blended. If too dry, add a few drops more water. Put some additional flour on the board and knead the dough about 5 minutes, or until smooth and elastic. Cover with plastic wrap and let rest 20 minutes.

Divide dough into 3 parts and roll each part until very thin. Dust top of rolled noodle dough lightly with flour. Fold dough over on itself and cut into ¼- to ½-inch wide strips. Separate and let dry.

Noodles can be used at once or dried and stored in a covered container. This recipe makes about 8 ounces.

To cook, boil 2 quarts water with 2 teaspoons salt. Add noodles and boil 5 to 15 minutes, depending on dryness of noodles. Serve buttered or use in a recipe.

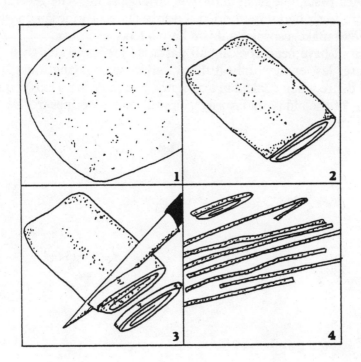

Spinach Noodles

These pretty noodles can be served with a sauce or buttered as suggested.

1 package (10 ounces) frozen chopped spinach, thawed	2 eggs
½ cup water	2 quarts boiling water
¼ teaspoon salt	1 teaspoon salt
1½ cups (about) all-purpose flour	¼ cup butter

Cook spinach with ½ cup water and salt, covered, in a 1-quart saucepan for about 5 minutes. Drain. Allow to cool and squeeze out all possible liquid. Chop fine.

Put flour on a board or other suitable work surface and make an indentation in center. Put in eggs and spinach and work flour into eggs and spinach with fingers to make a dough. It should not be sticky, so add a little additional flour if necessary. Bring dough together in a ball and let rest a few minutes. Clean off work surface and knead dough until smooth and elastic.

Cut dough into 2 or 3 pieces and roll each piece on a lightly floured surface until uniformly thin, about ¹⁄₁₆ inch. Lift dough with floured rolling pin and place each rolled piece on a clean cloth to dry on surface so that it will not stick to itself when folded to cut. This takes several hours, depending on humidity.

When dough is dry enough to cut, fold dough in half from long side. Cut into ½- to ¼-inch strips, toss lightly with fingers to separate, and unroll. Set aside to dry.

To cook, heat about 2 quarts water to boiling in saucepan and add 1 teaspoon salt. Add noodles and boil about 5 to 10 minutes, or until desired texture is reached. Drain and toss with ¼ cup butter. Makes 4 servings.

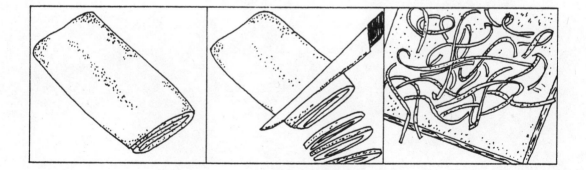

Saucy Macaroni Casserole

(sauce pictured between pages 72 and 73)

Prepare the sauce early in the day, refrigerate, but reheat before combining the casserole.

½ pound uncooked macaroni

1 cup grated cheddar cheese

Sauce

3 tablespoons vegetable oil
2 medium onions, chopped
1 clove garlic, chopped
½ pound ground beef
1 can (28 ounces) peeled,
   crushed tomatoes

1 teaspoon salt
Freshly ground pepper to taste
1 cup water
1½ teaspoons chili powder

Heat oil in skillet and cook onion and garlic until soft. Add beef and cook 3 to 5 minutes longer. Add tomatoes, salt, and pepper, and simmer, covered, about 30 minutes. Stir in water and chili powder.

When ready to cook, layer the sauce with the uncooked macaroni and cheese, starting with macaroni and ending with sauce and cheese, in a buttered 2-quart casserole. Bake, covered, 35 minutes. Uncover and bake 15 minutes longer. Makes 4 to 6 servings.

Quick version

Substitute 5 cups of your favorite commercial spaghetti sauce for this sauce.

Cottage Cheese Casserole

Ziti is another form of macaroni (or pasta). When combined in this casserole with cottage cheese and sour cream, it makes a tasty dish. Add buttered steamed zucchini, a small green salad, and hot bread and you have a good dinner.

½ pound ziti macaroni
3 quarts boiling water
2 teaspoons salt
¼ cup chopped onion
2 tablespoons olive or other
    cooking oil
¼ cup chopped fresh parsley

Dash Tabasco sauce
½ teaspoon salt
1½ tablespoons Worcestershire sauce
2 cups small-curd cottage cheese
2 cups dairy sour cream
½ cup buttered bread crumbs

Cook ziti in boiling water with 2 teaspoons salt for about 8 minutes, stirring once or twice. Drain.

Sauté onion in oil until tender. Mix with cooked ziti. Combine parsley, seasonings, cottage cheese, and sour cream, and stir into ziti and onions. Spoon into a buttered 2-quart casserole and sprinkle crumbs on top. Bake at 350°F for 30 to 35 minutes or until bubbly. Makes 4 servings.

Sausage Macaroni Bake

Black Jack's macaroni casserole can be prepared in advance and refrigerated.

1 tablespoon oil
1 garlic clove (peeled, whole)
1 large onion, chopped
¾ pound sweet Italian sausages,
    cut in pieces
1 pound macaroni

2 quarts boiling water
1 teaspoon salt
1 large can (1 pound, 13 ounces) whole
    tomatoes
1 tablespoon dried oregano
3 cups ½-inch cheddar cheese cubes

Heat oil in skillet and sauté garlic for about 2 or 3 minutes. Remove and discard garlic. Add onion to oil and sauté until translucent. Remove onion to a large casserole. Sauté sausage pieces. Remove, drain well.

Cook macaroni in boiling water with salt 6 to 8 minutes. Drain and cool it with cold water. Combine with the sausages, tomatoes, oregano, and 2 cups of the cheese cubes, stirring well. Spoon into the large casserole and put 1 cup cheese cubes on top. Bake at 325°F until cheese is melted and brown and casserole is bubbly, about 20 minutes. If the casserole has been prepared in advance and refrigerated, allow 40 minutes. Makes 6 servings.

from Black Jack, *Confidential Chat*

Rigatoni with Carbonara Sauce

If you don't often use the less-common pastas, you'll like the change offered by this recipe. A tomato-and-lettuce salad, crisp rolls, and fruit for dessert can make the meal.

1 pound rigatoni macaroni	½ cup dry white wine
3 quarts boiling water	3 eggs, lightly beaten
2 teaspoons salt	¼ cup grated Romano cheese
6 slices bacon, diced	¼ cup grated Parmesan cheese
2 tablespoons olive or other	¼ cup chopped fresh parsley
cooking oil	Additional Parmesan cheese

Cook rigatoni in boiling water with salt, stirring once or twice, for about 10 minutes. Drain and keep hot in a saucepan.

Meanwhile fry bacon in oil until crisp. Add wine and cook until wine has evaporated. Add bacon, eggs, and cheeses to hot cooked rigatoni and stir to coat. If the rigatoni is not hot enough to cook eggs, place saucepan over low heat for 1 minute, stirring. To serve, sprinkle with parsley and serve with additional Parmesan cheese. Makes 4 servings.

Lasagna

Lasagna can be prepared in advance, refrigerated, and heated when ready to serve. Meatless lasagna can be made by omitting the ground beef. With or without meat, this is a hearty dish, and usually a green salad, hot bread, and fruit suffice for a complete menu.

¾ cup chopped onion	½ teaspoon dried basil or 1½
1 garlic clove, chopped	teaspoons chopped fresh basil
3 tablespoons olive oil	1 whole clove, crushed
¾ pound ground beef	8 ounces lasagna noodles
1 can (8 ounces) tomato sauce	3 quarts boiling water
1 can (6 ounces) tomato paste	2 teaspoons salt
1 cup water	2 cups ricotta or small-curd cottage cheese
½ teaspoon dried oregano or 1½	½ cup grated Parmesan cheese
teaspoons chopped fresh oregano	8 ounces sliced mozzarella cheese

Sauté onion and garlic in olive oil until tender. Add meat and brown. Add tomato sauce, tomato paste, 1 cup water, herbs, and clove. Cover and simmer about 30 minutes.

Meanwhile cook lasagna in boiling water with salt about 10 minutes or until al dente. Drain.

Place half of lasagna in the bottom of a buttered 13×9-inch casserole. Spread half of the ricotta, Parmesan, and mozzarella cheeses over lasagna. Add half the meat sauce. Repeat layers. If you would like to save a few slices of mozzarella to put on top of the second layer of meat sauce, do so. Bake in 350°F oven 45 minutes. Makes 6 servings.

Egg Noodles (recipe on page 68)
with Sauce (recipe on page 70)

Noodles with Pesto

Pesto sauce keeps for several weeks, covered, in the refrigerator. If you are planning to do this, however, do not add cheese until serving time.

4 cloves garlic, minced
12 leaves fresh basil
Dash salt
²/₃ cup grated Parmesan cheese
½ cup olive oil

2 tablespoons pine nuts (optional)
1 pound egg noodles or 8 ounces
   spaghetti or linguine
2 quarts boiling water
2 teaspoons salt

The sauce called *pesto* is traditionally made in a mortar and pestle (hence the name), but this tradition was established before blenders. If you wish to use a mortar and pestle, use one with about a 2-cup capacity. Put garlic, basil, and dash of salt in mortar and mash with pestle until well blended. Add cheese and olive oil alternately a little at a time, pounding and mixing to blend after each addition. Add pine nuts, if desired, pounding and mixing until they are blended.

If you choose to use a blender (a food processor is a little too large for this operation), put in garlic (it need not be minced), basil leaves, a dash of salt, and a bit of the cheese and olive oil. Blend, then add remaining cheese and dribble in the remaining olive oil and optional pine nuts, blending until smooth. To serve, cook pasta (egg noodles, spaghetti, or linguine) in 2 quarts boiling water with 2 teaspoons salt until al dente: 6 minutes for noodles, 8 minutes for spaghetti or linguine. Drain and mix with pesto. Makes 4 servings.

Noodles Romanoff

January's Carnation says this dish is easy and elegant. It would make part of a buffet menu.

½ pound egg noodles
2 quarts boiling water
1 teaspoon salt
2 cups dairy sour cream
1 package (8 ounces) cream
   cheese, softened

¼ cup finely chopped onion
1 teaspoon Worcestershire sauce
½ teaspoon salt
Dash pepper
¼ cup grated Parmesan cheese
Paprika

Cook noodles in boiling water with 1 teaspoon salt until tender, 10 to 12 minutes. Drain well.

In a large bowl mix sour cream and cream cheese, blending well. Add onion, Worcestershire sauce, ½ teaspoon salt, and pepper. Transfer to a greased 1½-quart casserole or baking dish. Sprinkle top with Parmesan cheese and paprika. Bake at 350°F for 30 minutes. Makes 6 servings.

from January's Carnation, *Confidential Chat*

Egg Noodles Alfredo

This famous dish from Alfredo's restaurant in Rome is a grand way to use your chafing dish. But if you have no chafing dish, an electric skillet or a large heavy skillet or saucepan will do as well.

1 pound egg noodles, 1/8 or 1/4 inch wide	1/4 pound sweet butter, softened
2 quarts boiling water	2/3 cup heavy cream
2 teaspoons salt	1 cup grated Parmesan cheese
	Additional grated Parmesan cheese

Cook noodles in boiling water with salt until al dente, about 6 minutes. Drain.

Melt half the butter in a chafing dish or electric skillet set at low heat. Stir in the cream and 1/3 cup of cheese. Add hot noodles and with a fork and spoon toss noodles gently in a folding process, adding remaining cheese and butter. Mix and blend until noodles are well coated and creamy. Serve very hot with additional cheese sprinkled on the noodles. Makes 4 servings.

Sea Scallops with Spaghetti

A tasty change with spaghetti. Serve with a romaine, sliced radish, and black-olive salad with Italian dressing; crusty rolls; and for dessert, Neapolitan ice cream.

1 pound sea scallops, fresh or frozen	1 medium red onion, sliced
2 strips bacon	1 jar (15 ounces) meatless spaghetti sauce
1 small green pepper, seeded and diced	1/2 pound thin spaghetti
1/4 pound sweet Italian sausage meat	2 quarts boiling water
	2 teaspoons salt

If frozen, thaw scallops and cut into thirds or quarters. Cook bacon until crisp and reserve. In bacon fat, sauté green pepper, sausage meat, and onion until lightly browned. Remove from pan and sauté scallops until golden brown. Return pepper, sausage, and onion to skillet with scallops. Crumble bacon and add with spaghetti sauce, mixing well. Simmer 5 minutes.

Cook spaghetti in boiling water with salt 8 to 10 minutes. Drain. Serve with scallop sauce. Makes 4 servings.

Linguine with White Clam Sauce

This is one recipe where canned clams are really excellent, and this from a clammer. Served with a salad and hot crisp bread, it is a good quick dinner.

½ pound linguine
2 quarts boiling water
2 teaspoons salt
¼ cup olive or other cooking oil
1 large clove garlic, chopped
2 tablespoons flour
2 cans (7 ounces each) clams, or 1½
    cups minced raw clams with juice

¼ cup chopped fresh parsley
1½ teaspoons dried basil or 1½
    tablespoons chopped fresh basil
Salt and freshly ground pepper
    to taste

Cook linguine in boiling water with salt for about 10 minutes, stirring once or twice. Drain.

Heat oil and cook garlic about 1 minute. Add flour and juice from clams. Bring to a boil, stirring. Add clams, parsley, and basil and simmer 5 minutes, stirring. Taste and add salt and pepper. Serve over hot cooked linguine. Makes 4 servings.

Spaghetti with Meat Balls

Spaghetti and meat balls always seem to call for a good green salad, Italian bread, red wine, and fruit and cheese for dessert.

1 pound ground beef
1 clove garlic, chopped
2 tablespoons chopped fresh
    parsley
½ teaspoon salt
Freshly ground pepper to taste
2 slices white bread, crumbled
2 eggs
3 tablespoons chopped onion

¼ cup olive oil
1 can (1 pound, 12 ounces)
    tomatoes in puree
1 can (6 ounces) tomato paste
1½ teaspoons dried basil or 1½
    tablespoons chopped fresh basil
Freshly ground pepper to taste
½ pound thin spaghetti, cooked
Grated Parmesan cheese

Mix ground beef with garlic, parsley, salt, pepper, bread, eggs, and onion until blended. Shape into 12 to 16 meat balls. Put on a cookie sheet and chill in freezer about 30 minutes.

Heat oil in a large skillet and brown chilled meat balls on all sides. When browned, add tomatoes, tomato paste, basil, and pepper. Cover and cook over low heat for 1 to 1½ hours, stirring occasionally.

Cook spaghetti as directed. Serve meat balls with hot spaghetti and Parmesan cheese. Makes 4 servings.

Squash Tomato Sauce

Take advantage of summer vegetables to make this lovely light vegetable sauce for spaghetti. Adding whole wheat bread and a lettuce-and-bean-sprout salad will make a nourishing meal. If you prefer, use all zucchini.

1/4 cup oil
1 large onion, chopped
1 clove garlic, chopped
3 cups diced yellow summer
    squash (2 to 3 medium)
3 cups diced zucchini (2 to 3
    medium)
4 medium-size ripe tomatoes,
    peeled and diced*

Freshly ground pepper to taste
½ teaspoon each dried basil,
    oregano, and thyme; or 2
    teaspoons Italian seasoning
½ pound spaghetti or linguine
2 quarts boiling water
2 teaspoons salt
Grated Parmesan cheese

Heat oil in skillet and sauté onion and garlic until tender, not browned. Add squash, tomatoes, and seasonings. Bring to a boil, reduce heat, and simmer, covered, about 20 minutes. Uncover and simmer 5 minutes longer.

Cook spaghetti in boiling water with salt for 8 to 10 minutes while sauce is simmering. Drain. Serve with sauce and Parmesan cheese. Makes 4 servings.

In the winter, use 2 cups of canned tomatoes.

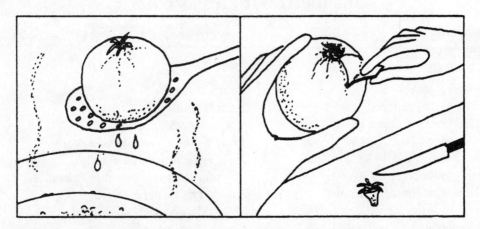

Put tomato into boiling water for thirty seconds, then drain. Cut around core with a knife, and discard. Peel away the skin with a knife or your fingers.

Spaghetti Sauce

This spaghetti sauce is excellent—and no, the spices have not been forgotten. The spoonful of cake crumbs, which smooths out the flavor, was a trick I learned from an Italian-American friend years ago. Use hot or sweet Italian sausage. Your choice.

1 tablespoon butter
2 tablespoons olive oil
2 tablespoons vegetable oil
1 large onion, finely chopped
1 carrot, finely chopped
1 stalk celery, finely chopped
¾ pound ground beef

¼ pound Italian sausage meat
⅔ cup dry white wine
4 teaspoons tomato paste
1¼ cups beef broth
1 tablespoon pound-cake crumbs
Salt and freshly ground pepper to taste
1 pound spaghetti, cooked as directed

Combine butter, olive oil, and vegetable oil in a large skillet. Add vegetables and sauté over moderate heat until lightly browned. Add beef and sausage and crumble and cook until lightly browned. Add wine, tomato paste, beef broth, and cake crumbs. Cover and simmer over low heat for 2 to 3 hours, stirring occasionally. Before serving, taste and add additional salt and pepper, if necessary. Serve over hot cooked spaghetti. Makes 4 to 6 servings.

Italian Spaghetti with Pork

Eliza sent Yrrej's recipe to Chat *when a reader asked for a repeat of the recipe. Her comment, "It's scrumptious."*

2 teaspoons olive oil
2 large onions, chopped
1 green pepper, seeded and chopped
2 cloves garlic, chopped
1 pound lean pork chops cut in
    very small pieces
1 can (6 ounces) tomato paste
1 tomato-paste can cold water
½ pound mushrooms, sliced, or
    1 can (4 ounces) sliced mushrooms

2 bay leaves
½ teaspoon dried thyme
1 pound spaghetti
3 quarts boiling water
2 teaspoons salt
¼ cup butter
1 or more cups grated Parmesan cheese

Heat oil. Add onion and green pepper. When onion is golden brown, add garlic. Cook on low heat for 5 minutes. Add meat. When brown, add tomato paste and cold water. Stir. Add mushrooms, bay leaves, and thyme. Cook slowly, covered, until meat is tender, adding additional water, if necessary.

Cook spaghetti in boiling water with salt for 8 to 10 minutes. Drain. Stir in butter and sauce. Add cheese. Makes 6 servings.

from Yrrej, *Confidential Chat*

Potato Gnocchi

Potato gnocchi, or dumplings, can be served with the same sauce as spaghetti. To my taste, though, they are better with melted butter and Parmesan and a meat dish.

2 pounds potatoes (about 6 medium)
Water to cover
2 cups (about) all-purpose flour
2 egg yolks, lightly beaten

½ teaspoon salt
2 quarts boiling water
Melted butter
Grated Parmesan cheese

Scrub potatoes and boil in water to cover until tender but firm, about 25 minutes.

Drain and peel immediately and rub through a ricer. Place potatoes on a well-floured surface and mix with flour. The mixture should be about ⅔ potatoes and ⅓ flour. Make an indentation in mixture and add egg yolks and salt. Mix and knead into a soft dough that is easily handled. Cut off small chunks of dough and roll quickly on a well-floured surface into finger-size rolls. Cut into 1-inch pieces. Press center of each piece with a finger. As they are made, put gnocchi on a floured board and sprinkle with flour to keep them from sticking together.

Boil a few gnocchi at a time in boiling water. Stir, and when gnocchi come to top, remove with a slotted spoon. Put into a serving dish and pour on some melted butter. Continue until all gnocchi are cooked. Sprinkle finished gnocchi with Parmesan cheese. Makes 4 to 6 servings.

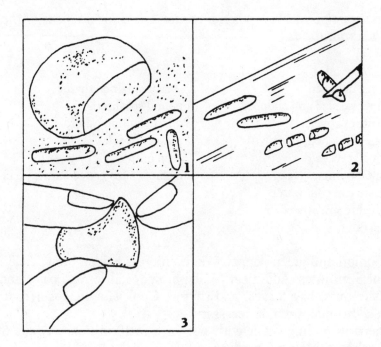

Noodle Spinach Bake

A tasty casserole to serve with baked ham or oven-baked chicken parts.

8 ounces medium or broad noodles
4 tablespoons margarine, divided
½ cup grated Parmesan cheese,
    divided
1 medium-sized onion, chopped

1 pound fresh spinach (or 1 10-ounce
    package frozen), cooked and
    well drained
Salt and pepper to taste
¼ cup bread crumbs

Cook noodles according to package directions until al dente; drain well. Toss with 1 tablespoon margarine and ¼ cup grated cheese. Set aside. In saucepan, melt 2 tablespoons margarine; add onion and cook until soft but not browned. Stir in spinach and cook, stirring over high heat until moisture has cooked off. Season with salt and pepper.

In a buttered casserole, place ⅓ of the noodles in an even layer; top with half the spinach mixture. Repeat again, then top with remaining noodles. Melt remaining butter; stir in bread crumbs and remaining cheese. Sprinkle evenly over noodles. Bake uncovered at 350°F for 20 to 25 minutes, until lightly browned. Makes 6 servings.

Noodle Mushroom Bake

Serve this with crisp-cooked broccoli and a platter of sliced tomatoes.

4 tablespoons margarine
2 cups sliced fresh mushrooms
1 teaspoon lemon juice
¼ cup grated Parmesan cheese
Salt and pepper to taste
8 ounces medium or broad noodles

2 eggs
1 cup milk
1 tablespoon flour
⅓ cup bread crumbs
1 tablespoon butter or margarine,
    melted

Melt the 4 tablespoons margarine in a heavy skillet. Add mushrooms and cook, stirring occasionally, for about 5 minutes. Add lemon juice, Parmesan, salt, and pepper. Set aside.

Cook noodles as directed on package, just until al dente; drain thoroughly. In a bowl, beat eggs, then add milk and flour, beating to mix well. Combine with the mushrooms, then fold in the noodles. Put into a buttered casserole. Mix bread crumbs with melted butter or margarine and sprinkle over top of casserole. Bake at 350°F for 30 minutes, until top is lightly browned and bubbly. Makes 6 servings.

Zucchini Ziti

Tasty and inexpensive, this makes a fine luncheon dish or can be part of a more substantial evening meal, accompanied by cold sliced meat or chicken.

1 pound ziti	2 cloves garlic, minced
3 or 4 small zucchini	1 teaspoon dried thyme
2 tablespoons margarine	Freshly ground pepper to taste
2 tablespoons olive oil	Grated Parmesan cheese

Cook ziti according to package directions just until al dente. While ziti is cooking, wash zucchini; cut off and discard ends. Cut zucchini into thin strips about 2 inches in length. Have remaining ingredients measured and ready to use.

When ziti tests done, drain very well. Put into large serving bowl. In a large skillet, heat margarine and olive oil until bubbly. Add zucchini and sauté, stirring constantly, for 2 minutes. Add the garlic and thyme and cook another minute. Sprinkle with pepper, then toss with the ziti in the bowl. Serve with a sprinkling of grated Parmesan. Makes 6 servings.

Summer Spaghetti Sauce

Fresh produce, whether from your own garden or a nearby vegetable stand, makes this sauce a pleasing change from tomato sauce.

4 ripe tomatoes, peeled and cut into wedges	1 teaspoon fresh basil, chopped
1 small eggplant, diced	½ teaspoon fresh tarragon, chopped
1 carrot, diced	1 clove garlic, minced
1 onion, chopped	Salt and pepper to taste
1 stalk celery, thinly sliced	1 pound spaghetti
⅓ cup fresh parsley, chopped	Grated Parmesan cheese

Put all ingredients, except spaghetti and cheese, into heavy pan. Cover and bring to a boil; lower heat and simmer uncovered, stirring from time to time, until vegetables are tender and sauce has thickened, about 30 minutes. Cook spaghetti as directed; drain well and serve topped with sauce and a sprinkling of Parmesan cheese. Makes 4 servings.

Spinach Lasagna

This always-popular casserole gets a bit of a nutritional boost from the addition of spinach.

2 tablespoons olive oil
1 medium onion, chopped
1 small green pepper, chopped
2 cloves garlic, minced
1 can (28 ounces) tomatoes
1 can (6 ounces) tomato paste
⅓ cup minced fresh parsley
½ teaspoon dried oregano

1 bay leaf
8 ounces lasagna noodles
1 package (10 ounces) frozen chopped
   spinach
1 pound ricotta cheese
1 egg
¾ cup grated Parmesan cheese
½ pound shredded mozzarella cheese

Heat oil in large skillet or heavy saucepan. Add onion, pepper, and garlic; sauté until tender. Do not allow to brown. Add tomatoes, tomato paste, parsley, oregano, and bay leaf. Stir well to mix, then simmer uncovered for 20 minutes, stirring occasionally. At end of cooking time, remove and discard bay leaf.

Cook spinach according to package directions; drain well. Cook noodles as directed; drain. Combine spinach, ricotta, egg, and ¼ cup of the Parmesan cheese. (Add salt and pepper to taste, if desired.) Lightly oil the bottom of a flat 9×13-inch baking dish. Place a single layer of the lasagna noodles on the bottom. Spoon a layer of the ricotta mixture over them, then top with a layer of the tomato sauce. Sprinkle with Parmesan and shredded mozzarella. Continue layering in this fashion, trying to make everything come out even. The top layers should be tomato sauce, then the two cheeses. Bake in a 350°F oven for about 45 minutes, until bubbly and lightly browned on top. Makes 8 to 10 servings.

Note: As with meat lasagna, this can also be securely wrapped, then frozen for later use. It's best to bring it back to room temperature, then bake as directed.

Eggs, Cheese, and Dairy

Numbers refer to pages where recipes appear in this book.

Eggs

Cheese

Dairy

*indicates a recipe variation

Eggs

Once one of our staple foods, today, as a result of advance research on cholesterol, eggs have a controversial place in our diet. Egg yolks are a prime source of cholesterol, and restrictions on their use are recommended by doctors and nutritionists. Egg whites do not contain cholesterol.

You should follow the advice of your doctor in this matter. Also, you can keep up-to-date on the latest information by consulting your state university extension service, whose trained nutritionists can help you.

Use more cereals for breakfast—hot oatmeal in winter, cold cereals with fruit during the summer. Limit eggs to two a week. And to reduce egg-yolk consumption, when preparing French toast, omelets, scrambled eggs, and such for breakfast, use one whole egg and one egg white instead of two whole eggs.

Grades found mostly at the grocers are AA and A. A yolk in the grade AA egg is higher, and the white will spread less when the egg is broken. Also the appearance of the shell can knock an egg from AA to A. For most uses, however, Grade A is as good as AA; and, in fact, after a week in the refrigerator, an AA egg will become an A egg.

Brown eggs are popular in New England, but nutritionists repeat over and over again that there is no difference nutritionally between a white and a brown. If white eggs are less expensive, buy them.

The old rule of thumb that if there is less than seven cents' difference between egg prices, the larger size is the best buy, still holds.

Remember that eggs are a perishable food and should be kept under refrigeration.

Cooking Eggs

Because the protein of eggs can become toughened with high heat, medium heat is recommended for all egg cooking.

Hard-Cooked Eggs: Use a teflon-coated, stainless-steel, or enamel pan. Cover eggs with cold water. As the water starts to boil, stir eggs with a wooden spoon to keep the yolks suspended in the middle as much as possible.

Eggs in the Shell: Put eggs into cold water and let come to a boil. Reduce heat and simmer for as long as you like your eggs—2 minutes for soft; 3 minutes, medium; and 5 minutes, well done. A pinch of salt added to water will help keep eggs from cracking. Crack eggs in half with a sharp knife and remove cooked eggs with a spoon (stainless steel, if possible, since eggs tarnish silver) into a small dish. If you have egg cups, cut off the sharp end of egg and place rounded end in the egg cup. The egg is then eaten with a spoon from the shell.

Poached Eggs: If you have an egg poacher, use it as directed. Otherwise, poach eggs in a skillet of lightly salted water. Let water come to a boil, drop in egg, reduce heat, and let egg poach 3 to 5 minutes. If you oil the skillet lightly before putting in the water, the egg will not stick to the bottom and the skillet will be easier to clean. The white coagulates closer to the yolk if you stir the water round and round before adding the egg (eggs). Some like to add a small amount of vinegar to the water to help coagulate the whites.

Fried Eggs: A teflon-lined skillet is good; and if you are not on a diet, even in a teflon skillet add a little fat for flavor. Heat over medium heat until fat is hot. Add eggs and fry to doneness desired. If you like the white over the yolk cooked, put a lid on the skillet for a few minutes.

Scrambled Eggs: For each egg, add 1 tablespoon water or milk and season to taste with salt and pepper. Mix with a fork until white and yolk are completely blended. One egg, scrambled, looks like such a small portion, that most people figure 1½ to 2 eggs per person. Cook in a small amount of margarine, stirring egg in from edges until doneness desired is reached.

French Omelets

Use an 8-inch skillet with sloping sides. An omelet party is fun, and they are so easily and quickly made that the guests can make their own while the hostess looks after toasted English muffins, coffee, etc. Put the various fillings in pretty bowls for omeleteers to mix and match.

The amount of fillings and eggs can easily be multiplied for a crowd. The fillings listed here are only suggestions. Bowls of bean sprouts, chopped fresh tomatoes, or green onions are a few more.

1 tablespoon butter or margarine	Dash salt
2 eggs	Dash freshly ground pepper
2 tablespoons water	

Fillings for 2 eggs—any one of the following:

¼ to ⅓ cup shredded cheese	2 tablespoons chopped green pepper
1 to 2 slices cooked crumbled bacon	2 tablespoons chopped cooked shrimp
2 fresh mushrooms, sliced	¼ cup yogurt or cottage cheese

Put butter in skillet over medium-high heat. Quickly mix eggs with water, salt, and pepper using a fork or whisk. Pour eggs into skillet and with a spatula, start drawing eggs in from outer edge to center. Tilt skillet so uncooked eggs will run to outer edges. Put filling (or fillings) you choose on one half of cooked omelet. Fold over other half and slide omelet onto plate. This cooking process should take only 1 to 2 minutes. Makes 1 omelet.

Note: Omelets should not be overcooked as they then break when you try to fold them. Also, when using fresh mushrooms or green peppers for filling, sauté for a few minutes in the margarine or butter, then remove before adding eggs to the pan. Add to omelet before folding.

Western Omelet

4 tablespoons butter or margarine	6 eggs
½ cup chopped onion	3 tablespoons milk
¾ cup chopped green pepper	½ teaspoon salt
¾ cup chopped smoked ham	Freshly ground pepper to taste

In 1 tablespoon of the butter, sauté onion and green pepper until tender. Combine with ham.

Beat eggs and milk enough to blend whites and yolks well. Season with salt and pepper. Heat remaining butter in a 10-inch skillet. Pour in eggs; sprinkle ham mixture over eggs. Pull cooked edges into center until all eggs are cooked to suit. Fold and slide onto platter. Makes 4 servings.

Cheese Soufflé

If you've been putting off making a soufflé, don't. They aren't that complicated, and once you've taken the plunge, you'll be sorry you didn't do it sooner. Just have the diners at the table before the soufflé comes out of the oven. A green salad with lots of tomatoes and hot bread go well with this dish.

6 tablespoons butter or margarine
½ cup all-purpose flour
½ teaspoon salt
Freshly ground pepper to taste
2 cups milk

¼ pound natural sharp cheddar cheese,
   shredded
3 tablespoons grated Parmesan cheese
Dash Tabasco sauce
4 eggs, separated

Heat butter in saucepan. Add flour, salt, and pepper and cook 1 or 2 minutes. Stir in milk and cook, stirring, until mixture comes to a boil and is thickened. Remove from heat and add cheeses and Tabasco. Stir until cheese melts.

Beat egg whites until very stiff. Beat egg yolks until thick and lemon colored. Fold yolks into cheese sauce, then fold in whites. Pour into a 1½-quart soufflé dish. Bake at 425°F for 25 minutes. Serve immediately. Makes 4 servings. If you like, serve soufflé with mushroom sauce (recipe below).

Mushroom Sauce

4 tablespoons butter or margarine
¾ cup sliced fresh mushrooms
2 tablespoons flour

Dash salt
Freshly ground pepper to taste
1¼ cups milk

Heat butter in saucepan and sauté mushrooms until they are tender and any liquid has evaporated. Stir in flour and seasoning and cook 1 to 2 minutes. Stir in milk and cook, stirring, until mixture boils and is thickened. Serve hot. Makes 1½ cups.

Swiss Cheese Pie

This is a dish that could go into either the egg or cheese category. It is the beloved of the cocktail circuit but was originally served with a light salad as a luncheon main dish.

<table>
<tr><td>¼ cup chopped green onion</td><td>3 eggs, well beaten</td></tr>
<tr><td>2 tablespoons butter or margarine</td><td>1 cup shredded Swiss cheese</td></tr>
<tr><td>1 unbaked 9-inch pie shell</td><td>½ teaspoon salt</td></tr>
<tr><td>2 cups light cream</td><td>Freshly ground pepper to taste</td></tr>
</table>

Sauté onion in butter until tender and spread on bottom of pie shell. Mix cream, eggs, cheese, and seasonings and pour over onions in pie shell. Bake at 425°F for about 40 minutes or until custard is firm in center.

Variation

Quiche Lorraine: Add 3 slices bacon, crisply cooked and crumbled, to onions.

Eggs Benedict

Chilled orange sections and hot tea add to eggs Benedict. Serves 2 or 4 people depending on appetites.

<table>
<tr><td>4 slices ham, cut to fit English muffins</td><td>2 tablespoons butter or margarine</td></tr>
<tr><td></td><td>4 poached eggs (page 85)</td></tr>
<tr><td>2 English muffins</td><td>1 recipe hollandaise sauce (page 116)</td></tr>
</table>

Grill ham and keep hot. Split English muffins, toast, and butter. Put on serving plates and top each with a ham slice, a poached egg, and hollandaise sauce. Makes 2 or 4 servings.

Cheese

There are so many fine American and imported cheeses, it is hard to know where to start.

The colonists brought their own methods of making their favorite cheeses when they settled. In 1851, the first cheddar cheese factory was established near Rome, New York. Today a great many of the cheeses that originated in Europe are made in this country. A recent ad by the cheese department of a large store claimed to have 180 varieties of cheese, so if I've left out any of your favorites, forgive me.

Cheeses are natural or processed. Natural cheese is made by the age-old method of separating curd from the whey of milk and continuing from there for various varieties. Pasteurized "processed" cheese is made by blending fresh and aged natural cheeses that have been shredded, mixed, and heated (pasteurized), after which no further ripening occurs. Processed cheese when melted is not stringy, melts easily, and is generally mild flavored.

Natural cheeses obtain their flavors (called ripening) from the kind of milk used (French Roquefort is made from sheep's milk, Norwegian Gjetost from goat's milk), bacterial culture, and molds.

Soft unripened cheeses such as cottage cheese do not undergo any ripening process and should be used fresh.

Firm unripened cheeses such as mozzarella ripen from the outside or rind of the cheese, toward the center. The bacteria or mold on the outside helps to fix the flavor of the cheese.

Soft ripened cheeses ripen from the interior as well as the exterior. Brie, Camembert, and Liederkranz are examples.

Firm ripened cheese ripens through the entire cheese, and ripening continues as long as the temperature is favorable. Vermont cheddar, Colby, Edam, Gouda, provolone, and Swiss (Emmentaler) are examples.

Very hard cheeses are Parmesan, Romano, and sapsago. They ripen slowly because of their low moisture content.

Other cheeses, such as blue (or "bleu"), Gorgonzola, Roquefort, and Stilton are ripened by veins of blue mold.

All natural cheese should be kept refrigerated. Cottage cheese, ricotta, and other soft unripened cheeses should be used within a few days after purchase.

Ripened or cured cheeses keep well in the refrigerator for several weeks if protected from mold contamination and drying out. Leave the original wrapper and protect cut surfaces with foil or plastic wrap.

Ends and pieces that have dried out may be grated, kept refrigerated in a covered jar, and used in cooking.

Smelly cheeses such as Limburger or Liederkranz should be stored in a tightly covered container.

Small pieces of cheese, 1 pound or less, can be frozen up to 6 months. Varieties that freeze well are brick cheeses, cheddar, Edam, Gouda, Muenster, Swiss, provolone, and mozzarella. Wrap cheese in freezer paper and label, seal, and date.

Except for cottage and cream cheese, all cheeses should be served at room temperature to bring out their distinctive flavor and texture. About 1½ hours should bring cheese to proper temperature depending on size of piece.

Neufchatel, Brie, Camembert, Limburger, Liederkranz, Bel Paese, Port du Salut, cheddar, Edam, Gouda, Swiss, Roquefort, blue, Stilton, Gorgonzola, fontina, Pont l'Eveque, and Muenster are among those that are good served with crackers and fruit for dessert.

Cooking cheeses include many of the above—such as Swiss, Edam, Gouda, Roquefort, blue, fontina, and cheddar—as well as processed cheeses, cottage cheese, cream cheese, ricotta, mozzarella, brick cheeses, Colby, provolone, Parmesan, and Romano.

Saturday Cheese Sandwich Special

This tasty sandwich spread can double as an hors d'oeuvre spread in a pinch.

2 tablespoons chopped onion
3 tablespoons chopped green pepper
1 fresh or canned chili pepper, seeded and chopped
2 tablespoons butter or margarine

1 small tomato, peeled and chopped (about ½ cup)
1½ cups grated American processed cheese
¼ teaspoon salt
2 tablespoons mayonnaise

Sauté onion, green pepper, and chili pepper in butter until tender, not browned. Add tomato and cook a few minutes longer. Cool and mix with cheese, salt, and mayonnaise to blend well. Makes about 2 cups. Use as a cold sandwich spread or broil on bread for a hot sandwich. It will store for several weeks, covered, in the refrigerator.

Swiss Cheese Fondue

A fondue party is loads of fun—it is informal, and since the host or hostess is an active participant, guests don't feel as though they are causing work. One fondue pot is enough for 4 persons, so if you plan to have more, borrow unless you already have more than one.

2 loaves crusty Italian or French bread
1 clove unpeeled garlic, cut in half
2 cups dry white wine
1 tablespoon lemon juice
1 pound natural Swiss cheese,
    shredded or cut in fine cubes*

3 tablespoons flour
3 tablespoons kirsch or cognac
Freshly ground nutmeg or pepper
    to taste

If you can buy long loaves of crusty bread, do so. Cut crosswise into 1½-inch slices and then cut each slice into pieces so that each piece has crust on one side. Allow bread to air-dry for about an hour and then cover with a clean cloth or plastic. For service arrange cubes in a bread basket lined with a bright napkin.

To make fondue:

Rub fondue pot on inside with cut garlic and discard garlic. Pour in wine. Set over heating unit of pot and heat to the boiling point. Add lemon juice. Sprinkle cheese with flour, mixing together, and add by spoonfuls to hot wine, stirring constantly with a wooden fork or spoon. Keep stirring until cheese is melted. Add kirsch or cognac and nutmeg or pepper and stir to blend.

Keep hot over heating unit. Each person in turn spears a piece of bread on a fork and twirls it in the fondue. Makes 4 servings.

Notes on Fondue

A crust forms in the bottom of the pan. Remove with a spatula and divide among the diners. Some think it is the best part of the fondue.

Serve a bowl of crisp vegetables with the fondue—a hearty dessert, such as an apple pie with ice cream. A Chablis or Riesling is a good accompaniment to the fondue.

*Half Swiss and half Gruyere cheese can be used also.

Presto Pizza

The Islander sent this recipe in answer to a request from Lady Glencora, and the baking-powder crust makes it "presto."

Crust

2¼ cups sifted all-purpose flour
1 tablespoon baking powder
1 teaspoon salt

⅓ cup shortening
¾ cup milk
2 tablespoons margarine, melted

Filling

⅓ cup chopped green pepper
2 tablespoons chopped onion
1 cup tomato sauce
½ cup tomato juice
½ teaspoon dried oregano

1 pinch garlic powder
⅔ cup grated mozzarella cheese
8 slices salami, cut up
½ cup grated Parmesan cheese

Mix flour, baking powder, and salt. Cut in shortening. Add milk and mix just enough to wet the dry ingredients. Place dough on lightly floured surface and knead gently 30 seconds.

Divide pizza dough in half. Press and pat each half into a 12-inch ungreased pizza pan. Brush with melted margarine.

In a mixing bowl, mix chopped pepper with onion, tomato sauce and juice, oregano, and garlic powder. Pour half over pizzas; reserve remaining half. Cover each pizza with grated mozzarella and pieces of salami. Pour remaining tomato sauce mixture over cheese. Sprinkle each pizza with ¼ cup grated Parmesan. Bake at 400°F for 15 minutes. Reduce heat to 300°F and bake 10 minutes more.

from The Islander, *Confidential Chat*

Dairy

Milk and milk products are an important part of the diet for most people. Calcium and vitamins are provided in good measure by the daily consumption of dairy products. However, the extra calories in whole milk, cream, ice cream, and such are not needed at all by those trying to control their weight.

Fortunately, choices are available in milks—skim, 1% and 2% fat—and adapting to them is quite easy. The use of reduced-fat milk in both cooking and drinking will lower both the calorie count and cholesterol intake.

An ever-increasing number of reduced-fat cheeses, yogurts, and even ice creams are available nowadays.

Milk, like eggs, is a perishable commodity and should be treated with respect. Depending on your family size and consumption of milk, the largest container you can use efficiently will be the least expensive per ounce. Buy milk from a store that keeps it well refrigerated and get it into your refrigerator as soon as possible. Watch the use date on the container and buy the milk with the latest date.

Milk is sold in many forms, and the following kinds are widely available:

Homogenized whole milk has been subjected to enough pressure so that the milk fat remains evenly distributed throughout the milk. Most homogenized milk has vitamin D added. It can be used for drinking or cooking.

Skim milk has had its butterfat removed. This removal of fat is the only difference between skim and whole milk. Skim milk can be used for drinking or cooking.

Low-fat milk is whole milk with all but 1 or 2% of the fat removed. It is a little richer to the taste than skim milk but lower in calories than homogenized whole milk. It can be used for drinking or cooking.

Other kinds of milk in the dairy department are **buttermilk** and **chocolate milk**.

In the grocery department you can find other milk products, such as the following:

Sweetened condensed milk is a mixture of whole cow's milk and sugar, with about 60% of the water removed. It is canned under pressure, has excellent keeping qualities, and can be used for sweetening coffee and for making ice cream and desserts. Refrigerate after opening.

Evaporated milk is whole milk with about half the water removed and with vitamin D added. The milk is homogenized to distribute the fat evenly, pasteurized before it is put into the can, and sterilized after the can is sealed. It comes in 13-ounce and 6-ounce cans, sometimes referred to as tall and small cans. In the can, evaporated milk will keep for up to a year if stored in a cool place.

Evaporated milk also comes in a low-fat variation with both vitamins A and D added. This product contains only $\frac{1}{4}$ of 1% fat.

Evaporated milk can be used straight from the can; and in fact if regular evaporated milk is partially frozen it whips very well. It can also be diluted with water or with other liquids to add flavor. After opening, refrigerate any left in the can at once.

Nonfat dry milk is skim milk with the water removed. It is fortified with vitamins A and D. It comes in powder and granular form and should be reconstituted with water according to directions on the package. Keep opened package in a cool, dry place.

Reconstituted, it can be used in any recipe where regular milk is called for. Some recipes call for dry milk mixed with the dry ingredients without reliquefying.

Cultured buttermilk powder is available for use in recipes calling for buttermilk. It does not reconstitute as a beverage, so directions on the package should be followed. Refrigerator storage after opening is required.

Cream comes in several degrees of richness. Heavy or whipping cream is used mainly for whipped cream and has not less than 30% butterfat. "All-purpose" cream can also be whipped. Light cream, for coffee or cooking, is not less than 18% butterfat.

Half-and-half is a mixture of half milk and half cream and contains 10 to 12% butterfat.

Dairy sour cream is light cream soured by culture or starter. It has a thick texture and a characteristic tartish flavor.

Yogurts take up a big space in the dairy department. There are so many varieties and flavors that it would be impractical to discuss them. Plain yogurt with no flavorings added (other than the bacilli that make yogurt) is used most in cooking. Yogurt can be made of regular, skim, or low-fat milk and will generally indicate on the carton which milk is used. A culture is introduced into the milk which, on standing, produces the texture and flavor of yogurt.

Yogurt

If you make your own yogurt, it costs about half what you pay for commercial yogurt; and it is so simple to make. These are the directions for making 1 quart of yogurt from 1 quart of whole milk. It will be necessary to buy a small container of plain yogurt to have a starter.

1 quart whole milk	¼ cup plain yogurt

Bring milk to a full, rolling boil. Let it come to the top of the pan, but be careful it doesn't boil over. Cool the milk to 110°F. Stir occasionally so a skin does not form on top of the milk. When it has reached 110°F, take 1 cup of the warm milk and blend into the plain yogurt. Return this to the remaining milk and gently stir until mixed well. Pour into 2 pint containers or a china or glass bowl; cover.

The yogurt must now be kept in a warm place, 110 to 120°F, to incubate. One way is to turn the oven to lowest temperature (150°F) for 2 or 3 minutes, turn oven off, and place yogurt in oven. If there is a light in the oven, turn it on. Or if your oven has a pilot light, this will keep the oven warm enough. Or set a bowl of boiling water in the oven beside or below the yogurt. It will take 6 to 8 hours for the yogurt to set. If you think the oven is getting too cool, replace the boiling water.

Makes 1 quart yogurt. Store, covered, in refrigerator, where it will keep about 2 weeks. Save ¼ cup yogurt to start the next batch.

This yogurt may be used any way commercial yogurt can be used. Serve it with fruit, honey, or maple syrup, or use in recipes calling for yogurt.

Variation

For a less rich yogurt, use 2 cups whole milk and 2 cups liquid nonfat milk.

Pancakes

Pancakes, since they use milk, seem an ideal set of recipes for this dairy section.

We have always had a love affair with pancakes, or hotcakes as they are also called, and a breakfast or supper of hotcakes and sausage with butter and real maple syrup is tops.

There are plenty of good pancake mixes on the market, but if you don't make them that often and don't want an open box hanging around your cupboard—or if you prefer the made-from-scratch flavor—they are easy to make.

Pancakes

Pancake preparation can be quick and easy if you measure out the dry ingredients the night before. Then you can simply add egg, oil, and milk in the morning.

1½ cups all-purpose flour
3½ teaspoons baking powder
½ teaspoon salt
3 tablespoons sugar

1 egg, well beaten
3 tablespoons oil or melted shortening
1 cup (about) milk

Mix flour with baking powder, salt, and sugar in a bowl. In another bowl, combine egg, oil, and milk. Add to flour and stir just enough to moisten the dry ingredients. Do not beat.

Heat griddle so that drops of water bounce off it, or to 400°F. Swipe some oil across griddle, and use a ¼ cup measure full of pancake batter to make each pancake. Cook until tops begin to rise and bubbles dot surface; turn and brown on other side, about 3 minutes altogether. Makes about 12 4-inch pancakes.

Variations

Blueberry Pancakes: Add 2 tablespoons more sugar to dry ingredients. Add 1 cup berries, stirring carefully just to mix them in.

Corn Pancakes: Add to the batter 1 cup canned whole-kernel corn, drained, or 1 cup fresh corn or frozen corn cut off the cob, thawed.

Clam Pancakes: Omit sugar from recipe; add 1 cup drained, chopped raw clams and 1 teaspoon grated onion to batter.

Men's Favorite Griddle Cakes

White Moonflower's griddle cakes are quick and easy to make, and Canadian bacon goes well with them. The amount of baking powder is correct.

2 cups whole wheat flour
1 egg
½ teaspoon salt
1 tablespoon sugar

2 tablespoons baking powder
1½ cups milk
2 tablespoons butter, melted

Select the best whole wheat flour, one that has excellent flavor and is ground fine. Sift the flour, but also add the bran, which does not go through the sifter. Beat the egg, add the salt and sugar, then the sifted flour, baking powder, milk, and finally the butter. Beat well and drop by large spoonfuls on hot griddle. When light and fluffy, turn the griddle cakes to brown the other side. Makes 15 to 16.

from White Moonflower, *Confidential Chat*

Oatmeal Pancakes

Oatmeal pancakes make a fine supper dish with butter, syrup, and bacon. Serve fruit salad for dessert.

1 cup uncooked quick or old-
    fashioned oatmeal
¾ cup all-purpose flour
1 tablespoon baking powder

½ teaspoon salt
1 cup milk
1 egg
2 tablespoons oil

Combine oatmeal, flour, baking powder, and salt in a medium-sized bowl. Stir until well mixed. Beat together milk, egg, and oil and stir into dry ingredients until just moistened. Heat griddle to 400°F and lightly grease. Fill a ¼-cup measure with batter and pour on hot griddle. Turn pancakes when tops begin to rise and edges look cooked. Makes about 10 4-inch cakes.

Chicken Crepes

Crepes are always spectacular to serve, but not that difficult to make. The crepes can be made way in advance and frozen, or the day ahead and refrigerated.

Crepes

½ cup all-purpose flour
1 egg
1 egg yolk
⅛ teaspoon salt

1 teaspoon sugar
1 cup milk
2 tablespoons butter, melted

Chicken Filling

⅓ cup butter
½ cup flour
1½ cups half-and-half
1 cup well-seasoned chicken broth
Salt and freshly ground pepper
    to taste

2 cups finely chopped cooked
    chicken or turkey
½ cup chopped fresh mushrooms
2 tablespoons dry sherry
½ cup dairy sour cream

Crepes: Put flour in a bowl. Add all remaining ingredients and beat with whisk until very smooth. Chill for two hours. Grease a 6- or 7-inch crepe skillet and heat over moderate heat. Pour in about 2 tablespoons batter and tilt skillet so a thin layer is formed. Brown on one side only and remove to a wire rack to cool. Makes 16 crepes. When cooled, separate with pieces of plastic or wax paper, overwrap, and store overnight or freeze.

Chicken Filling: Heat butter and flour together in a saucepan for 2 minutes. Stir in half-and-half and broth and cook and stir until mixture boils and is thickened. Season to taste.

Divide sauce into 2 equal parts. In one half stir chicken, mushrooms, and sherry. Cool. Put a spoonful of this filling on the uncooked side of each crepe and roll crepe around filling. Place seam side down in one or two buttered flat casseroles or baking dishes the right size to hold crepes in one layer.

Into the remaining sauce stir the sour cream. Pour over the filled crepes. Bake at 400°F for 25 minutes or until bubbly. Makes 4 to 6 servings.

Soups

Numbers refer to pages where recipes appear in this book.

*indicates a recipe variation

Soups

Soup is one of my favorite foods, particularly if it is homemade. I try always to keep something on hand with which to make soup, however simple. If you want to get into soup making, there are ways to make it a fairly effortless project.

When the soup base is meat or chicken stock, always make it the day before you need the soup so that it can be chilled overnight for easy removal of the fat.

Save liquid from vegetables to use in soup stock. A clean coffee can with a plastic cover is a good container. Keep it in the freezer and add liquid as it accumulates. Don't save strong-flavored cooking water such as that from cabbage, broccoli, and related vegetables unless you are particularly fond of it as a flavor; then save it separately from the more mild vegetables.

Everything is a candidate for the soup pot in my kitchen—leftover gravy, vegetables, bones from boning a steak or chicken. When I go shopping, I canvass the meat and poultry department for chicken necks, pork or beef bones, and lamb breasts or bones. All make a good stock base for soup. And in fact if you mix up the kinds of meat and chicken in making the stock, it seems to me to have a better flavor. When you find these soup-making items you can freeze them for future use.

Leftover vegetables also go into the soup. When preparing asparagus, snap off the tender tips and peel the tougher ends (not the very tough bottoms, but the part in between the tough bottom and the top you cook), and make cream of asparagus soup.

If you have a food processor, it is a great help in preparing soup. Vegetables can be processed to soup size in a jiffy or pureed for cream soups in a hurry.

Garnishes for Soup

- Crisp ready-to-eat cereal (not sweetened)
- Snipped chives or parsley
- Croutons, bought or homemade (toast buttered bread slices in a 300°F oven until lightly browned, trim, and cut into small squares; season, if you like, with garlic or savory salt)
- Popcorn
- Thin lemon slices
- Sour cream or yogurt

Soup Stock

After the stock has been cooked and strained, taste it to see if it has a good strong flavor. If it seems a little weaker than you'd like, add some beef or chicken bouillon cubes or boil the stock to concentrate it a bit more. (With power costs what they are, it is actually less expensive to add bouillon cubes.) But remember that you are going to add vegetables and other things to the stock which will help bring up the flavor.

Beef, pork, or chicken bones
    (about 2 to 3 pounds)
2 quarts water
1 onion, peeled
1 carrot, peeled

1 stalk celery
1 bay leaf
6 peppercorns
$\frac{1}{2}$ teaspoon salt

Cover bones with water, add remaining ingredients, and bring to a boil. If there is much scum that appears on the liquid after it begins to boil, skim it off and discard. Reduce heat, cover, and simmer. Beef or pork bones take about 3 hours or longer. Chicken- and lamb-bone flavor will be extracted with $1\frac{1}{2}$ to 2 hours of simmering. Cool stock enough to handle and strain out bones and vegetables. Chill stock and bones separately overnight. (If bones have little or no meat on them, they can be discarded.) Remove fat from chilled soup and discard. This should make about $1\frac{1}{2}$ quarts stock.

Chicken Stock

A fine clear stock can be made by following the above method, using various chicken parts—backs, necks, and wings. To make a richer, as well as a thrifty stock, however, make it a rule in your kitchen never, never to throw away the carcass and skin from a roast chicken or turkey. If not needed right away, put stock into containers and freeze. It is then ready to use for soup or in recipes that call for stock.

1 chicken or turkey carcass
1 medium onion, chopped

2 stalks celery with tops
Salt and pepper to taste

Break up carcass and put into a large pot that has a tight-fitting cover. Add remaining ingredients, then enough water to cover. Put on lid, place pan over high heat, and bring to boil. Lower heat and allow to simmer 2 to 3 hours, until stock is rich and tasty. Strain; chill and remove fat. Makes about 1 quart.

Clam Chowder

Massachusetts clam chowder is famous worldwide. In its original form it was always made with diced salt pork, and most commercially prepared clam chowder has salt pork. At home, today, some homemakers use bacon instead. It is more likely to be on hand since it has many other uses. Another question is whether to add a whiff of thyme or not, and that is a matter of taste.

If you open and clean your own clams, strain the juice through cheesecloth to remove sand and possibly bits of shells. Wash the clams well and chop in a blender or food processor. Be certain to taste the clam chowder before adding salt; clams are inclined to be salty, so additional salt may not be needed.

4 slices bacon, cut up, or 4 table-
    spoons diced salt pork*
1 medium onion, chopped
1 to 2 tablespoons flour
2 cups strained clam juice
1 medium potato, peeled and diced
Pinch of dried or powdered
    thyme (optional)

1 cup milk
1 cup chopped clams
Salt and freshly ground pepper
    to taste
Pilot crackers

Slowly cook bacon or salt pork in a 1½-quart saucepan until pieces are crisp. Add onion and cook, stirring, until tender but not browned. Stir in flour, then clam juice. Add potato (and thyme if desired), bring to a boil, cover, and simmer 15 minutes or until potatoes are tender. Stir in milk and reheat (but do not boil). Add clams and again reheat, but do not boil. Taste, and if needed, add salt and pepper. Clam chowder is sometimes served with a bit of butter floating on top; but in any event, serve with pilot crackers. Makes about 1 quart.

If you use salt pork, remove the pieces from saucepan after frying and reserve. Sprinkle on top of clam chowder in bowls.

Vegetable Soup

If there is cooked meat left from making the stock, chop it finely and add to the soup.

1 medium onion, chopped
1 stalk celery, chopped
2 carrots, peeled and diced
2 tablespoons butter or margarine

2 tablespoons uncooked rice
1 cup canned tomatoes, chopped
1 quart beef stock
Salt to taste

Sauté onion, celery, and carrots in butter for 5 minutes, stirring. Add remaining ingredients and simmer, covered, 30 minutes. Makes about 6 cups.

New England Fish Chowder

Ask at the fish market for chowder fish. These are smaller pieces left from cutting up big fish and generally sell for much less money. Check for bones, however, and remove any before adding to chowder. Fish should be cooked quickly to retain its best flavor and texture.

4 slices bacon, cut up, or ¼ cup
    diced salt pork
½ cup chopped onion
½ cup chopped celery
2 cups cubed potatoes (2 to 3
    medium)
1½ cups boiling water
1 bay leaf (optional)
¼ teaspoon dried thyme

1 teaspoon salt
4 cups milk
¼ cup flour
¼ cup butter or margarine
1 pound chowder fish or
    boneless white fish fillets cut
    in 1-inch pieces
Pilot crackers

Cook the bacon or salt pork in a large saucepan with onion and celery until bacon is crisp and onion tender. Add potatoes and boiling water, bay leaf, thyme, and salt and cook, covered, until potatoes are tender, about 15 minutes. Add milk. Cream flour and butter together to make a roux and stir into chowder. Bring to a boil, stirring, and simmer 1 minute. Add fish and simmer 1 minute longer. Remove from heat and let stand covered about 10 minutes. Serve with pilot crackers. Makes 10 cups.

Fish Chowder #2

This is my version of fish chowder for those on low-calorie diets.

3 slices bacon, cut up
½ cup chopped onion
1½ cups cubed potatoes (2 medium)
2 cups boiling water
½ teaspoon salt

½ cup nonfat dry milk powder
    or granules
2 tablespoons flour
½ to ¾ pound chowder fish, cut up
Paprika

Cook bacon with onion until bacon is crisp and onion tender. Add potatoes, water, and salt and cook, covered, until potatoes are tender, about 15 minutes. Mix dry milk with flour and stir into potatoes. Bring to a boil and simmer, stirring, 1 minute. Add fish and simmer 1 minute. Remove from heat and let stand, covered, 10 minutes before serving. Serve with a sprinkling of paprika. Makes 6 cups.

**Broiled Scallops and Bacon
(recipe on page 126)**

Oyster Stew

In many homes, oyster stew was a special Christmas Eve treat when I was growing up. Its savory goodness comes to mind, however, on any cold and blustery day.

1 pint shelled fresh oysters
1/4 cup butter
Oyster liquor
3 cups milk, scalded

1 cup cream, scalded
1/2 teaspoon salt
Dash white pepper
Oyster crackers

Drain and reserve oyster liquor. Check oysters and remove any pieces of shell. Heat butter. Add oyster liquor and oysters and heat just until oysters begin to curl on the edge. Combine with hot milk, cream, salt, and pepper. Serve with oyster crackers. Makes about 5 cups or 4 servings.

Corn Chowder

New England has always been famed for its corn chowder. It can be made with canned or frozen corn, or with corn freshly cut from the cob. It is a hearty chowder, which, with a sandwich and fruit, would make a satisfactory lunch or supper.

1/4 cup diced salt pork or 4 slices
    bacon, diced
1 medium onion, chopped
4 cups diced, peeled potatoes
1 cup water
3 cups milk

2 cups corn (fresh, canned
    whole kernel, or frozen,
    thawed)
3/4 teaspoon salt
Freshly ground pepper to taste
2 tablespoons chopped fresh parsley

Fry salt pork or bacon about 2 minutes. Add onion and continue to fry until onion is soft but not browned. Add potatoes and water and simmer, covered, about 20 minutes, or until potatoes are tender. Add milk, corn, salt, and pepper and continue cooking over low heat for 10 minutes. Serve sprinkled with fresh parsley. Makes 6 servings.

Lamb Barley Soup

Lamb barley soup can be the centerpiece for a luncheon or supper meal. Add lots of bread and butter, milk to drink, and fruit for dessert.

1½ pounds breast of lamb
1 quart water
1 teaspoon salt
6 peppercorns
1 small onion
1 stalk celery
¼ cup regular barley

½ cup chopped onion
½ cup chopped celery
½ cup chopped carrots
1 cup stewed tomatoes
¼ cup chopped fresh parsley
Salt to taste

Combine lamb breast in a saucepan with water, salt, peppercorns, 1 small onion, and 1 stalk celery. Bring to a boil and simmer, covered, for about 2 hours. Do this the day before making the soup. Strain broth and refrigerate lamb breast and broth separately.

To make soup, remove fat from broth. Measure broth and add water if necessary to make 4 cups. Cook broth and barley together, covered, for 1 hour. Meanwhile, remove lamb meat from bones and dice. Add with all remaining ingredients to lamb broth and barley and cook, covered, another 30 minutes. Makes 6 to 7 cups.

Lentil Soup

Lentil soup is really heartwarming. Serve it with pita-bread sandwiches and hot tea.

3 tablespoons butter
¾ cup chopped onion
1 medium carrot, peeled and
    chopped
½ pound (1 cup) dried lentils,
    washed

4 cups beef stock, or 3 beef bouillon
    cubes dissolved in 4 cups water
½ teaspoon salt
Freshly ground pepper to taste
½ teaspoon ground cumin
1 tablespoon lemon juice

Heat butter in a 6-cup saucepan and sauté onion and carrot until tender but not browned. Add lentils, beef stock, salt, pepper, and cumin. Bring to a boil, cover, and simmer over low heat until lentils are tender, about 1 hour. If desired, puree soup in a blender or processor. Add lemon juice. Reheat to serve. Makes 1½ quarts.

Split Pea Soup

Whenever I buy a smoked pork shoulder, I ask the meat man to cut off the hock end, which I save for soup. It makes wonderful split pea or bean soup. A good homemade soup is always better if you follow this two-day process.

1 smoked pork hock	1 medium onion, chopped
6 cups water	¼ teaspoon ground thyme
1 cup dried green split peas	Salt and freshly ground pepper
1 carrot, peeled and diced	to taste
1 stalk celery, diced	

The day before you plan to make the soup, cover the pork hock with the water and simmer several hours until tender. (If you wish, put an onion, a stalk of celery, a few peppercorns, and a piece of bay leaf in with the pork hock.) Drain liquid into a container and refrigerate overnight so that the fat can be taken off. Cool the pork hock enough to handle. Remove skin and fat and cut any meat on bone into fine dice and refrigerate to add to soup.

Next day, skim fat from the broth and strain it. Sort and wash split peas and combine with broth, carrot, celery, onion, and seasonings. Bring to a boil and simmer, covered, about 1 hour or until split peas are tender. Add diced ham to soup. This makes about 1½ quarts of soup. Can be stored for several days in the refrigerator.

This soup freezes well, so if the quantity is too large, freeze a container for future use.

Variation

Bean Soup: Omit split peas. Sort and soak 1 cup dried pea beans in water overnight. Cook in broth for about an hour before adding vegetables; then proceed as directed.

Black Bean Soup

This makes a particularly good soup with which to start a meal. This recipe can be halved and it freezes well.

1 pound dried black beans	1 beef bouillon cube
Water to soak	2 tablespoons lime juice
½ cup chopped onion	2 bay leaves
½ cup chopped green pepper	¼ cup dry sherry
2 tablespoons butter or margarine	Salt and freshly ground pepper
1 ham hock (about 1 pound)	to taste
7 cups water	1 hard-cooked egg

Wash and sort beans, cover with double their volume of water, and soak overnight.

Next day, drain beans. Sauté onion and green pepper lightly in butter. Add to beans with ham hock, 7 cups water, bouillon cube, lime juice, and bay leaves. Bring to a boil and simmer, covered, about 1½ hours or until beans are tender. Remove ham hock and bay leaves and let soup cool slightly. (Use any meat on ham hock for sandwiches or other use; discard bay leaves.) Puree soup in small quantities until smooth. When all soup is pureed, taste for seasoning, reheat, and add sherry. Chop hard-cooked egg fine and use as a garnish. Makes about 2 quarts.

Herbed Beef Soup

When there is a bargain in ground beef or some in the freezer you wish to use up, herbed hamburger soup is one delicious answer. It is hearty for lunch or supper.

½ to ¾ pound ground beef	1 can (1 pound) stewed tomatoes
1 large onion, chopped	2 tomato cans water
2 or 3 stalks celery	½ teaspoon each dried basil,
2 large peeled carrots	oregano, and thyme; or 1½
1 potato, peeled	teaspoons Italian seasoning
Several sprigs fresh parsley	1 teaspoon salt

In a 2½-quart saucepan, fry crumbled ground beef until lightly browned. Pour off accumulated fat.

In a food processor or grinder, process onion, celery, carrots, potato, and parsley until chopped fine (or chop fine by hand). Also chop up any large pieces of tomato. Add vegetables to ground beef along with water, herbs, and salt. Bring to a boil and simmer, covered, for about 2 hours. This makes 8 cups of thick soup. It freezes very well.

Onion Soup

One of the real treats of the soup world is onion soup. As a starter you need a strong, well-flavored beef stock and plenty of onions. If you haven't time or the ingredients to prepare a homemade beef stock, buy canned condensed beef bouillon and dilute it only half strength. For onions, use either sweet Spanish onions or the red Italian.

The classic service for onion soup is in a 1-cup earthenware casserole dish that can go into the oven. The absence of such service wouldn't stop me from making onion soup, though.

2 tablespoons butter or olive oil	1 long thin loaf French bread
2 cups sweet onion slices	6 to 8 tablespoons grated Parmesan
2½ cups beef stock	cheese
½ teaspoon sugar	

Heat butter or oil in a heavy 6-cup saucepan. Add onions which have been cut on the bias so they are not full rings. Cook and stir until onions are limp but not browned. Add beef broth and sugar. Bring to a boil and simmer, covered, about 10 minutes.

Meantime, cut French bread in about 1-inch-thick slices and toast on both sides in a broiler.

To serve, put a ladle of soup in dish, add a piece of toasted bread and sprinkle liberally with cheese. Fill the dish with soup and put in another piece of toast and pile on the cheese. Either bake at 375°F for about 15 minutes or run under the broiler until cheese is melted. Serve with remaining bread and additional Parmesan cheese. Makes 1 quart soup.

Baked Bean Soup

This recipe, found in an old Cape Cod cookbook, makes use of leftover Boston baked beans. It is a good soup for a cold night. Hot dogs on buns and coleslaw would go well with it.

2 cups Boston baked beans	1 teaspoon prepared mustard
1 stalk celery cut in 1-inch pieces	3 tablespoons water
½ small onion	2 beef bouillon cubes
4 cups water	Salt and freshly ground pepper
1 cup canned tomatoes	to taste
1 tablespoon flour	

Combine beans, celery, onion, 4 cups water, and tomatoes in a 2½-quart saucepan. Cover and simmer 30 minutes. Put through a food mill or puree in a processor or blender. Mix together flour, mustard, and 3 tablespoons water and stir into bean mixture. Add bouillon cubes and reheat, stirring, until bouillon cubes are dissolved and mixture boils. Taste and add salt and pepper as needed. Makes 5½ cups.

Chilled Zucchini Soup

A summer treat when zucchini is plentiful. Serve with cold chicken sandwiches made on whole wheat bread and radishes.

2 large zucchini
1 medium onion
½ green pepper
1½ cups chicken broth
¼ teaspoon dried basil or ¾
    teaspoon fresh basil

¼ teaspoon dried rosemary or ¾
    teaspoon fresh rosemary
1½ cups milk
½ teaspoon salt
Freshly ground pepper to taste
Lime wedges

Scrub and cut off stem end of zucchini. Slice zucchini, onion, and green pepper. Cook in chicken broth until tender. Cool slightly and puree in processor or blender. Add herbs, milk, and salt and pepper; chill. Serve with a wedge of lime. Makes 4½ cups.

Gazpacho

A great concoction to keep on hand in the refrigerator. Makes a fine light lunch, a satisfying afternoon snack, or a delicious first course on a hot summer night.

4 slices firm bread, torn into pieces
4 large ripe tomatoes, peeled, cored,
    and chopped
2 cucumbers, peeled and chopped
1 green pepper, seeded and chopped
1 onion, peeled and chopped

1 cup water
¼ cup olive oil
Juice of 1 lemon
2 cloves garlic, minced
Fresh parsley, chopped

In a large bowl, combine bread, 3 of the tomatoes, 1 cucumber, and half the green pepper and onion. Stir in water and oil; cover and refrigerate for an hour.

Blend half the mixture at high speed for 6 to 8 seconds; repeat with the remaining half. Stir in lemon juice and garlic. Taste, adding salt and pepper as needed. Cover and refrigerate 2 to 3 hours. Place remaining chopped vegetables and parsley in small bowls and serve as accompaniments, to be sprinkled onto each serving. Makes 1½ to 2 quarts.

Homemade Tomato Soup

Until you make homemade tomato soup, you've forgotten how good it tastes. Serve it with a grilled cheese sandwich and a tossed salad.

5 tablespoons chopped onion
2 tablespoons butter or margarine
3 tablespoons ground oat flour*
¼ teaspoon salt
2¼ cups milk

1 can (16 ounces) whole
   tomatoes, undrained
1 can (15 ounces) tomato puree
1 teaspoon sugar
1 bay leaf

Sauté onion in butter in a 3½-quart Dutch oven or saucepan until tender. Blend in oat flour and salt. Remove from heat. Gradually stir in milk, tomatoes, and puree. Add sugar and bay leaf. Break up tomatoes with a wooden spoon. Cook over medium heat, stirring occasionally, until thickened. Remove bay leaf to serve. Makes 6 cups. If soup becomes too thick on standing, add additional milk.

About 5 tablespoons uncooked oatmeal ground in the blender for about 1 minute should make 3 tablespoons oat flour for the soup. If you make a larger amount of oat flour, store unused portion in a tightly covered container in a cool place up to 6 months.

Vichyssoise

Vichyssoise is the French name for cold potato soup. There are richer versions made with heavy cream, but this recipe is delicious without being too caloric.

4 leeks
1 small onion, chopped
¼ cup butter or margarine
3 or 4 potatoes

3 cups chicken broth
¾ cup half-and-half
Salt and white pepper to taste
Snipped chives

Clean leeks carefully of sand. Use only the white part and cut crosswise into thin slices. Sauté leeks and onion in butter in a 2-quart saucepan until tender but not browned. Peel potatoes and cut into thin slices. (There should be 2 cups or more.) Add potatoes and chicken broth to leeks and onions in saucepan and cook, covered, until potatoes are very tender, about 30 minutes. Cool slightly and puree in processor or blender until smooth. Add cream and salt and pepper to taste. Chill. Serve very cold in soup cups garnished with snipped chives. Makes about 1¼ quarts.

Cold Cucumber Soup

Crisp, fresh summer cucumbers make this no-cook soup extra special.

2 or 3 medium cucumbers
2 cups plain yogurt

½ teaspoon salt (or to taste)
Fresh mint sprigs

Cut ends from cucumbers; discard. Cut six thin cucumber slices; reserve. Cut remaining cucumber into chunks and put half into blender with ¼ cup yogurt. Cover and blend until smooth. Repeat with remaining cucumber, then return first half to blender with salt and remaining yogurt. Blend on low speed until smooth. Cover and refrigerate 1 hour or longer. Garnish with reserved cucumber slices and mint sprigs. Makes about 1 quart.

Mushroom Soup

Using light cream will give a richer, creamier soup. Milk lowers the calorie count and still produces a fine-tasting soup.

½ pound mushrooms
2 shallots, finely minced
4 tablespoons butter or margarine

¼ cup flour
2 cups chicken stock
1 cup light cream or milk

Trim and discard ends of mushroom stems. Chop remaining stems fine; slice mushrooms, cutting slices in half if mushrooms are large. Melt butter or margarine in heavy saucepan; add mushrooms and shallots, stirring continually with wooden spoon for 4 or 5 minutes. (One tablespoon of finely minced onion may be substituted for the shallots.) Sprinkle flour into pan; stir quickly to dissolve flour in mushroom juices. Stir in chicken stock and allow to come to low boil, stirring constantly. When thickened, stir in cream or milk, mixing thoroughly. Do not allow to boil after adding cream or milk. If soup seems too thick, add a little more stock or milk. Taste, and if needed, add a bit of salt or pepper. Makes about 1 quart.

Sauces

Numbers refer to pages where recipes appear in this book.

Sauces

Today sauces do not take such a prominent part in our cooking, since many are high in calories and difficult to prepare. According to hearsay, sauces reached such a high accord in classic cookery because they were used to enhance the slightly gamy flavor of meat, fish, and fowl that was necessarily stored without refrigeration.

But I've included a few easy-to-prepare sauces that you might like to have in your cooking repertoire.

Mustard Sauce For Fish

When you are broiling or pan frying fish with no additions, serve this mustard sauce on the side. It is particularly good with mackerel and bluefish.

1 tablespoon prepared brown mustard   1/4 cup butter or margarine, melted

Mix mustard with a small amount of melted butter. Gradually add remaining butter and heat. Makes 1/3 cup.

Make Your Own Mustard

If you love hot mustard, make your own from dry mustard. Either this or English style mustard, below, is good with Chinese dishes.

6 tablespoons dry mustard   3 tablespoons water, white
                                        wine, or stale beer

Blend mustard with liquid to make a paste. If you like a little thinner mustard, add more of the chosen liquid. Makes about 1/3 cup.

English Style Mustard

1/2 cup dry mustard   2 tablespoon cider vinegar
1/4 teaspoon salt   1 teaspoon oil
1/2 teaspoon sugar   1/2 teaspoon horseradish
1 tablespoon hot water

Mix mustard, salt, and sugar. Add hot water and blend in remaining ingredients. Chill. Store, covered, in refrigerator. Makes 1/3 cup.

Hollandaise Sauce

Used for green vegetables such as asparagus or broccoli, this sauce is also one of the ingredients in eggs Benedict (page 89). A blender or a food processor makes this adaptation of the classic hollandaise sauce easy to prepare. Use the variations suggested below for compatible meat dishes.

3 egg yolks
2 tablespoons fresh lemon juice
¼ teaspoon salt

Dash white pepper
½ cup butter, softened
½ cup boiling water

Put egg yolks, lemon juice, salt, pepper, and butter in blender or processor. Whirl or process to mix. Keep machine running and slowly add boiling water until blended. Remove to a small bowl or pan and cook over hot water, stirring constantly, until thick and custardlike. Makes 1½ cups.

Variations

Mint: Add 1 tablespoon chopped fresh mint or 1 teaspoon crushed dried mint.

Chive: Add 2 tablespoons finely chopped chives.

Dill: Add 2 teaspoons chopped fresh dillweed or 1 teaspoon crushed dried dillweed.

Béarnaise Sauce

Béarnaise sauce is one of the components of Chateaubriand steak. This recipe is an adaptation of the classic French béarnaise. It is a variation of hollandaise, so if you master one, it is easy to make the other. Béarnaise is good with roast beef, lamb, or veal, too.

3 egg yolks
1 tablespoon fresh lemon juice
1 tablespoon tarragon vinegar
½ teaspoon onion salt
Dash freshly ground pepper
½ cup butter, softened

½ cup boiling water
3 teaspoons chopped fresh
  tarragon or 1 teaspoon
  crushed dried tarragon
2 teaspoons chopped fresh parsley

Put egg yolks, lemon juice, vinegar, onion salt, pepper, and butter in blender or processor. Whirl or process to mix. Keep machine running and slowly add boiling water until blended.

Remove to a small bowl or pan and cook over hot water, stirring constantly, until thick and custardlike. Stir in tarragon and parsley. Makes 1½ cups.

Green Sauce

Serve well chilled with cold shellfish or meat.

1 cup mayonnaise
¼ cup chopped fresh parsley
½ cup finely chopped chives

½ cup finely chopped watercress
1 tablespoon grated onion
1 tablespoon tarragon vinegar

Mix mayonnaise lightly with all remaining ingredients. Store, covered, in the refrigerator. Makes about 2 cups. Will keep for about 2 weeks in refrigerator.

Polly's Savory Apple Jelly Sauce

A delicious spicy sauce to serve with ham, lamb, or roast duck or goose.

½ teaspoon dry mustard
¼ teaspoon ground cloves
½ teaspoon cinnamon

2 tablespoons vinegar
1 jar (8 ounces) apple or crabapple jelly

In a small saucepan mix spices and vinegar. Blend in jelly and cook over low heat until jelly is melted and flavors blended, stirring constantly. Makes about 1 cup.

Horseradish Cream Sauce

A natural to serve with ham, pork, or cold roast beef.

½ cup dairy sour cream
4 tablespoons drained horseradish

1 teaspoon lemon juice

Combine sour cream with horseradish and lemon juice. Mix lightly and store, covered, in refrigerator. Makes ¾ cup.

Fresh Mint Sauce

The best sauce for roast lamb, as taught to me in my mother's kitchen. In those days, getting the mint leaves fine enough to suit her was a chore. Now, the food processor does it in no time.

4 cups fresh mint leaves, packed ½ cup (about) white vinegar
½ cup sugar

Put half the mint leaves into the food processor fitted with the metal blade. Process until very fine; put into a bowl. Repeat with remaining mint. With large spoon, press sugar into the leaves so that juice from mint will melt sugar. When all sugar is incorporated, add enough vinegar to give sauce a spoonable consistency. Here is where your own taste must be used—if the sauce seems too vinegary to you, add a little more sugar and some water. This sauce will keep indefinitely in the refrigerator. Makes about 2 cups.

Fresh Tomato Sauce

When there are plenty of good locally grown tomatoes available, make this light and tasty sauce, which can be served with many dishes.

2 pounds ripe fresh tomatoes 1 clove garlic, chopped
3 tablespoons butter or margarine ½ teaspoon salt
½ cup finely chopped onion Freshly ground pepper to taste
½ cup chopped green pepper
1½ tablespoons finely chopped
    shallots or green onions

Remove core from tomatoes and cut remaining tomatoes into cubes. Heat butter and sauté onion, pepper, shallots, and garlic until onion is soft. Add tomatoes, salt, and pepper and continue cooking about 10 minutes.

Puree in blender or food processor until smooth. Push through sieve with wooden spoon to remove seeds. Reheat to serve. Makes about 2 cups. This sauce could be served on fish, pasta, over poached eggs, or with shellfish.

Orange Raisin Sauce

This tangy sauce is good with baked ham, roast duck, or goose.

1 cup seedless raisins
1 cup orange juice
½ cup water
6 tablespoons brown sugar

1 tablespoon cornstarch
1½ tablespoons grated orange rind
¼ teaspoon salt
1 tablespoon cider vinegar

Combine raisins, orange juice, and water in a 1-quart saucepan. Cover and simmer 10 minutes. Mix brown sugar, cornstarch, orange rind, and salt. Stir into raisin mixture and cook and stir until thickened and clear. Mix in vinegar. Serve hot. Makes about 1½ cups.

Yogurt Cucumber Sauce

Serve with cold lamb or roast beef or as a garnish for chilled soups or sliced tomatoes.

1 cup seeded and finely
    chopped cucumbers
2 cups plain yogurt
1 clove garlic, finely chopped
    (optional)

¾ tablespoon chopped fresh dill-
    weed or ½ teaspoon crushed
    dried dillweed
Salt and freshly ground pepper
    to taste

Mix cucumber with yogurt, garlic, dill, and salt and pepper. Store, covered, in refrigerator for several hours before using. Makes about 3 cups. Will keep several weeks under refrigeration.

Creamy Mustard Sauce

Serve this sauce hot with fish, ham, or beef. It is also fine with broccoli or cauliflower.

3 tablespoons margarine
2 tablespoons all-purpose flour
1 teaspoon dry mustard
Salt and pepper to taste

1 egg yolk
1 cup milk
1 tablespoon lemon juice

In a heavy saucepan, melt butter; then stir in flour, mustard, salt, and pepper. Cook, stirring constantly, for a minute or so. Remove from heat. In a small bowl, beat egg yolk; then add milk and mix well. Stir into the first mixture, return to heat, and cook about 3 minutes, until smooth and thickened. Remove from heat and stir in lemon juice, mixing well. Makes about 1¼ cups.

Quick Vegetable Sauce

This is almost too easy to be so good. Spoon it over crisp-cooked broccoli, green beans, cauliflower, and such.

½ cup sour cream
½ cup mayonnaise

Grated Parmesan cheese

Combine sour cream and mayonnaise, mixing well. Put cooked vegetable into shallow baking dish; spoon sauce over top and sprinkle lightly with the cheese. Put under broiler just long enough to brown top lightly, 3 or 4 minutes. Makes about 1 cup.

Seafood

Numbers refer to pages where recipes appear in this book.

Shellfish

Finfish

Shellfish

In our area, the most popular shellfish are lobster, clams, oysters, bay and sea scallops, shrimp, and mussels. Crabs and conch are sometimes available, particularly the crabs that are found in the lobster traps.

Shellfish, like finfish, are fragile and must be bought and stored with great care. Lobsters should be alive and wiggling when purchased, clams and mussels tightly closed. Always purchase shellfish at a reliable source. If you are purchasing any kind of finfish or shellfish that cannot be gotten to your refrigerator within a reasonable time, say an hour, bring along a simple ice chest with ice in it to protect the fish en route.

Easy Souffled Clams

This recipe is easy to prepare and very good for lunch or a light supper. Serve with a green vegetable and a simple lettuce-and-tomato salad.

2 cups soft whole wheat bread
    crumbs (about 3 slices)
2 cups chopped fresh clams

2 tablespoons grated onion
1/2 cup melted butter or margarine
1 cup clam juice

Put 1/3 of the bread crumbs in the bottom of a well-buttered 1-quart casserole. Mix clams with onion and spoon in 1/2 clams. Repeat layers, ending with crumbs. Pour over melted butter and clam juice. Bake at 375°F for 45 minutes. Makes 4 servings.

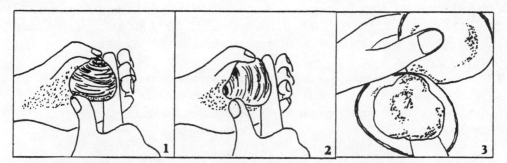

Scrub clam shells to remove mud and dirt. Place clams in the freezer for an hour to relax the muscle that holds the two shells closed. Hold the clam firmly in one hand. Insert the side of the blade of a clam knife next to the hinge. Turning the clam, work the knife around the shell to the opposite side of the hinge. Pry open the shell, scrape the meat from the top shell, and slip the knife underneath the meat to release it from the bottom shell.

Clam Pie

Had I not read a clam pie recipe in a national magazine in which the clams were (1) steamed 8 to 10 minutes to open them; (2) cooked by themselves for 15 minutes; (3) cooked 15 minutes more with vegetables (carrots and potatoes); and finally (4) baked 35 to 40 minutes at 425°F, this recipe might not have appeared. Those poor clams. Okay, so here is mine.

Pastry for a 2-crust 9-inch pie	½ cup evaporated milk
3 cups ground raw quahog or	¼ teaspoon freshly ground
sea clams	pepper
½ cup finely chopped onion	¼ teaspoon dried thyme
1 cup fine cracker crumbs	

Line a 9-inch pie plate with pastry. Mix clams, onion, cracker crumbs, evaporated milk, and seasonings. Spoon into pie shell. Cover with pastry and seal edges. Cut several slits in top.

Bake at 425°F for about 50 minutes or until nicely browned. Serve hot or cold. Makes one 9-inch pie.

Baked Stuffed Lobster

Perhaps because the first time I ate lobster on Cape Cod it was a baked stuffed lobster, it is still my favorite way to prepare it at home. This recipe was given to me years ago by a friend who is a native of Massachusetts. I have made it many times with no failures—and that is important since lobster has become a special-occasion luxury. This recipe is for two lobsters. It is easily multiplied for four, but the number is qualified by how many you can get into your oven. Eight is my limit.

2 lobsters, 1½ pounds each	2 teaspoons Worcestershire sauce
30 round crackers, finely	Lobster liver or tomalley
crushed (1 cup of cracker crumbs)	Additional melted butter
¼ cup butter, melted	Lemon wedges

Ask at the fish market to have lobsters split and cleaned. ("Cleaned" means only that they will take out the stomach, which is near the front feelers.) The liver, a grayish green, goes into the stuffing. Wash the lobsters and place, cut side up, in a baking pan.

Mix crumbs, butter, Worcestershire sauce, and lobster liver until well blended. Divide between body shells. Bake at 400°F for 25 minutes. Serve with additional melted butter and lemon wedges. Makes 2 servings.

Boiled Lobsters

When boiling lobster, it is okay to leave the little wooden pegs in the claws, and if the fish market has used rubber bands to keep the lobster from pinching, leave them on, too. Remove both before serving the lobster.

For each 1½-pound lobster use about 3 quarts water and about 2 tablespoons salt. Many people living near the shore swear by ocean water for boiling lobster.

Bring the water to a boil, catch the lobster from behind the head, and plunge it into the water. Cover and let simmer about 8 minutes. Remove from water and place lobster on its back on a cutting surface. Use a large heavy knife and a mallet and split the lobster from end to end. Remove the stomach (which is at the claw end) and the intestinal vein. Do not discard either the liver (or tomalley) or, if the lobster is female, the roe, called coral because of its color. They are delicious. If desired, the coral can be saved for later use. It freezes well.

Serve the lobster with plenty of melted butter and lemon wedges. Accessories are small forks for picking the lobster out of small crevices, nutcrackers for cracking the claws, and lightly dampened guest towels for sticky fingers.

A "bone" plate, platter, or any suitable large container that everyone can reach is good for parking the shells.

Boiled lobster meat can be chilled to use for any number of lobster dishes as well.

Steamed Lobster

Some prefer to steam rather than boil lobster, so we include the directions for steaming.

Put 2 to 3 inches of water in a pot large enough to hold the lobsters. Bring the water to a boil, put in lobsters, cover, reduce heat and steam as follows:

1 pound	18 minutes
1¼ pound	20 minutes
1½ pounds	25 minutes
2 to 3 pounds	30 minutes

Broiled Scallops and Bacon

(pictured between pages 104 and 105)

New Bedford fishermen bring in sea scallops from George's Bank. When they are plentiful, dip in lemon juice and freeze.

1 pound sea scallops, fresh or
    frozen and thawed
¼ cup honey
¼ cup soy sauce

¼ cup lemon juice
8 slices bacon
4 cherry tomatoes

Remove any shell pieces from scallops. Rinse and drain. Mix honey, soy sauce, and lemon juice and marinate scallops in mixture for several hours in the refrigerator. Drain off sauce and reserve. Meanwhile, cook bacon slices over moderate heat about 4 minutes. Remove from fat.

Put scallops and bacon on 4 skewers, stringing bacon around and between scallops. Top each skewer with cherry tomato. Grill about 3 inches from heat for 5 to 7 minutes, basting with sauce and turning to brown all sides. Makes 4 servings.

Scallop Salad Plate

Cold scallops are very good and when marinated in an oil-and-vinegar sauce, they are delicious. If you like, add deviled eggs to this cold plate. Serve with breadsticks.

1 pound sea scallops
2 cups dry white wine
2 sprigs parsley
1 small onion, sliced
2 sprigs fresh thyme or ½
    teaspoon dried thyme
½ cup oil

2 tablespoons lemon juice
½ teaspoon salt
Freshly ground pepper to taste
Crisp lettuce
Sliced cucumbers
Sliced fresh tomatoes
Mayonnaise

Cut sea scallops into 3 or 4 pieces; wash and drain. Combine wine with parsley, onion, and thyme in a skillet. Bring to a boil, cover, and simmer 10 minutes. Add scallops and simmer 3 to 5 minutes. Let cool in liquid. When cooled, drain and mix with oil, lemon juice, salt, and pepper. Chill in refrigerator for several hours.

Drain and arrange on crisp lettuce. Garnish with sliced cucumbers and tomatoes and serve with a bowl of mayonnaise for those who wish it. Makes 4 servings.

Scallops with Linguine

With a tossed green salad, crisp hot bread, and cheese and crackers, a good meal.

1 pound cape or sea scallops
¼ cup butter or margarine
1 clove garlic, minced
½ teaspoon salt
Freshly ground pepper to taste

1 tablespoon chopped fresh
    basil or 1 teaspoon dried basil
½ cup chopped fresh parsley
1 pound cooked linguine

If sea scallops are used, cut each in 4 pieces. Wash scallops and dry. Heat butter in skillet and add garlic and salt. Cook until garlic is lightly browned. Add scallops, pepper, basil, and parsley and cook, stirring, about 5 minutes. Serve with hot cooked linguine. Makes 4 servings.

Steamed Mussels

Mussels have gained new popularity. They are a product of our East Coast waters and as tasty as steamers according to some. Serve with lots of Italian or French bread.

2 quarts mussels
¼ cup dry white wine
2 sprigs fresh thyme or ½
    teaspoon dried thyme

2 sprigs parsley
Melted butter or margarine
Lemon wedges

Scrub mussels well with a stiff brush to remove the pieces of eel grass and seaweed that might be attached to them, as well as their own fibrous "beards." Discard any that feel heavy as they are probably filled with dirt. Rinse well.

Put wine, thyme, and parsley in a large saucepan. Add mussels and cover. Bring to a boil and cook 2 to 3 minutes or until mussels are opened. Discard any that do not open.

Serve mussels and broth in flat bowls with melted butter and lemon wedges. Makes 4 servings.

Curried Shrimp

This shrimp is actually better if prepared in advance, refrigerated, and reheated at serving time. Serve chopped peanuts, toasted coconut, chutney, mandarin oranges, and chopped green onions in small bowls. Everyone helps themselves to whatever accompaniment they wish.

1 pound raw shrimp in shell
4 tablespoons butter or margarine
1 clove garlic, finely chopped
1 medium apple, cored, peeled, and diced
2½ tablespoons flour
1 tablespoon curry powder
½ teaspoon chopped fresh gingerroot
¼ teaspoon sugar
1⅔ cups chicken broth
Salt and freshly ground pepper to taste
2 to 3 cups hot cooked rice

Peel, devein, and wash shrimp. Drain well.

Heat butter in a 1½-quart saucepan and slowly sauté garlic, onion, and apple until tender but not browned, about 10 minutes. Stir in flour, curry powder, gingerroot, and sugar and cook for 1 minute.

Slowly stir in chicken broth and continue stirring until mixture boils and is thickened. Taste and add salt and pepper as needed.

Add shrimp and cook 3 to 5 minutes. Serve over hot cooked rice. Makes 4 servings.

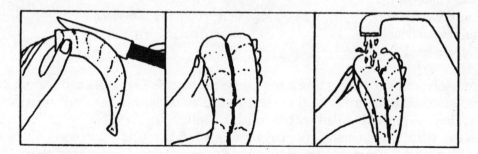

Peel off soft shell of shrimp. Using a sharp paring knife make a shallow cut down the back of the shrimp, exposing the black vein. Hold shrimp under running water to wash the vein away. You may need to use the tip of your knife to scrape the vein away.

Shrimp and Mushrooms

Steamed snow peas would go well with the shrimp and mushrooms. Serve a sherbet for dessert.

1 pound raw shrimp in shell	¼ cup dry sherry
¾ pound fresh mushrooms	½ teaspoon salt
4 green onions	Freshly ground pepper to taste
4 tablespoons butter	1 cup plain yogurt
1 tablespoon oil	2 cups hot cooked rice
¼ cup chopped fresh parsley	

Peel, devein, and wash shrimp. Drain well. Brush mushrooms, if necessary, and cut off stem ends. Slice onions.

Heat butter and oil in a 10-inch skillet and cook onions for several minutes. Add mushrooms and cook and stir about 10 minutes over moderate heat. Add parsley, sherry, salt, and pepper and bring to a boil. Stir in shrimp and cook a few minutes longer until shrimp turn pink. Add plain yogurt and heat, but do not boil. Serve with hot cooked rice. Makes 4 servings.

Scalloped Oysters

Scalloped oysters make a lovely winter supper dish. Serve with noodles, broccoli, and a grape-and-apple salad.

1 pint fresh oysters	Freshly ground nutmeg to taste
½ cup butter or margarine	2 cups soft bread crumbs
1 teaspoon grated onion (optional)	¼ cup oyster liquor
Freshly ground pepper to taste	¼ cup cream

Drain oysters, saving liquor. Take out any shell pieces that might be present.

Melt butter in a saucepan; add onion, pepper, and nutmeg and mix well. Stir in the bread crumbs.

Put half of crumb mixture in a buttered 1-quart flat baking dish. Spread oysters on crumbs and top with remaining crumbs. Mix oyster liquor and cream and pour over all. Bake at 375°F for 30 to 35 minutes. Makes 2 to 4 servings, depending on appetites.

Pan Fried Oysters

If you wish to stretch the pan fried oysters, serve with soft scrambled eggs, toasted English muffins, and lots of coffee, for a brunch or breakfast meal.

1 pint fresh oysters	½ cup vegetable oil
1 large egg	Salt
2 tablespoons light cream	Freshly ground pepper
¾ to 1 cup freshly rolled saltine cracker crumbs	Lemon wedges

Drain oysters and remove any shell. Beat egg lightly with cream. Dip oysters in egg, then in cracker crumbs. Let air dry on waxed paper about 10 minutes.

Heat oil in a large skillet. When hot, add oysters and cook quickly until nicely browned. Sprinkle with salt and pepper and serve with lemon wedges. Makes 2 to 4 servings, depending on appetites.

Finfish

When buying fish remember that fresh fish has no odor. The amount to buy per person depends on the amount of bones and other waste matter in the fish. This guide may help.

Whole	¾ pound
Dressed or pan dressed	½ pound
Fillets or steaks	⅓ pound
Portions	⅓ pound
Canned	⅙ pound

Fish may be purchased fresh, frozen, or canned. **Fresh fish** should have firm flesh, not separating from the bone. Eyes should be bright and clear on a whole fish.

Frozen fish should be adequately wrapped and have been held at 0°F or below while in storage. It should have no odor.

Canned fish includes tuna, salmon, mackerel, and sardines. Tuna comes in "fancy" or solid form, the most expensive, and used where appearance is important, such as on a cold fish plate; chunk, smaller pieces ideal for salads or casseroles; and flaked or grated, great for sandwiches or canapes. Salmon is canned by species. The differences are in color, texture, and flavor. In order of price, the grades are red or sockeye; Chinook or king salmon; medium red, coho, or silver salmon; pink salmon; chum or keta salmon. Mackerel and sardines are each one species.

The basic ways to cook fresh or frozen fish are to bake, broil, pan fry, poach, or steam. I recommend that frozen fish always be thawed before cooking. Let the frozen fish stand in the refrigerator overnight or for 4 to 5 hours, depending on thickness of fish. Thawing can be hastened under cold, running water.

The sign of doneness of fish is when it flakes easily with a fork. Try separating the flesh of raw fish into flakes; it is impossible. But when the fish is cooked, the flesh separates easily; and regardless of the method of cooking, this test will always be true. The cardinal sin for fish cookery is overcooking.

These facts may help you if you are new to purchasing and cooking fish:

Fillets of sole or flounder are interchangeable in recipes. Cod, haddock, pollock, ocean catfish, and hake are interchangeable in recipes. Schrod (or scrod) is young cod or haddock. Bluefish and mackerel can be substituted for each other. When you go into the fish market and see "whitefish" on sale, ask the fish man what kind of fish it is. There is no fish called whitefish, except a small freshwater fish, so varieties of less-known fish are sold as whitefish. Often, for example, it is ocean catfish, which is one of my very favorite fish. So then I buy extra and freeze it.

Broiled Fish

Fish cooks so quickly that you should have all the rest of the meal ready before the fish goes in the broiler to cook.

1½ to 2 pounds fillets of cod, haddock, bluefish, mackerel, or flounder

3 to 4 tablespoons lemon juice
2 to 3 tablespoons butter, softened or melted
½ cup plain or seasoned dry bread crumbs

Place fillets, skin side down, on greased broiler pan. Dribble lemon juice generously over fish; spread with softened or melted butter. Sprinkle with bread crumbs. Broil 8 minutes or until fish flakes. Makes 4 servings.

Variation

Omit butter and crumbs. Broil fish for 4 minutes. Spread with ½ cup mayonnaise and broil 4 minutes longer.

Pan Fried Fish

Pan frying fish is still one of the most popular methods of cooking fish. The simplest method is to dredge the fish in seasoned flour, shaking off any excess before putting it into hot oil. For a crisper coating, try this recipe.

1½ to 2 pounds skinless, boneless fillets of cod, haddock, pollock, ocean catfish, flounder, or hake
2 tablespoons milk
1 egg

½ teaspoon salt
1 cup dry bread or cracker crumbs or cornmeal
Oil for frying (about ¼ cup)
Lime or lemon wedges

Wash fish and cut in serving-size pieces. Beat together milk, egg, and salt. Dip fish in egg and then in crumbs. Let fish air dry 10 or 15 minutes on waxed paper. Heat oil (about ⅛ inch deep) in large skillet. Fry fish over moderate heat, turning carefully to brown both sides, about 6 to 8 minutes in all. Makes 4 servings. Serve with lime or lemon wedges.

Steamed Fish

Steamed fish can be served as is with parsley butter or used in fish casseroles or salads.

Put the fish in a steamer rack with enough water below it to create a good steam. Cover and bring to a boil and steam fish 5 to 8 minutes, depending on thickness.

Poached Fish

Poaching fish is one of the better ways to cook it, to my mind. The cooked fish can be served with lemon butter and parsley; it can be chilled to make into fish salad; a whole poached fish can be skinned, covered with mayonnaise, and decorated with sliced stuffed olives, parsley, lemon slices, radish slices, or any compatible decoration you choose and be the centerpiece of a buffet supper; or the cooked fish can be flaked and creamed.

2 cups water or dry white wine,
    or 1 cup each
½ lemon, sliced
1 small onion, thinly sliced
½ teaspoon salt

3 peppercorns
2 sprigs parsley
2 pounds fillets or steaks of cod,
    flounder, haddock, turbot, salmon,
    or other fish

Combine liquid, lemon, onion, salt, peppercorns, and parsley in a skillet large enough to hold fish in a single layer. Simmer, covered, 10 minutes. Add fish. Simmer, covered, 5 to 10 minutes, depending on thickness of fish. Remove to platter and serve in any way desired. Makes 4 servings.

Bluefish with Tomato Sauce

You might want to serve spaghetti with butter with the bluefish. Mixed green salad and Italian bread would be good, too.

Bluefish fillets for 4 (about 1½
    to 2 pounds)
2 tablespoons all-purpose flour
½ teaspoon salt
Freshly ground pepper to taste
1 egg, beaten
1 tablespoon water
½ cup seasoned dry bread
    crumbs

¼ cup oil
4 to 5 medium fresh
    mushrooms, sliced
4 whole green onions, chopped
2 ripe tomatoes, peeled and
    diced (about 1½ cups)
2 teaspoons Italian seasoning
Additional seasoned bread crumbs
3 tablespoons grated Parmesan cheese

Wash and dry fillets. Dip in flour that has been mixed with salt and pepper, then in egg beaten with water, and finally in seasoned bread crumbs. Let breaded fillets air dry about 10 minutes on waxed paper. Heat oil in a 10-inch skillet and pan fry fillets quickly to brown both sides, 4 to 5 minutes. Place in an oiled flat casserole.

    In same skillet, sauté mushrooms and green onions for about 5 minutes. Add tomatoes and Italian seasoning and cook until tomatoes are soft and sauce begins to reduce a little. Pour over fish in casserole. Measure any seasoned crumbs left from breading fish and add enough to make ⅓ cup. Sprinkle over tomato sauce. Sprinkle cheese over crumbs. Run dish under broiler and heat until cheese melts and is nicely browned. Makes 4 servings.

Baked Stuffed Striped Bass

The striped bass was here when the Pilgrims arrived and helped keep them going. It's really quite a sight to serve one whole (head and all), but even if you have the head cut off, it's still a beauty to serve.

1 dressed striped bass (about 3 pounds)	6 tablespoons butter or margarine
1 teaspoon salt	1 quart dry bread cubes
Freshly ground pepper to taste	1 egg, beaten (optional)
½ cup chopped celery	½ teaspoon dried rosemary
¼ cup chopped onion	¼ teaspoon dried thyme

Wash fish inside and out and pat dry. Sprinkle inside of fish with ½ teaspoon of the salt, and pepper. If you have a bake-and-serve platter, grease it well and place fish on that. If you do not, choose a pan long enough to hold fish, grease well, and lay a double strip of heavy-duty foil down the pan so that the ends of the foil extend up over the ends of the pan. (The foil folded in half lengthwise should be a wide enough strip.) Grease foil and place fish on that.

Sauté the celery and onion in 4 tablespoons of the butter until tender. Add the remaining salt and all the rest of the ingredients (if egg is used the stuffing is softer and clings together; without egg, it is drier) and mix well. Stuff inside of fish, but put any leftover stuffing in bottom of pan and bake with fish. Spread fish with remaining 2 tablespoons butter. Bake at 350°F for 45 to 55 minutes or until fish flakes easily with a fork. If an aluminum foil strip was used, lift fish by ends of foil and transfer to platter. Carefully remove foil from under fish. To serve, cut fish down to backbone and serve some fish and stuffing. Then turn fish and cut from other side. Makes 4 servings.

Stuffed Fillet of Flounder

Tastily stuffed flounder fillets are company fare. Serve with a green vegetable, and a lettuce-and-tomato salad, French bread, and chilled pineapple with creme de menthe for dessert.

1 small onion, finely chopped	1 tablespoon lemon juice
4 tablespoons butter or margarine	½ teaspoon salt
½ cup fresh mushrooms, chopped	2 pounds fillet of flounder
3 cups soft bread crumbs	Melted butter or margarine
3 tablespoons chopped fresh parsley	

Sauté onion in butter until tender. Add chopped mushrooms and sauté gently another 2 or 3 minutes. Mix in crumbs, parsley, lemon juice, and salt. If mixture seems too dry, add 2 or 3 tablespoons of water or white wine.

Codfish Provincetown

The combination of ingredients here makes a fine sauce with the fish. Serve rice baked in the oven with the fish, a lettuce salad, and lots of Portuguese bread.

1 pound fresh or frozen codfish
2 tablespoons softened butter or margarine
1 clove garlic, finely chopped
1 medium onion, finely chopped
1 medium tomato, peeled and chopped

½ teaspoon salt
½ teaspoon dried tarragon
Freshly ground pepper to taste
¼ cup dry white wine
½ cup bread crumbs

If frozen codfish is used, thaw. Place fish in a flat buttered casserole. Mix all remaining ingredients except crumbs, and spoon over fish. Sprinkle crumbs on top. Bake at 350°F for 30 minutes or until fish flakes easily. Makes 2 or 3 servings.

Baked Cod with Vegetables

Serve with steamed rice and a fresh fruit salad.

1 green pepper
1 medium onion
1 ripe tomato
1½ pounds cod fillets
½ teaspoon salt

Freshly ground pepper to taste
½ cup tomato juice
2 tablespoons butter or margarine
½ teaspoon paprika
1 cup plain yogurt

Remove seeds from green pepper and slice. Slice onion and tomato. Place half of vegetable slices in a well-buttered 9×9×2-inch flat casserole. Arrange cod fillets on top of vegetables and sprinkle with salt and pepper. Place remaining vegetables on top of fish, pour over tomato juice, dot with butter, and sprinkle with paprika. Bake at 350°F for 15 to 20 minutes; then cover with yogurt and continue baking until yogurt is heated through. Makes 4 servings.

Batter Fried Fish

Use any white fish fillets except flounder or sole, which are too delicate for batter frying.

³/₄ cup all-purpose flour
½ cup flat beer or lemon-lime
    carbonated beverage
2 teaspoons oil
1 egg, separated

1 pound boneless fish fillets
    (cod, haddock, ocean catfish, hake)
Oil for frying
Lemon wedges

Mix flour, liquid, and oil. Let stand in refrigerator for several hours. Beat egg yolk and white separately and fold first yolk, then white, into flour mixture.

Cut fish fillets into serving pieces and dip in batter. Fry in about 2 inches oil heated to 375°F in an electric skillet or heavy skillet. Turn to brown both sides. Total frying time is about 5 minutes. Drain on paper towels. Serve at once with lemon wedges. Makes 4 servings.

Quick 'n' Easy Fried Fish

If you like to fry fish this way, strain and save oil in a separate container, covered, in the refrigerator. By adding a little new oil each time, it can be reused several times before discarding. (Use cod, haddock, ocean catfish, or hake)

1½ to 2 pounds fish fillets about
    ³/₄ inch thick
Water
½ teaspoon salt

Lemon pepper
1½ cups (about) dry pancake mix
Oil for frying
Tartar sauce (recipe below)

Tartar Sauce

1 cup mayonnaise
¼ cup drained pickle relish

1 tablespoon lemon juice

Cut fish into serving-size pieces. Dip in cool water. Sprinkle with salt and lemon pepper and roll in dry pancake mix. Heat enough oil or shortening to cover the bottom of a heavy skillet or electric skillet to 1½ to 2 inches in depth to 375°F. Add prepared fish and fry, turning to brown both sides, for a total of 4 to 5 minutes. Drain on paper towels. Serve with tartar sauce. Makes 4 servings.

Tartar Sauce: Mix mayonnaise with drained pickle relish and lemon juice. This makes 1¼ cups. Store unused portion, covered, in refrigerator.

Mustard Broiled Atlantic Mackerel

This fish is found in the waters off New England and the middle Atlantic Ocean. Mackerel is an oily fish, which if given a good shot of lemon juice, lots of freshly ground pepper, and just a dash of salt is quite good when broiled. It is abundant in June, August, and September and is in fairly good supply in July, October, and November. Its size varies from 1/2 to 2 1/2 pounds and the flesh is dark. Any recipe that is good for mackerel is good for bluefish and vice versa.

1 large mackerel (2 pounds) or two 1-pound mackerel, dressed	Freshly ground pepper to taste
	1 teaspoon prepared mustard
1 tablespoon oil	2 tablespoons butter, softened
1/2 teaspoon salt	2 tablespoons chopped fresh parsley
4 tablespoons lemon juice	

Split fish in middle of back and lay, skin side down, on greased broiler rack.

Mix oil, salt, 2 tablespoons of the lemon juice, and pepper and rub on flesh side of fish. Broil, 4 inches from source of heat, about 5 minutes.

Meanwhile, cream mustard, butter, 2 tablespoons lemon juice, and parsley together. Spread on broiled fish and place under broiler another 2 minutes or until topping is melting and beginning to brown. Makes 4 servings.

Baked Fish and Leeks

The delicate flavor of leeks nicely complements the equally light savoriness of fish. Serve with brown rice and julienned carrots for an eye-appealing dinner.

2 medium-sized leeks, thinly sliced	2 pounds haddock, sole, pollock, or other firm white fish
2 tablespoons butter or margarine	
Salt and pepper to taste	1/2 cup buttered bread crumbs
1 cup dry white wine	

Sauté leek slices in the butter or margarine for 2 to 3 minutes. Sprinkle lightly with salt and pepper, then stir in the wine. Simmer about 5 minutes. Place fish fillets in single layer in lightly oiled baking dish. Pour leek-wine mixture over, then sprinkle with buttered bread crumbs. Bake at 350°F for 20 to 30 minutes. Timing depends on thickness of fillets, which should flake easily when done. Makes 6 servings.

Lemon Baked Fillets

Serve with a bowl of small, red-skinned potatoes, boiled and dressed with a bit of melted butter or margarine; green or wax beans; and a platter of thick-sliced summer tomatoes.

1½ pound cod fillets (or other
    firm fish)
¼ cup margarine, melted

2 tablespoons lemon juice
¼ cup flour
Salt and pepper

Cut fish into serving-size pieces. Combine margarine and lemon juice in a shallow dish. Put flour with a sprinkle of salt and pepper on a sheet of waxed paper. Dip fish pieces into margarine mixture, then into flour. Put in lightly greased baking dish; pour any remaining margarine over fish. Sprinkle with a bit of paprika, if desired. Bake at 350°F for 20 to 25 minutes, or until fish flakes easily when tested with a fork. Makes 4 servings.

Spiced Mako Steaks

Mako shark steaks are comparable to swordfish in taste but are lower in price. Marinate as directed here and then broil for a fine entree.

½ cup vegetable oil
1 tablespoon lime juice
2 or 3 drops Tabasco sauce
1 clove garlic, minced
1 tablespoon minced onion

1 tablespoon minced fresh parsley
1 tablespoon Dijon-style mustard
Salt and pepper to taste
2 pounds mako shark steak

Combine thoroughly all ingredients, except fish, in a shallow dish large enough to hold the shark. Add shark and turn carefully, lightly rubbing marinade into the fish. Cover and let stand about an hour, turning once or twice during that time. Preheat broiler. Lightly oil pan, place steak on it, and broil about 2 inches from heat for 5 minutes. Turn carefully, baste, and broil another 4 to 5 minutes, until fish flakes easily when tested with a fork. Makes 6 servings.

Oven "Fried" Fish

Any firm fish fillets may be prepared in this popular and tasty fashion. Have lemon wedges and tartar sauce ready. Good with hot steamed rice and crisp-tender broccoli.

2 pounds fresh fish fillets
  (haddock, cod, pollock, etc.)
3/4 cup milk
1 cup bread crumbs

1/4 cup grated Parmesan cheese
1/4 teaspoon dried thyme
1/4 cup melted butter or margarine

Cut fillets into serving-size pieces. Dip each in milk, then in mixture of the bread crumbs, cheese, and thyme. Place in single layer in oiled baking dish. Drizzle melted butter or margarine over fish. Bake at 425°F for 10 to 12 minutes, until fish flakes easily. Makes 4 servings.

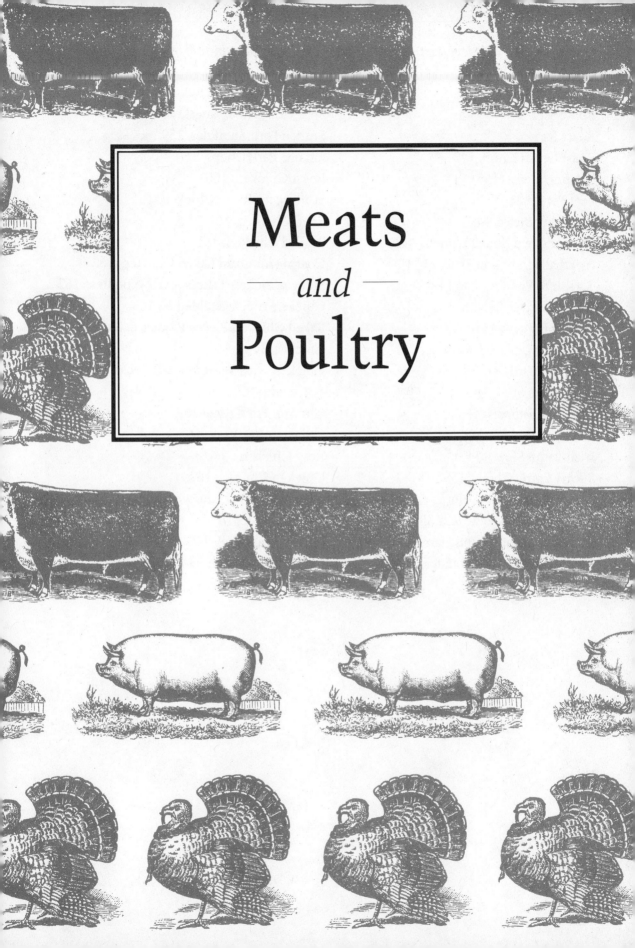

Meats
— *and* —
Poultry

Meats and Poultry

It is no secret that this is the most expensive part of our meals. But, as we are reminded constantly, we should all be consuming less animal fat—particularly less red meat—to help keep cholesterol levels down.

We turn, then, to increased use of poultry and fish in menu planning. Unfortunately for the budget, as demand for these foods has increased, so have prices. It is thus apparent that very realistic adjustments must be made in menu planning for two extremely important reasons: health and budget.

To accomplish this, we look first at serving smaller portions of meat, poultry, and fish, with compensating increases in other parts of the meal. No one wants to go away from the table still hungry or unsatisfied after a meal. So, what to do?

Think of restaurant meals. You are offered appetizer, soup, salad, and bread before you ever get to the "main course." If you order these, you get to the entree with the keenness of your appetite already blunted, so a smaller serving of meat, poultry, or fish will satisfy.

Adapt this principle for home menu planning. Serve a cup or small bowl of soup as a starter. Follow with a good husky salad and perhaps a whole-grain bread. Then a main course consisting of a small portion of meat, accompanied by good fresh vegetables and a baked potato, will almost seem like too much.

At first glance, this might seem like more work for the person preparing meals. But we get back again to that vital word: *planning*. Keeping soup stock in the freezer is a great help. Soups in endless variety can then be quickly readied, with a potful of vegetable soup, for example, becoming the first course for a couple of meals.

Lentil and bean soups make wonderful weekend lunches, and any leftovers can be served with dinner an evening or two later. Small portions can be tucked in the freezer, too, for later use.

When buying meats, make the most of "specials" offered. But also be aware of cost per serving. That is to say, look carefully at edible yield. A bone-in chuck, for instance, may have an appealing price, but it may well turn out that a boneless cut will have a lower cost per serving, which is what counts in budget planning.

Poultry comes in all forms nowadays, but buying the whole bird is still the most economical. Either cook the bird whole or do your own cutting to suit your needs. It is not difficult to remove the legs and thighs with a good, sharp knife. Use these for oven-baked dishes, then poach or bake the breast for slicing or casserole dishes. Remember, the extra parts go into the soup pot!

Turkey parts can be a great help in menu planning, particularly for small families. While facing a whole turkey may be a bit much, a roasted turkey breast makes a tasty dinner with as many "fixings" as you like. Then there's the bonus of slices for lunch sandwiches, casserole dishes, turkey pie, soup, and such.

Hamburger is turned to very often for quick and easily prepared meals. Do select the package with the least fat content. It may seem more expensive at first glance, but remember that there is less waste in fat that cooks off, and the better grades have the least cholesterol.

Make the effort to work new recipes into your meal plans regularly. Libraries have both cookbooks and current magazines that can give you new ideas. Many ethnic recipes use small amounts of meat and poultry to produce delicious dishes. Simplified Chinese recipes are very helpful in using lots of vegetables and rice with small amounts of protein.

By keeping new dishes coming to your table, you'll find that meal preparation can be far more fun, and the results will be satisfying to everyone.

Roasting Meats

Roasting is cooking meats with dry heat and is a method usually reserved for tender cuts that do not need any aid in tenderizing.

Roast Beef

4- to 6-pound standing rib of beef

Place rib bone side down in a roasting pan. Roast at 300°F for 25 minutes per pound for rare, 30 minutes per pound for medium, and 35 minutes per pound for well done. Allow meat to stand at room temperature for 15 minutes before carving. If using a meat thermometer, place it so it does not touch bone or fat. The temperatures are:

Rare	110°–120°F
Medium	130°–140°F
Well done	150°–160°F

A rolled rib weighing 5 to 7 pounds should be roasted at 300°F, 32 minutes per pound for rare, 38 minutes per pound for medium, and 48 minutes per pound for well done.

Roast Pork

3- to 5-pound center cut loin

Place bone side down in a roasting pan. Roast at 350°F for 30 to 35 minutes per pound. Pork should always be well done. The internal temperature with a meat thermometer should be 170°F. Be certain the thermometer is not touching bone or fat.

Roast Leg of Lamb

3 to 8 pound leg of lamb

Place lamb on rack in roasting pan. Roast at 325°F for 25 minutes per pound for rare, 30 minutes per pound for medium, and 35 minutes per pound for well done. The internal temperature with a meat thermometer should be:

Rare	140°F
Medium	150°F
Well done	170°F

Be certain the thermometer does not touch fat or bone.

Broiling Meats

Place the meat (steaks or chops) on a greased or oiled broiler rack set over the drip pan to catch any fat. The surface of the meat should be about 3 inches from source of heat.

1-inch steaks	medium 20	rare 15
1½-inch steaks	medium 30	rare 25
2-inch steaks	medium 45	rare 35

If there is ever any question of the steak overcooking (or undercooking), don't hesitate to cut into the center to check.

Beef Pot Roast

Pot roast is a great favorite and this recipe is one of the best. A 3- or 4-quart heavy pan with a tight lid will pay for itself over and over again through use in cooking good meat recipes. If you like a smooth gravy, force the cooked vegetables through a sieve or puree them in the food processor before making the gravy. The trivet or rack called for in this recipe is part of its success.

3 tablespoons flour
1 teaspoon salt
Freshly ground pepper to taste
4 pounds beef bottom round
2 to 3 tablespoons oil

1 cup beef bouillon
1 medium onion, cut up
1 carrot, peeled and cut up
2 stalks celery, chopped

Gravy

Liquid from pot roast
3 tablespoons flour
1/2 cup water

1/2 cup dry white wine
Salt and freshly ground pepper
   to taste

Mix 3 tablespoons flour, salt, and pepper. Rub into beef. Heat oil in a Dutch oven or casserole large enough to hold meat comfortably. Brown roast on all sides. Remove meat from pan and pour off excess fat. Put a trivet or rack in bottom of pan and return meat. Add bouillon, onion, carrot, and celery and bring to a boil. Cover, reduce heat so liquid will just simmer, and cook about 3 hours or until meat is tender.

Remove meat to a platter and keep hot. Slightly mash vegetables in liquid.

To make gravy: If there seems to be an excess of fat on liquid, remove as much as possible. Mix the additional 3 tablespoons flour with 1/2 cup water until smooth. Add with wine to liquid in pan and cook and stir until mixture boils and is thickened. Taste and season with salt and pepper if needed. Slice beef and serve with gravy. Makes 8 servings.

Company Steak

A chuck steak does nicely for this recipe. Put 4 potatoes in to bake the last hour and fifteen minutes, and a casserole of sliced zucchini with butter, salt, and pepper. Heat some rolls—and for dessert, icy cold pears with Camembert cheese.

2 tablespoons oil
2 pounds (about) bone-in chuck
   steak
$\frac{1}{2}$ teaspoon salt
Freshly ground pepper to taste
1 large clove garlic, chopped

1 can (14$\frac{1}{2}$ ounces) whole
   tomatoes in juice
4 or 5 fresh mushrooms, sliced
1 teaspoon dried oregano
$\frac{1}{2}$ teaspoon dried basil
$\frac{1}{2}$ cup seasoned dry bread crumbs

Put 1 tablespoon oil in bottom of large shallow baking dish that can be covered. Trim excess fat from steak and place in dish. Spread remaining oil over steak and sprinkle with salt, pepper, and garlic

Spoon tomatoes over steak, crushing with fork. Add mushrooms, oregano, and basil. Cover and bake at 350°F for 1$\frac{1}{2}$ hours. Test with fork, and when tender, remove cover, sprinkle with crumbs and bake for 30 minutes longer, uncovered. Makes 4 servings.

New England Boiled Dinner

Choose the leanest piece of corned beef available, and as this meat shrinks during cooking, pick a large piece. Leftovers can be used for sandwiches or for a fine hash at another meal.

1 corned brisket of beef (about 4
   pounds)
Water to cover
1 onion
6 carrots, peeled
6 potatoes, peeled

12 small onions or 6 small
   turnips, peeled
1 medium head cabbage
Prepared mustard
Horseradish
Vinegar

Wash brisket and put into an 8-quart Dutch oven. Cover with cold water and add the onion. Bring to a boil. Reduce heat and simmer, covered, until meat is tender, 3 to 3$\frac{1}{2}$ hours. Remove meat to platter. Add carrots, potatoes, and small onions or turnips. Cook 15 minutes. Trim cabbage and cut into 6 wedges. Add to vegetables and continue cooking 15 minutes longer. Slice corned beef crosswise of the grain and serve 2 slices corned beef with a potato, carrot, onion (or turnip), and cabbage wedge. Always serve mustard, horseradish, and vinegar with a New England boiled dinner. Makes 6 servings with corned beef left over.

Meatballs in Onion Sauce

Delicious and different, served with hot noodles. For vegetables, try fresh green beans and a bowl of crisp coleslaw with shredded carrots.

2 large sweet Spanish onions
¼ cup margarine, divided
1½ pounds lean ground beef
½ cup dry bread crumbs
1 egg
¼ cup milk

2 tablespoons ketchup
½ teaspoon salt
¼ teaspoon pepper
3 tablespoons flour
1 teaspoon paprika
1½ cups beef bouillon

Peel and slice onions, then separate into rings. There should be about 3 cups. Melt 2 tablespoons of the margarine in heavy skillet; add onion and cook slowly until tender. Do not allow to brown. Remove onion and reserve.

Combine ground beef with bread crumbs, egg, milk, ketchup, salt, and pepper. Form into 1½-inch balls. Melt remaining margarine in skillet onions were cooked in. Add meatballs and brown lightly on all sides. Remove meatballs.

Blend flour and paprika into drippings in pan. Gradually add bouillon and cook, stirring constantly, until thickened. Return onions and meatballs to skillet and mix gently. Cover and simmer 20 minutes. Makes 6 servings.

Yorkshire Pudding-Pie

This is an adaptation I made many years ago from a truly old recipe. (My adaptations are usually ways to get yet one more meal from a small amount of leftover beef, lamb, chicken, or turkey.) It can also be made with a half pound or so of hamburger.

1 cup flour	2 eggs
½ teaspoon salt	2 tablespoons butter or oil
2 cups milk	

Preheat oven to 450°F. Mix flour and salt in bowl; make well in center and add milk and eggs. With eggbeater, beat vigorously until batter is smooth and bubbly. Put the butter or oil in a 2½-quart casserole. Place casserole in oven until butter or oil is sizzling hot. Pour half the batter into casserole, place in oven, and bake until puffed and set, about 15 to 18 minutes. The batter will bake into funny humps and peaks, but that's all right. Remove from oven, pour on meat-filling mixture (see below), then top with remaining batter. Return to oven for another 20 to 25 minutes. The top should be crispy brown. Serve cut in wedges. (Leftovers are good as next day's lunch and may be served cold.) Makes 4 servings.

Filling:

Grind or coarsely chop leftover beef, lamb, chicken, or turkey—you should have about 2 cups when ground. Heat 1 cup of leftover gravy in saucepan, stir in meat and warm thoroughly. If there is no gravy left over, make some by melting 2 tablespoons butter in small saucepan, stirring in 2 tablespoons flour until smooth, then adding 1 cup chicken stock, chicken bouillon, or beef bouillon. Cook, stirring, until smooth. If using hamburger, brown in a skillet, then use beef bouillon to prepare gravy. Small amounts of leftover vegetables may also be added to meat.

Beef Casserole Superb

With its delicately balanced herbs this casserole is a great dish. Serve with hot buttered noodles, crusty bread, and hearts of lettuce. It's a good way to make use of your slow cooker and have the meal ready without last-minute fuss.

¼ cup flour
½ teaspoon salt
Freshly ground pepper to taste
2 pounds boneless stew beef
¼ cup butter or margarine
2 cans (8 ounces each) tomato
    sauce
1 cup dry red wine
1 teaspoon salt
2 teaspoons Worcestershire
    sauce

½ teaspoon dried rosemary
1 tablespoon chopped fresh
    basil or 1 teaspoon dried basil
¾ teaspoon dried dillweed
1 cup small whole onions
2 cups (10 to 12) sliced medium
    mushrooms
1 jar (6 ounces) marinated
    artichoke hearts, drained
Hot buttered noodles

Mix flour with ½ teaspoon salt and freshly ground pepper. Roll meat pieces in flour. Heat butter in skillet and brown meat, transferring to slow cooker as browned. When all meat is browned, heat tomato sauce in skillet and scrape browned crust from bottom. Pour over meat in cooker. Add to cooker the wine, 1 teaspoon salt, Worcestershire, herbs, small onions, and mushrooms. Cover and set on low. Cook for 7 hours. Thirty minutes before end of cooking time add artichokes. Serve with hot buttered noodles. Makes 6 servings.

If you do not have a slow cooker, brown floured meat in butter in a 2-quart Dutch oven over low heat, add tomato sauce, wine, salt, Worcestershire sauce, rosemary, basil, dill, onions, and mushrooms and cook, covered, over low heat for 1½ to 2 hours or until meat is tender. Add artichokes the last 15 minutes of cooking.

Stretch Burgers

If you prefer, these burgers can be broiled. If broiled three inches from source of heat, they take about the same length of time as pan fried. French fries would be good with them.

1 slice white bread, crumbled
½ teaspoon garlic salt
Freshly ground pepper to taste
½ teaspoon Worcestershire
    sauce

3 tablespoons dry red wine
¾ pound ground beef
1 tablespoon butter or
    margarine

Combine bread, garlic salt, pepper, Worcestershire, and wine in a bowl and blend well. Add ground beef and lightly mix with bread and seasonings. Shape into 4 patties. Heat butter in skillet and pan fry patties, about 8 minutes for medium, turning to brown both sides. Makes 4 servings.

Beef and Eggplant Casserole

This casserole can be prepared in advance, refrigerated, and baked when needed. If refrigerated, add about 10 minutes to the baking time in the recipe. Served with parslied rice, crusty hot bread, and grape-and-celery salad, it would make a tasty meal.

1 medium eggplant
½ cup (about) butter or margarine
¾ pound ground beef
1 teaspoon salt
Freshly ground pepper to taste
½ teaspoon nutmeg

¼ teaspoon cinnamon
2 cloves garlic, chopped
2 medium onions, chopped
2 tomatoes, peeled
Paprika

Peel eggplant, cut in half lengthwise, and cut into ½-inch slices. Heat part of butter in a skillet and sauté eggplant slices until nicely browned on both sides. Transfer to paper towels to drain, as browned. Add additional butter as needed.

When eggplant is all browned, put ground beef in skillet and cook, stirring, until all red color is gone. Mix salt, pepper, spices, and garlic into beef. Spoon beef from skillet into another dish. Add remaining butter and brown onions lightly.

To assemble casserole: In a buttered flat 5-cup casserole arrange half the eggplant slices. Spoon in meat. Slice tomatoes and arrange on top of meat. Put in remaining eggplant and top it with onions. Sprinkle with paprika. Bake at 350°F for 30 minutes. Makes 4 servings.

Family Meat Loaf

The only outstanding thing about this meat loaf is that it is good. Sweet potatoes and a casserole of sliced carrots and celery can go into the oven to bake at the same time.

1 medium onion, chopped
2 slices bread (caraway rye is
    good), cut up
1 egg
1 teaspoon Worcestershire
    sauce
2 to 3 sprigs parsley, chopped

1 teaspoon salt
1/4 cup water
3 tablespoons chili sauce or
    ketchup
1 1/2 pounds ground beef
2 slices bacon (optional)

Gravy

3 tablespoons fat from meat
    loaf
Juices from meat loaf
Additional water
3 tablespoons all-purpose flour

1 or 2 beef bouillon cubes
    (optional)
Salt and freshly ground pepper
    to taste

Combine onion, bread, egg, Worcestershire sauce, parsley, salt, water, and chili sauce. Mix to blend well. Add to ground beef and mix with a fork or fingers until evenly distributed. Pack lightly into a 9×4-inch loaf pan. Lay bacon slices lengthwise along top. Bake at 350°F for 1 hour. Remove meat loaf to platter. Plenty for 4 with leftovers.

To make gravy: Pour 3 tablespoons of the fat accumulated in the bottom of the pan into a saucepan. Skim off remaining fat and discard. Pour meat loaf juices into a measuring cup and add water to make 2 cups.

Add all-purpose flour to saucepan and stir over moderate heat until bubbly. Gradually add water and juices, stirring, and cook and stir until gravy boils and is thickened.

Taste and if gravy seems to need more flavor, add 1 or 2 beef bouillon cubes. Stir until dissolved. Taste again and add salt and pepper to taste. Makes 2 cups.

Variations

Omit bread and add 1/2 cup uncooked oatmeal.
Omit bacon and spread top of loaf with additional ketchup or chili sauce.
Omit 1/2 pound of beef and grind or chop 1/2 pound kielbasa and add to meat loaf.

White Veal Stew

Sometimes one exchanges time for money, and making a veal stew from veal neck bones is one of those times. But it is an excellent stew.

3 to 4 pounds veal neck bones
    with meat
2 cups water
½ teaspoon salt
6 peppercorns
Good-sized sprig of tarragon or
    ½ teaspoon dried tarragon
½ cup dry white wine
Additional water if needed
½ cup frozen small white
    onions

1 medium carrot, peeled and
    diced
2 medium potatoes, peeled and
    cut in half
¾ cup cooked peas, drained
3 tablespoons butter or margarine
3 tablespoons flour
Salt and freshly ground pepper
    to taste

The day before you wish to serve the white veal stew, cook neck bones with 2 cups water, ½ teaspoon salt, peppercorns, and tarragon until meat is tender, about 2 hours. Cool enough to handle, then remove meat from bone and cut into dice. Discard bones. Strain liquid. Refrigerate veal and liquid overnight.

Before serving time, measure liquid; add liquid from peas (if any), wine, and, if necessary, water to make 2½ cups. Put into a saucepan and cook onions, carrots, and potatoes until tender. Add peas and veal. Cream butter and flour together to make a roux. Add to stew and cook until mixture boils and is thickened, stirring carefully. Taste and add salt and freshly ground pepper, if necessary. Makes 3 to 4 servings.

Veal with Peppers

Serve this savory combination with hot linguine and a mixed salad on the side.

1 pound veal scallopini
¾ cup white-wine Worcestershire
    sauce, divided
2 tablespoons vegetable oil

1 large green pepper, seeded and
    cut into thin strips
1 tablespoon cornstarch

Cut veal into narrow (about 2×1-inch) strips. Put into bowl and mix with 2 tablespoons of the Worcestershire; set aside. Heat oil in skillet, add pepper strips, and toss to coat with oil. Add veal strips and sauté, stirring often, until peppers are just crisp-tender and veal is lightly browned. Combine remaining Worcestershire sauce with cornstarch; stir into pan and continue cooking gently until sauce is thickened, another 3 to 4 minutes. Makes 4 servings.

Chopped Veal Parmigiana

One of my friends who is a great cook persuaded me to try the frozen chopped veal, since regular veal is expensive. I did and this recipe resulted. When you eat it, it's obviously chopped veal, but good. The secret is for once not to thaw the meat before cooking.

1 package (16 ounces) frozen
    chopped veal "steak"
3 tablespoons flour
1 egg
1 tablespoon water
¼ teaspoon salt
Freshly ground pepper to taste

¾ cup plain dry bread crumbs
3 tablespoons grated Parmesan
    cheese
3 tablespoons oil
1 cup tomato sauce
4 slices mozzarella cheese

Do not thaw veal steaks. Coat all over with flour. Beat egg, water, salt, and pepper together lightly. Dip coated steaks in egg mixture, then in bread crumbs that have been mixed with Parmesan cheese, coating both sides and edges.

Heat oil in a large skillet over high heat and brown veal quickly on both sides. As browned, remove to a greased flat baking pan. Spoon tomato sauce over browned steaks and top each with a slice of mozzarella cheese. Bake at 350°F for 25 to 30 minutes. Makes 4 servings.

Irish Lamb Stew

The late Maura Laverty, of Irish cookery fame, says of Irish Lamb Stew, "the potatoes should be cooked to a pulp." You can make more than one layer of meat and potatoes and onion, if you wish, but always end with potatoes.

3 pounds lamb stew meat with
    bones or 2 pounds boneless
1 cup frozen small white onions
1 tablespoon chopped fresh
    parsley

1½ tablespoons chopped fresh
    thyme or 1½ teaspoons dried thyme
1 teaspoon salt
4 potatoes
Water to cover

Put lamb in a 2½-quart saucepan. Add onions, parsley, thyme, and salt. Peel potatoes, cut in halves, and place on meat and onions. Put in water just barely to cover meat. Bring to a boil, reduce heat, and simmer for about 1½ hours or until meat is tender. Makes 4 servings.

Savory Lamb Chops

Serve buttered orzo and steamed broccoli with the chops. Bake pears for dessert while the chops are baking.

4 shoulder lamb chops
1/4 cup all-purpose flour
1/2 teaspoon salt
Freshly ground pepper to taste
1 tablespoon Worcestershire sauce

2 tablespoons tomato paste
1/2 cup plain yogurt
4 tablespoons chopped fresh
    parsley

Rub chops with flour, salt, and pepper which have been mixed. Place in a buttered flat baking dish. Mix Worcestershire sauce, tomato paste, and yogurt and pour over chops. Bake at 350°F for 1 hour or until tender. Serve with sauce and sprinkle with chopped parsley. Makes 4 servings.

Lamb and Vegetable Hotpot

A marvelous combination of lamb and vegetables. Serve with plenty of crusty bread, with a fresh fruit compote for dessert.

1 1/2 pounds lamb cubes
2 large onions, thinly sliced
1/2 pound green beans, sliced
2 large potatoes, peeled and
    sliced
2 large carrots, peeled and
    sliced
2 ripe tomatoes, peeled and
    sliced

2 large green peppers, seeded
    and cut into strips
1 1/2 teaspoons salt
Freshly ground pepper to taste
1/2 cup butter or margarine
1/2 cup hot water

Fill a 2 1/2-quart Dutch oven with 2 layers each of meat and vegetables in the order listed, sprinkling with salt and pepper and dotting with butter between the layers. Pour over the hot water. Cover tightly and cook over low heat for about 1 1/4 hours or until meat and vegetables are tender.

To serve, dig down into the pot so that something of everything is in each serving. Makes 4 servings.

New England Baked Ham Slice

Put sweet potatoes in the oven to bake with the ham. Rolls—heated during the last part of the baking time—and apple salad could finish up the menu.

1 inch-thick center-cut ham
    slice (1½ pounds)
10 cloves
1 tablespoon prepared brown
    mustard

½ cup white grape juice or
    apple cider
¼ cup pure maple syrup

Put ham slice into a greased flat casserole and stud fat on edges with cloves. Spread mustard over ham slice. Mix grape juice and maple syrup and pour over ham. Bake at 400°F for about 45 minutes or until ham is browned and bubbly. Serve sliced with pan juices. Makes 4 servings.

Scalloped Potatoes and Ham

A good way to use up a small amount of leftover ham. Baked butternut squash seasoned with pepper and a dash of powdered cloves, and a bowl of crisp coleslaw, are good accompaniments for this dish.

3 medium potatoes
Water to cover
1 cup diced cooked ham

2 medium onions, sliced
1 stalk celery, sliced

Sauce

2 tablespoons butter or
    margarine
2 tablespoons flour
½ teaspoon dry mustard
1 teaspoon salt

Freshly ground pepper to taste
1½ cups milk
½ cup buttered dry bread
    crumbs

Cook potatoes in water 20 minutes. When cool enough to handle, peel and slice. Layer potatoes, ham, onions, and celery in a buttered 6-cup casserole.

To make sauce: Melt butter in saucepan and stir in flour, mustard, salt, and pepper. Gradually add milk and cook and stir until mixture boils and is thickened. Pour over food in casserole, digging down with a fork so sauce gets to bottom. Bake, covered, at 350°F for 30 minutes. Uncover, sprinkle with crumbs, and bake 10 minutes longer. Makes 4 servings.

Boiled Cured Pork Shoulder Dinner

A boiled dinner is one of my favorite meals, and very often a cured pork shoulder can be bought at a good price, which makes it an even stronger favorite. I ask the butcher to cut off the hock end and use it for split pea soup (page 107).

4³/₄ pounds (about) cured pork
    shoulder
Water to cover
1 onion stuck with 2 whole
    cloves (optional)
4 whole potatoes, peeled
4 carrots, peeled and cut in half
    lengthwise

1 cup small whole onions
4 cabbage wedges
Prepared mustard
Horseradish
Vinegar

Put pork shoulder in a saucepan and cover with cold water. Use a pan in which the shoulder fits neatly so it won't drown in the water. If necessary turn it from time to time. If you like a spicier flavor, add an onion with two whole cloves stuck in it. Bring to a boil, reduce heat, and simmer, covered, 2½ to 3 hours or until meat is tender when pierced with a fork.

Remove meat (and onion, if used) from broth and keep warm. Discard onion.

Put potatoes, carrots, and small onions in broth. Cover and boil 15 minutes. Place cabbage wedges on top of vegetables and continue cooking 15 minutes longer or until potatoes and carrots are tender.

If meat has cooled, slice and place slices on top of cabbage long enough to reheat.

Serve with mustard, horseradish, and vinegar. Makes 4 servings, with bone for soup and pieces of meat left over for salad and for sandwiches.

Pork Chops with Wine

Mashed sweet potatoes and fried green tomatoes would taste good with these pork chops.

4 pork chops (about 1 pound
   in all)
1 tablespoon oil
1 clove garlic, chopped

1 beef bouillon cube
½ teaspoon dried tarragon
½ cup dry sherry

Trim fat from pork chops. Heat oil in a 10-inch skillet and brown chops on both sides. Add remaining ingredients. Cover and cook over low heat for about 45 minutes or until chops are tender. Check occasionally to see that there is enough liquid. If not, add more wine or water. Makes 4 servings.

Pork Chops and Sauerkraut

Buttered noodles and cranberry sauce along with rye bread will round out the menu for these spicy pork chops.

4 pork chops
1 tablespoon prepared brown
   mustard
1 small clove garlic, finely
   chopped

1 teaspoon caraway seed
½ teaspoon salt
Freshly ground pepper to taste
1 can (20 ounces) sauerkraut

Trim fat from pork chops and fry slowly to grease skillet; when fat is crisp, discard. Mix mustard, garlic, caraway, salt, and pepper and spread on pork chops. Brown in pork fat in skillet over medium heat, about 30 minutes, turning to brown on both sides. Pork should be completely cooked. Remove from skillet and quickly heat sauerkraut in same skillet. Serve with pork chops. Makes 4 servings.

Stuffed Pork Shoulder

If you like to make your own soup, it really pays to learn to bone meat; and the bones from a pork shoulder make delicious broth for soup. In any event, this stuffed pork shoulder is a good main dish. Bake sweet potatoes and a casserole of broccoli at the same time.

4 pounds (about) fresh pork
    shoulder, boned
1 large onion, chopped
$\frac{1}{4}$ cup butter or margarine

1 tablespoon poultry seasoning
$\frac{1}{2}$ teaspoon salt
3 cups soft bread crumbs
1 egg, beaten

Gravy

2 tablespoons flour
$1\frac{1}{2}$ cups water
Salt and freshly ground pepper
    to taste

1 chicken bouillon cube
    (optional)

If you bone the pork shoulder yourself, leave it flat. If it has been boned at market, cut string and unroll.

Sauté onion in butter until tender. Add poultry seasoning, salt, and bread crumbs and mix well. Stir in egg. Spread on pork and roll up. Either retie or fasten with skewers.

Place on rack in a pan and roast at 325°F for $2\frac{1}{2}$ to 3 hours or until meat thermometer registers 170°F. Remove meat from oven and let stand 10 minutes. Meanwhile, make gravy.

To make gravy: Stir 2 tablespoons flour into pork's pan juices. Add $1\frac{1}{2}$ cups water and cook and stir until mixture boils. Season to taste. (If gravy does not have enough flavor, add a chicken bouillon cube.)

To serve pork, carefully remove skin and as much fat as possible. Cut crosswise into slices. Makes 6 servings, with leftovers.

Orange Pork Chops

Serve steamed rice, peas and celery, lettuce wedges, and rolls with these perky chops.

4 pork chops
1 medium onion, chopped
³/₄ cup orange juice
2 teaspoons grated orange rind

2 tablespoons honey
¹/₂ teaspoon salt
Freshly ground pepper to taste

Trim fat from pork chops and slowly fry in skillet until there is enough fat in which to brown chops. Remove fat pieces and brown chops on both sides, cooking onion at the same time. Add remaining ingredients and cook, covered, over low heat until chops are tender, about ¹/₂ to 1 hour. Serve chops with any juices in pan. Makes 4 servings.

Roast Chicken

An unstuffed chicken cooks more quickly than one that is stuffed. Peel potatoes, cut in half, and roast in the pan with the chicken the last 45 to 50 minutes. Creamed carrots and a fruit salad can be served with the chicken.

1 roasting chicken (about 4 pounds)
1 tablespoon butter or margarine
1 teaspoon dried tarragon

Salt and freshly ground pepper
¹/₄ cup butter or margarine
3 tablespoons fresh lemon juice

Wash and dry chicken. Mix 1 tablespoon butter and tarragon and put inside chicken. Season inside and out with salt and pepper.

Place chicken on rack in roasting pan, breast side down. Melt ¹/₄ cup butter and mix with lemon juice. Brush chicken all over with the mixture. Roast at 350°F for 1 hour, brushing every 15 minutes. Turn chicken breast side up and continue roasting another hour, brushing as before, using pan juices as they accumulate. Chicken should be roasted about 30 minutes per pound. The leg joint should move easily when done; another test for doneness is to prick chicken to see if the juices are running clear and yellow with no trace of pink or red.

Remove chicken, breast side up, to a platter and let stand 15 minutes before carving. Reduce pan juices about ¹/₃ and serve in a separate dish.

A 4-pound chicken should serve 6.

Stuffing for Roast Chicken

If you prefer to stuff the chicken (some people think it gives the meat a better flavor), this is a good basic recipe.

½ cup butter or margarine
¾ cup chopped celery
¼ cup chopped onion
4 cups soft bread crumbs

½ teaspoon salt
1 teaspoon poultry seasoning
½ teaspoon dried sage

Heat butter in a large skillet and sauté celery and onion until tender, but not browned. Add remaining ingredients and toss over low heat until they are well mixed and bread is lightly toasted. This makes enough stuffing for a 4-pound chicken. Double this recipe for a medium-sized turkey.

Fried Chicken

This is one way to fry chicken. There are many, but this is a simple recipe that brings out the chicken flavor.

1 broiler-fryer chicken (2½ to 3
   pounds)
¼ cup all-purpose flour
½ teaspoon salt

Freshly ground pepper to taste
¼ cup butter or margarine
¼ cup vegetable oil

Disjoint chicken. Save bony pieces such as back and neck for soup. (I also cut the third joint off the wings.) Wash chicken pieces and dry. Mix flour, salt, and pepper and dip chicken in mixture. Heat butter and shortening in a large skillet and fry chicken over moderate heat 30 minutes, turning with tongs once or twice. Do not crowd pieces; use 2 skillets, if necessary. Makes 4 servings.

Broiled Chicken

Chicken quarters or halves are usually broiled. Wash and dry well. Cut off the third joint (wing tip). Brush your chosen seasoning on chicken and place on oiled broiler rack. Broil skin side up first. Surface of chicken should be at least 4 inches from source of heat. Broil 15 minutes, turn, and broil 15 minutes on other side.

If broiling pieces, surface of pieces should be 3 inches from source of heat. Brush pieces with butter or marinade and turn frequently. Broil about 20 minutes altogether.

Coating for Oven Baked Chicken

A make-your-own coating for chicken that is very good.

<table>
<tr><td>½ cup flour</td><td>½ teaspoon salt</td></tr>
<tr><td>½ cup very fine dry bread crumbs</td><td>1 teaspoon garlic salt</td></tr>
<tr><td>2 tablespoons cornstarch</td><td>1 teaspoon dried minced onion</td></tr>
<tr><td>2 teaspoons sugar</td><td>1 teaspoon paprika</td></tr>
<tr><td>2 teaspoons instant chicken
    bouillon granules</td><td></td></tr>
</table>

Mix all ingredients very well. Store in a covered container. This makes about 1⅓ cups, or enough for two 2½ to 3-pound cut-up chickens.

To use, coat the pieces of a 2½- to 3-pound chicken with 2 to 3 tablespoons oil. Put about ⅔ cup of the coating (half of this recipe) in a plastic bag and add 2 pieces of chicken at a time. Shake to coat. Continue to coat all pieces. Place in a single layer in a greased shallow pan. Bake at 400°F for 20 minutes. Turn and bake 25 minutes longer. Makes 4 servings.

Spicy Chicken Fillets with Noodles

A mixture of piquant flavors accents this dish. Accompany this with steamed snow peas.

<table>
<tr><td>1 teaspoon grated lemon rind</td><td>8 ounces medium noodles</td></tr>
<tr><td>1 teaspoon grated orange rind</td><td>¼ cup milk</td></tr>
<tr><td>¼ cup orange juice</td><td>½ cup plain low-fat yogurt</td></tr>
<tr><td>1 tablespoon soy sauce</td><td>Salt and freshly ground pepper to taste</td></tr>
<tr><td>1 garlic clove, put through press</td><td>2 green onions, thinly sliced</td></tr>
<tr><td>4 boneless, skinless chicken fillets</td><td>2 tablespoons vegetable oil</td></tr>
<tr><td>1 cup (about) plain dry bread crumbs</td><td></td></tr>
</table>

Mix together grated rinds, orange juice, soy sauce, and garlic. Put chicken in a flat dish and spread with seasoning mixture. Let stand, turning once, for about 1 hour. When ready to cook, cover fillets with bread crumbs and let air-dry on waxed paper for 10 to 15 minutes. Cook noodles as directed. Drain; mix with milk and yogurt. Season to taste with salt and pepper. Garnish with onions. Keep warm. Heat oil in a teflon-coated skillet. Sauté chicken fillets on both sides, over medium heat, until nicely browned, about 4 minutes on each side. Serve with noodles. Makes 4 servings.

Chicken and Vegetable Pie

Make this tasty dish with either chicken or turkey left over from another meal. Parboiled sliced carrots (2 or 3) and small canned onions may be used in place of the canned mixed vegetables.

3 tablespoons butter or margarine
¼ cup flour
1 can (16 ounces) mixed
    vegetables
1 cup chicken broth (about)
1 cup milk (about)

¼ teaspoon nutmeg
2 cups diced cooked chicken
Salt and freshly ground pepper
    to taste
Pastry for 1 crust (page 273)

Heat butter in saucepan. Add flour and cook until bubbly. Drain vegetable liquid into measuring cup and add chicken broth and milk so total liquid is 2 cups. Stir liquid into flour mixture and cook and stir until sauce boils and is thickened. Add nutmeg, vegetables, and chicken. Taste and add salt and pepper, if needed. Spoon into a flat 1-quart casserole. Roll pastry to fit and mark into 4 triangles with knife or pastry cutter. Place on chicken mixture. Bake at 425°F for 30 minutes or until crust is lightly browned and filling is bubbly. Makes 4 servings.

Baked Chicken Pieces Piquante

Put 4 baking potatoes and a casserole of green beans in the oven to cook with the chicken.

1½ pounds chicken pieces
¼ cup butter or margarine
1 tablespoon sugar
½ teaspoon salt
1 tablespoon flour
⅓ cup water

2 teaspoons Worcestershire
    sauce
1½ tablespoons lemon juice
¼ cup vinegar
Dash Tabasco sauce
Paprika

Wash and dry chicken pieces. Place in a single layer in a buttered flat pan, skin side down.

Melt butter with sugar and salt. Stir in flour and all remaining ingredients except paprika. Brush half of sauce on chicken.

Bake at 375°F for 30 minutes. Turn chicken, spread with remaining sauce and sprinkle with paprika. Continue baking for 15 minutes or until chicken is done. Serve hot. Makes 4 servings.

Chicken Birds

It's easier to bone a leg than a breast, and these birds are nifty. You might want to try your favorite bread stuffing, too. And cold, they make good picnic fare.

8 chicken legs, boned
½ cup chopped mushrooms
¼ cup chopped celery
1 green onion, chopped
2 tablespoons butter or margarine
1 cup cooked rice
½ teaspoon salt

Freshly ground pepper to taste
½ teaspoon crushed dried
    tarragon
3 tablespoons butter or
    margarine, softened
½ cup Chablis

To bone chicken legs, use a sharp knife and cut along one side of chicken from thigh end down. With knife, work around bone to release flesh. Cut loose at bottom.

Put leg meat between two pieces of plastic wrap and flatten with a mallet.

Sauté mushrooms, celery, and onion in 2 tablespoons butter until tender. Mix with rice, salt, pepper, and tarragon. Spread a layer of the rice mixture on the flesh side (not skin side) of chicken and roll up. Put seam side down in a buttered casserole. Spread chicken with softened butter and pour Chablis into pan. Bake at 350°F for 1 hour or until chicken is tender and lightly browned. Baste with wine several times during baking. Makes 4 servings.

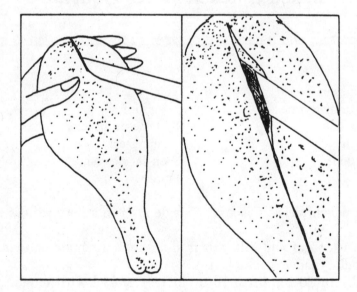

Boning a chicken leg

Chicken with Vegetables, Chinese Style

Whenever you have a stir-fry dish, be sure everything is ready before you start to cook.

8 broiler-fryer chicken thighs*
¼ cup cornstarch
¼ cup oil
⅛ teaspoon garlic powder
1 large ripe tomato cut into chunks
⅓ cup sliced water chestnuts
½ cup fresh sliced mushrooms

1 cup bean sprouts
1 cup coarsely chopped green
    onion, both green and white
1 cup celery, sliced on the bias
¼ cup soy sauce
2 to 3 cups hot cooked rice

Skin chicken, remove meat from bone, and cut into 1-inch dice. (Use skin and bones to make chicken broth.) Mix chicken pieces with cornstarch. Heat oil in a large skillet or wok. Stir-fry chicken quickly to brown. Sprinkle with garlic powder. Stir in vegetables. Sprinkle with soy sauce. Cover and cook 5 minutes. Serve over hot cooked rice. Makes 4 servings.

*3 boneless breast halves could be used instead of thighs. Cut into thin strips.

Chicken Fried Rice

A light and satisfying dish. Boneless turkey breast can also be used for this dish.

4 tablespoons vegetable oil
½ cup minced onion
1 pound boneless chicken breast,
    cut into 1-inch cubes
2 cups cooked rice (at room
    temperature)

1 cup frozen peas
2 eggs, lightly beaten
6 scallions (all of the white
    and some of the green), chopped
2 tablespoons soy sauce (or to taste)

Heat oil in wok or heavy skillet; add onion when oil is hot and stir-fry 2 to 3 minutes, just until soft and golden. Add chicken and stir-fry for 3 to 4 minutes, or until chicken turns white. Add rice and peas, stirring to heat thoroughly. (Peas do not need to be cooked first.) Push mixture to side of pan. Add a little more oil to pan, then pour in beaten eggs, stirring for about 30 seconds. Stir contents of pan together quickly, then add scallions and soy sauce, again stirring briefly. Makes 4 servings.

Chicken Paprikash

A deservedly popular dish, suitable for a family meal as well as for serving to guests. Hot noodles, fresh green beans with slivered almonds, and a cool jellied salad complete the meal.

1 chicken (about 3 pounds), cut up	¼ cup oil
1 cup flour	1 clove garlic, coarsely chopped
2 teaspoons paprika	¼ cup dry white wine
1 teaspoon minced fresh basil leaves (or ¼ teaspoon dried)	2 tablespoons white-wine Worcestershire sauce
	1 cup dairy sour cream

Wash and dry chicken. In a plastic bag, mix flour, paprika, and basil. Shake chicken pieces in this mixture to coat evenly. Heat oil in skillet; add chicken pieces and garlic and brown evenly. Discard garlic. Mix together wine and Worcestershire; pour over chicken. Cover and cook over low heat until chicken is tender (about 35 minutes). Remove chicken and keep warm. Blend sour cream into skillet, stirring continually until sauce is warm, but do not allow to boil. Pour over chicken, sprinkling with a dash of paprika, if desired. Serves 6.

Rosy Chicken

There's lots of savory flavor in this Hungarian-style dish. Serve with hot noodles or rice, accompanied by broccoli or green beans for both color and texture appeal.

1 broiler (about 3 pounds), cut up	2 tablespoons Hungarian paprika
2 tablespoons vegetable oil	Salt and pepper to taste
2 tablespoons butter or margarine	1 cup sour cream
4 onions, chopped	1 tablespoon flour

Put chicken in a large bowl; cover with cold water. Heat oil and butter or margarine in a Dutch oven that has a tight-fitting cover. Sauté the onions slowly until they are transparent, but do not allow to brown. Sprinkle in the paprika and stir well, mixing all ingredients very thoroughly. Drain chicken, but do not dry.

Place in the pan, spooning the paprika-onion mixture over the pieces. Season with salt and pepper, cover, and cook slowly for half an hour. Check the pan then to see if more liquid is needed. If so, add ¼ cup of chicken broth, stock, or water. Continue slow-cooking for at least another half hour, until chicken is very tender.

When chicken is done, in a small saucepan, heat the sour cream gently; mix in flour. Do not allow to boil. Place chicken on warmed serving platter. Pour sour cream into the paprika sauce, blending well. Let it simmer gently a minute or two; then spoon the sauce over the chicken. Top with a light sprinkling of additional paprika, if desired. Makes 6 servings.

Chicken Chunks

A homemade version of the popular fast food, ready to go from freezer to table in just minutes.

4 whole chicken breasts,
   boned and skinned
½ cup dry bread crumbs
⅓ cup grated Parmesan cheese

½ teaspoon garlic salt
1 teaspoon dried thyme
1 teaspoon dried basil
½ cup melted margarine

Cut each breast half into 6 or 8 chunks. Combine crumbs, cheese, garlic salt, thyme, and basil. Dip chunks into melted margarine, then into crumb mixture. Place on foil-lined cookie sheet and freeze. When frozen, transfer to freezer bags and store in freezer until needed. Bake frozen chunks at 400°F for 18 to 20 minutes. Makes 6 to 8 servings.

from The Bohemian Girl, *Confidential Chat*

Cornish Game Hens with Vegetables and Rice

A meal in itself. Heat garlic bread with hens the last 15 minutes. Serve cranberry sauce, and for dessert, fresh or frozen peaches and ice cream.

2 Cornish game hens (about 1½
   pounds each), thawed
1 medium onion
1 small green pepper
½ cup fresh sliced mushrooms
1 teaspoon salt
Freshly ground pepper to taste

½ teaspoon dried rosemary
¾ cup uncooked rice
¾ cup dry white wine
¾ cup chicken broth
2 tablespoons butter or
   margarine, softened

Split hens in half. Wash and dry. Dice onion; seed and dice pepper. Combine with mushrooms, salt, pepper, rosemary, rice, wine, and broth and mix well. Spoon into a buttered flat casserole. Lay hens, skin side up, on top of rice and vegetables. Spread hens with 1 tablespoon of the butter. Bake at 350°F, covered, for 45 minutes. Uncover, brush hens again with additional butter, and bake 15 minutes longer. Fluff rice with fork before serving with hens. Makes 4 servings.

Turkey Scallopini

Turkey parts are readily available at most meat counters. For this recipe, a package of thin-sliced breast meat is ideal, but you can also use a skinless, boneless turkey breast and cut it on the bias into thin slices. If the package contains more than is needed for one meal, simply wrap the extra pieces individually in plastic wrap, overwrap, seal, date, and freeze.

4 turkey scallopini (about ¾
   pound altogether)
Salt and freshly ground pepper
   to taste
3 tablespoons (about) flour
1 egg, beaten

1 tablespoon water
1 cup (about) dry bread crumbs
2 tablespoons oil
4 tablespoons butter or margarine
1 tablespoon lemon juice
¼ cup dry white wine

Place scallopini between pieces of waxed paper or plastic wrap and flatten with a mallet until thin, but do not break the flesh. Season to taste with salt and pepper and dip in flour. Mix egg with water and dip floured scallopini in egg mixture and then in crumbs, coating both sides well. Let air dry on paper 10 minutes.

Heat oil and butter in a large skillet and quickly sauté breaded scallopini on both sides to brown nicely. Remove to platter and keep warm as they are browned. When all are browned, pour off most of fat in skillet, add lemon juice and wine, and swirl in skillet until hot. Pour over scallopini to serve. Makes 4 servings.

*Scallopini slices can also be made from boneless chicken breast. Both turkey and chicken breast cut more easily if allowed to stand in freezer 1 hour. Cut chicken down side of breast. Pieces will not be as large as turkey, but handle in the same manner.

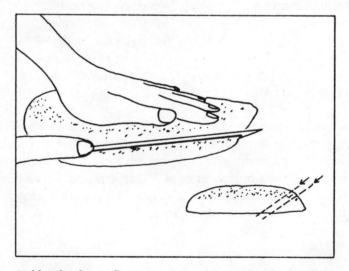

Hold turkey breast flat on cutting surface. With a sharp knife, cut slices on a bias.

Turkey Breast with Sour Cream

For a special meal, serve this with steamed rice, green beans amandine, and fresh cranberry-orange relish.

1 turkey breast (about 3 pounds)	½ cup dry white wine
2 tablespoons butter or margarine	¼ teaspoon dried oregano
2 tablespoons finely minced onion	¼ teaspoon dried rosemary
1 cup sliced fresh mushrooms	Freshly ground pepper to taste
2 tablespoons flour	1 cup dairy sour cream
1 cup milk (or half-and-half)	Paprika

Bone and remove skin from turkey. Cut turkey meat into 6 equal parts. Sauté onion in butter or margarine until barely tender, then add mushrooms and sauté 3 to 4 minutes. Sprinkle with flour, stirring carefully to mix well. Stir in milk and cook, continuing to stir, until thickened. Stir in wine, oregano, rosemary, and pepper.

Place turkey pieces in a flat, buttered casserole and cover with sauce mixture. Bake, covered, at 325°F for 1 hour. Remove cover, gently stir in sour cream, sprinkle with paprika, and bake 20 minutes longer. Makes 6 servings.

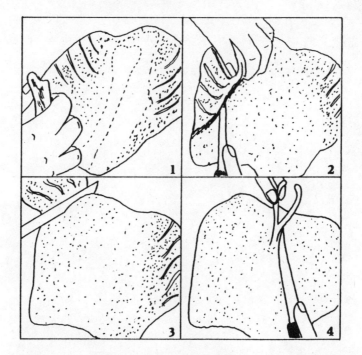

Place turkey breast skin side down. Cut along both sides of breast bone to loosen it. Pull up on the breast bone to remove. Work your knife underneath the rib bones on one side while pulling up on them. Cut rib bones off at outside edge. Repeat on other side. Remove wish bone near center of breast. Turn breast over and pull skin off with your fingers.

Timetable for Roasting Turkey

Remove giblets from turkey and wash turkey inside and out. Drain and dry with paper towels. Plan ¾ cup stuffing per pound for birds 10 pounds and over and ½ cup per pound for smaller birds. Season cavity of turkey with salt, pepper, and poultry seasoning. Loosely pack stuffing into turkey neck and cavity. Place turkey on a rack in a shallow roasting pan, breast side up. If you have a meat thermometer, insert it in the thickest part of the thigh, being careful that it does not touch the bone. Place turkey in a preheated 325°F oven.

Size	Stuffed	Unstuffed
6–8 pounds	3–3½ hours	2½–3 hours
8–12 pounds	3½–4½ hours	3–4 hours
12–16 pounds	4–5 hours	3½–4 ½ hours

If turkey becomes too brown before it is done, cover lightly with foil during last half hour of roasting time. The turkey is done when the meat thermometer registers 180 to 185°F. If you do not have a thermometer, using a folded paper towel, pinch the thigh. It should feel soft. Prick the skin and the juices should run clear.

Dried Legumes
— *and* —
Cereals

Numbers refer to pages where recipes appear in this book.

Dried Legumes (Beans)

Cereals

Dried Legumes (Beans)

In this category you will find a great variety of beans, some carried in the supermarket, others at specialty food stores. They include beans such as navy beans, also known as California or Michigan pea beans; red kidney beans; pinto beans; black turtle or just plain black beans; cranberry beans; lima and baby lima beans; blackeye beans, also known as black-eyed peas; garbanzo beans, also called chick-peas; Great Northern (a larger variety of navy beans); red beans; soybeans; white kidney beans, also known as cannellini; green or yellow split peas; and lentils.

After purchasing, the dried beans will keep almost indefinitely in a tightly covered container in a dry place.

If buying canned beans, keep them in a cool place (below 70°F) and mark date of purchase on can in order to use first, just as you would with any canned product.

Cooked beans should be stored in refrigerator, covered; they will keep four to five days. Cooked beans can also be frozen in a covered, vapor proof container, as long as six months.

With the exception of split peas and lentils, dried beans should be soaked before cooking to restore water lost in drying. There is a long-soak and a quick-soak method.

Long-soak method: To 1 pound dry beans add 6 cups water and 2 teaspoons salt. Let stand overnight. Drain. Beans soaked this way cook more quickly and retain their shape better. A rule of thumb is to use 2 to 3 cups water for each 1 cup beans.

Quick-soak method: To 1 pound dry beans add 6 to 8 cups hot water. Bring to a boil, cover, and cook 2 minutes. Remove from heat and let stand an hour or so. Drain, then cook.

To cook 1 pound soaked beans, place in a large saucepan. Cover with 6 cups hot water. Simmer with the lid tilted until beans are tender. Add additional hot water if needed. Test beans frequently during cooking. They are done when fork tender. One pound dry navy beans equals 6 cups cooked. As a rule of thumb, 1 cup dry beans equals 2 to 3 cups cooked beans.

Cooking Time & Yields for Beans

(based on pre soak)

1 Cup Dry Measure	Water	Cooking Time	Yield
Black beans (turtle beans)	4 cups	1½ hours	2 cups
Black-eyed peas	3 cups	½ hour	2 cups
Chick-peas (garbanzo)	4 cups	2 hours	2 cups
Great Northern beans	3½ cups	1½ hours	2 cups
Kidney beans	3 cups	1½ hours	2¼ cups
Lentils & split peas	3 cups	¾ hour	2¼ cups
Limas	2 cups	1 hour	1¼ cups
Baby limas	2 cups	1 hour	1¾ cups
Pea beans	3 cups	1½ hours	2 cups
Pinto beans	3 cups	2 hours	2 cups
Red beans	3 cups	3 hours	2 cups
Soybeans	4 cups	3 hours or longer	2 cups

Boston Baked Beans

This recipe comes from Boston's Durgin-Park restaurant. I have made these baked beans many times and they are delicious. If this quantity is too much for your family, baked beans freeze nicely in covered containers. Thaw completely before heating.

1 pound dried pea (navy) beans
12 cups cold water
2 teaspoons salt
½ pound salt pork
1 medium whole onion
4 tablespoons brown sugar
⅓ cup molasses

1 teaspoon dry mustard
½ teaspoon salt
¼ teaspoon freshly ground
  pepper
2 cups boiling water, or more if
  needed

Sort beans to remove any stones or dirt. Wash. Soak beans overnight in 6 cups of the cold water to which 2 teaspoons salt have been added. In the morning, drain. Add about 6 cups water, bring to boil, and parboil 10 minutes.

Drain in a colander and rinse well with cold water. Cut piece of salt pork in half through its rind and cut each half into 1-inch squares. Put onion and half of the salt pork in bottom of a 2-quart bean pot. Spoon in beans. Mix sugar, molasses, dry mustard, ½ teaspoon salt, and pepper with the 2 cups boiling water. Pour over beans. Press remaining salt pork into beans. If necessary, add additional boiling water to make liquid come just to top of beans. Bake in a 300°F oven for 5 hours, adding water as necessary. Makes 1½ quarts.

Baked Rice and Beans

Sautéed cherry tomatoes, spinach salad, and rye bread could finish the menu.

3 slices bacon, cut in half
½ cup chopped onion
6 tablespoons ketchup
2 tablespoons brown sugar
1 teaspoon Dijon-style mustard

½ teaspoon salt
Freshly ground pepper to taste
1½ cups cooked rice
1 can (15 ounces) pinto beans

In a 10-inch skillet, cook bacon until about half done. Remove bacon. Add onions to skillet and cook until soft but not browned. Mix in remaining ingredients. Spoon into a buttered 6-cup casserole. Arrange bacon strips on top. Bake, uncovered, at 350°F for 30 to 35 minutes. Makes 4 servings.

Baked Beans with No Molasses

Beanpot Barbie sent this recipe in to Chatters at the request of Hoppy.

1 cup dried pea (navy) beans
Water to cover
1 medium onion, chopped fine
1 teaspoon salt
1 teaspoon dry mustard

½ box (1 firmly packed cup)
   dark brown sugar
¼ pound salt pork scored on
   one side
½ cup ketchup

Wash and sort beans. Soak overnight in water to cover. In the morning, drain and add fresh water. Cover and simmer until soft, about 30 to 40 minutes. Pour into a 1-quart bean pot; add just enough water to cover beans; then stir in all the remaining ingredients. Cover and bake at 300°F for 5 to 7 hours. Uncover the last hour to let liquid thicken. If you have a crockery slow cooker, cook on low for about 8 hours. Makes 8 servings.

from Beanpot Barbie, *Confidential Chat*

Chick-Pea and Vegetable Stew

Served with a tossed green salad and whole wheat French bread, this skillet dinner is good fare.

¼ cup oil

2 medium onions, thickly sliced

1 can (20 ounces) chick-peas (garbanzos)

2 cloves garlic, sliced

3 medium potatoes, peeled and thinly sliced

2 large ripe tomatoes, peeled and coarsely chopped

1 teaspoon Italian seasoning

1½ tablespoons tomato paste

½ teaspoon salt

Freshly ground pepper to taste

2 cups hot water, or more if needed

Heat oil in a 3-quart Dutch oven and fry onions until soft. Drain chick-peas and add with the garlic to the onions. Fry until garlic is lightly colored. Add potatoes and fry, turning, until they are lightly browned. Mix in the tomatoes. Mix Italian seasoning, tomato paste, salt, and pepper in 2 cups hot water. Add to food in Dutch oven. Bring to a boil and simmer gently, covered, until potatoes are soft, about 20 minutes. Stir from bottom occasionally and add additional hot water, if necessary, just to cover. Makes 4 servings.

*To use dried chick-peas, soak 1 cup overnight and cook as directed until tender.

Netta's Southern Baked Beans

This version of baked beans is a real pleaser. Prepare in advance, refrigerate, and bake when needed.

1 small green pepper

1 small onion

1 fresh tomato

½ teaspoon each freshly ground pepper, dry mustard, and paprika

1½ tablespoons dark corn syrup

1 tablespoon Worcestershire sauce

1 can (28 ounces) pork and beans

Seed and chop green pepper. Chop onion; peel and chop tomato. Mix pepper, mustard, and paprika with corn syrup and Worcestershire sauce. Combine all ingredients with beans and spoon into a buttered 6-cup casserole. Bake at 300°F for 1 hour. Makes 4 to 6 servings.

Bourbon Baked Beans

Definitely a dish for adults, but a family adaptation could be made simply by omitting the bourbon. So good for buffets, served with sliced baked ham, a sturdy salad, and hot rolls.

4 cans (13 ounces each) baked beans
4 oranges, thinly sliced
1 lemon, thinly sliced
1 cup raisins

1 cup molasses
¼ teaspoon ground ginger
½ cup bourbon

Combine all ingredients except bourbon. Put into a bean pot or large casserole. Gradually add bourbon and carefully mix to blend. Bake at 300°F for 45 to 50 minutes. Serves 8.

Vegetarian Casserole

This answers a request for barley recipes and is also a fine dish for vegetarians.

¼ cup butter or margarine
½ pound mushrooms, sliced
1 small onion, chopped
½ pound barley
2½ cups chicken or vegetable
   bouillon (or stock)

½ cup cottage cheese
½ cup sour cream
1 tablespoon chopped scallions
   or chives
1 tablespoon minced parsley
Salt and pepper to taste

Heat butter or margarine in large skillet. Sauté sliced mushrooms for 10 minutes, until golden but firm. Remove from pan. Sauté chopped onion just until soft. Add barley to skillet; stir until light brown. Pour in bouillon or stock, cover pan, and simmer until barley is tender, about 40 minutes or more. Add more water or stock if needed.

Return mushrooms to pan; add cottage cheese, sour cream, scallions or chives, parsley and season to taste with salt and pepper. Transfer mixture to baking dish. Bake at 325°F for 1 hour. Cover dish with foil for last 20 minutes if top is browning too much. Sprinkle with additional parsley before serving. Makes 8 to 10 servings.

from MJB, *Confidential Chat*

Soybean Casserole

Soybeans take a lot of cooking but they are good. A carrot slaw and whole wheat bread would taste good with the beans, with cheese for dessert to help the protein.

½ pound dried soybeans	1 can (6 ounces) tomato paste
3 cups water	1½ teaspoons prepared
1 teaspoon salt	mustard
3 tablespoons finely minced	16 frozen small white onions
chutney, preferably mango	3 tablespoons molasses

Wash and sort soybeans. Cover with 3 cups water and salt and soak overnight. In the morning, pour off the soaking water and cover with water to about 2 inches above the beans. Heat to boiling and simmer 3 to 4 hours or until beans are tender. Drain, reserving 2 cups of the liquid. Mix the chutney, tomato paste, mustard, onions, and molasses with the reserved liquid. Simmer with the beans until the sauce has slightly thickened. Spoon into a 1-quart bean pot or casserole and bake at 325°F for 1½ hours. Makes 4 servings.

Lentil and Tomato Salad

Hot pita bread and butter would complement this salad, and orange sherbet with creme de menthe would be fine for dessert.

1 large Spanish onion, finely	1 teaspoon salt
chopped	1 teaspoon Dijon-style mustard
2 tablespoons oil	Freshly ground pepper to taste
1 clove garlic, finely chopped	1 medium tomato, chopped
1 bay leaf	½ green pepper, seeded and
5 cups water	chopped
½ pound dried lentils, washed	1 medium tomato, sliced
2 tablespoons lemon juice	2 tablespoons chopped fresh
¼ cup oil	parsley

In a 2-quart saucepan, sauté onion in 2 tablespoons oil until tender but not brown. Add garlic, bay leaf, water, and lentils and simmer, covered, until lentils are tender but not mushy, 35 to 40 minutes. Drain and remove bay leaf.

Mix together lemon juice, ¼ cup oil, salt, mustard, and pepper. Mix with drained warm lentils and chill. When ready to serve, mix in chopped tomatoes and green peppers.

Put in a bowl and garnish top with sliced tomatoes and chopped parsley. Makes 4 servings.

Barley with Lentils

A very filling dish that combines a popular legume and cereal. Serve whole wheat bread, and fruit for dessert.

¼ cup butter or margarine
¾ cup chopped celery
1 cup chopped onion
4 cups water
¾ cup dried lentils, washed
2 cans (1 pound each) tomatoes
   in puree

¾ cup barley
½ teaspoon dried basil
1½ teaspoons salt
Freshly ground pepper to taste
½ teaspoon garlic salt
½ cup shredded zucchini

Heat butter in a 3-quart Dutch oven and sauté celery and onion until tender but not browned. Add water and lentils and simmer, covered, for 20 minutes. Add tomatoes, barley, basil, and seasonings and simmer, covered, for about an hour. Stir often and add additional water if needed. Add zucchini and cook 5 minutes longer. Makes 6 servings.

Lentil Curry

Serve with cherry tomatoes, celery sticks, chopped peanuts, and whole wheat rolls. For dessert, broiled canned peaches with sour cream.

½ pound dried lentils
4 cups water
3 tablespoons butter or margarine
2 medium onions, chopped
1 tart cooking apple, peeled,
   cored, and diced
1 tablespoon flour

1 tablespoon curry powder
1 teaspoon sugar
½ teaspoon salt
Freshly ground pepper to taste
1 teaspoon apricot jam
2 teaspoons lemon juice
2 cups hot cooked rice

Wash lentils and soak in water for 6 hours. Simmer them in the soaking water until just soft and still whole, about 20 minutes. Heat butter and fry onion and apple until just soft. Stir in flour and curry powder. Add lentils and liquid, sugar, salt, pepper, apricot jam, and lemon juice, and cook 10 minutes longer. Serve at once over rice. Makes 4 servings.

Baby Lima Beans in Tomato Sauce

This dish could be a main course; with it you might serve broccoli and a Waldorf salad. The salad could double for dessert.

2 cups dried baby limas*
6 cups water
1 teaspoon salt
3 slices bacon, finely chopped
1 can (1 pound) tomatoes
½ green pepper, chopped
¼ cup firmly packed brown
    sugar
¼ cup chopped onion
¼ teaspoon chili powder, or to
    taste
1 tablespoon vinegar

Wash and sort lima beans and soak overnight in 6 cups of water with salt. Drain. Cover with water about 1 inch over beans and simmer, covered, about 1 hour, until tender. Drain.

Fry bacon until crisp. Remove from skillet and drain on paper towels. Add all remaining ingredients, including beans, to pan and simmer about 25 minutes or until thickened. Serve sprinkled with bacon. Makes 4 servings.

If dried baby lima beans are not available, use regular dried limas.

Split Peas with Lamb Chops

You might want to bake some apples for dessert while the chops are baking. A bowl of crisp celery and radishes in lieu of salad, and rye bread and butter, go with the main dish.

1½ cups dried split peas
4 cups water
½ teaspoon salt
Freshly ground pepper to taste
1 medium onion, sliced
4 medium carrots, peeled and sliced
½ teaspoon dried rosemary
4 shoulder lamb chops
3 tablespoons flour
2 tablespoons butter or
    margarine

Sort and wash split peas. Combine with water, salt, pepper, onion, carrots, and rosemary in a saucepan. Cover and simmer 15 minutes. Spoon into a buttered flat casserole.

Trim fat from chops and dredge chops in flour. Heat butter in skillet and brown chops on either side. Place chops on top of peas and bake at 350°F for 45 minutes or until chops are tender. Makes 4 servings.

Cannellini with Tomatoes

Serve these delicious beans with almost any dinner. They are truly good.

2 cans (20 ounces each)
    cannellini (white kidney
    beans)*
2 medium tomatoes, peeled
1½ tablespoons chopped fresh
    basil or 1½ teaspoons dried

1 medium onion, chopped
2 tablespoons olive oil
Salt and freshly ground pepper
    to taste

Drain beans. Chop tomatoes and combine with basil, onion, and olive oil in a saucepan. Cook over low heat, stirring, until tomatoes are slightly cooked. Add beans and mix lightly. Heat until beans are hot. Makes 4 to 6 servings.

*If you can purchase dried cannellini beans, about 1½ cups dry beans, soaked and cooked, are needed.

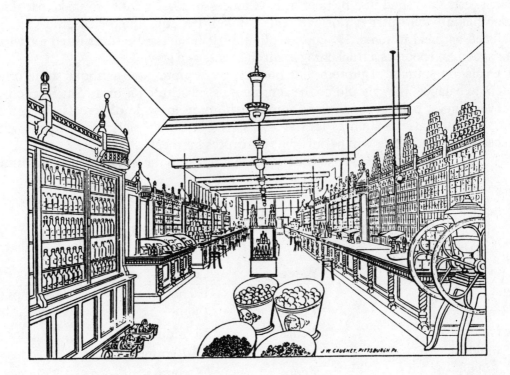

Cereals

All important civilizations were founded on the cultivation and use of one or another of the cereal grains. The Mideast cultivated wheat, barley, and millet. The ancient cultures of the Orient were based on rice. The Inca, Maya, and Aztec civilizations depended on corn.

Cultivation of cereal grains began so long ago that its early history is lost. But we do know that cereals have been man's most important food plants since the dawn of history.

They include rice, wheat, oats, barley, corn, rye, sorghum grain, and millet. Whole grains are concentrated sources of needed nutrients.

We buy them in varying forms, such as cracked wheat or bulgur, oatmeal, cornmeal, rye flour, and many other products. Rice probably comes in as many variations at the consumer level as any of the cereals: white milled rice, brown rice, converted rice, parboiled or instant rice, and innumerable combinations of rice and seasoning, some dried, some frozen.

Brown rice is particularly popular because it retains the bran layer which gives it a nutlike flavor and higher nutritive value.

Oatmeal, long a popular cereal and ingredient for everything from meat loaf to cookies, can be ground in a blender or food processor for 1 minute to make oat flour, which has all the nutrition of oatmeal. It takes 1½ cups uncooked quick or old-fashioned oatmeal to make 1¼ cups oat flour. Oat flour can be substituted for white flour spoon for spoon as a thickening agent in sauces and gravies.

Cereals are sources of protein, but not complete protein; so without some other protein to balance, they should not be considered a substitute for meat. Small amounts of cheese, eggs, fish, or meat can complete the protein cycle of cereals. Or cereal-legume combinations such as lentils and barley or brown rice, or split peas with cracked wheat or bulgur, will be suitable substitutes for meat.

Whatever natural cereals you choose will add interest to the menu and be healthful.

Cooking Time & Yields for Grains

1 Cup Dry Measure	Water	Cooking Time	Yield
Barley	3 cups	1¼ hour	3½ cups
Brown rice	2 cups	1 hour	3 cups
Buckwheat	2 cups	15 minutes	2½ cups
Bulgur wheat	2 cups	15–20 minutes	2½ cups
Cracked wheat	2 cups	25 minutes	2⅓ cups

For milled, converted, parboiled, or instant rice, follow directions on package. Generally rice doubles in quantity in cooking.

Sweet Rice

Rice is such a versatile grain that it works equally well for main dishes, salads, or desserts. If you prefer to chill this dessert, you may.

1 cup uncooked rice
3½ cups milk
½ teaspoon salt
5 tablespoons butter or margarine

¼ cup raisins
¾ cup chopped dates
½ teaspoon almond extract

Combine rice, milk, salt, and 2 tablespoons of the butter in a 2-quart saucepan. Bring to a boil. Stir once. Cover and cook over low heat until milk has been absorbed, about 50 minutes, stirring occasionally. Heat 3 tablespoons butter in a skillet and sauté raisins and dates for a few minutes. Stir into rice with almond extract. Serve warm with additional milk, if desired. Makes 4 servings.

Fried Rice

A tasty way to use up the last of a pork roast. Top with strips of fried egg if you want a more Chinese-style dish.

2 tablespoons peanut oil
1 small onion, minced
1 clove garlic, minced
1½ to 2 cups finely chopped
    cooked pork

1 cup uncooked rice
1¾ cups water or chicken stock
2 tablespoons soy sauce
Pepper to taste

Heat oil in large skillet; add onion and garlic and sauté 3 to 4 minutes. Stir in pork and continue to sauté another 5 minutes, until meat is lightly browned. Stir in rice; sauté 3 or 4 minutes. Add water or chicken stock, soy sauce, and pepper. Bring to boil, cover, and simmer gently 25 to 30 minutes, until rice is tender and all liquid has been absorbed. Makes 4 servings.

Brown Rice Medley

A nice rice dish for a buffet table.

2 medium carrots
3 tablespoons oil
¾ cup sliced green onion
2 cups sliced, cored, unpeeled
  apple

2 cups cooked brown rice
½ teaspoon salt
⅓ cup raisins
1 tablespoon sesame seeds

Peel and thinly slice carrots. Sauté in oil, stirring, for about 10 minutes. Add onion and apple and continue cooking 10 minutes. Add rice, salt, and raisins and cook and stir until rice is hot. Lightly mix in sesame seeds. Makes 4 servings.

Rice Pilaf

Rice pilaf is good with lamb or chicken.

1 cup rice
1 medium onion, chopped
3 tablespoons oil
2 ripe tomatoes, peeled and
  diced

2 cups water
2 beef bouillon cubes
Salt and freshly ground pepper
  to taste

Cook rice and onion in oil until rice is lightly browned, about 10 minutes, stirring constantly. Add all remaining ingredients and simmer, covered, over low heat about 20 minutes or until all liquid is absorbed. Let stand, covered, another 20 minutes over very low heat until rice is dry and fluffy. Stir from bottom 2 or 3 times with a fork. Makes 4 to 6 servings.

Bulgur Pilaf

Pilaf made from cracked wheat or bulgur fits nicely into a menu including lamb or chicken.

2 tablespoons oil
1 small onion, chopped
1 cup cracked wheat or bulgur

½ teaspoon salt
2 cups chicken broth

Heat oil in a 1-quart saucepan and sauté onion and cracked wheat until onion is tender and wheat lightly browned. Add salt and broth and simmer, covered, 20 to 25 minutes or until broth is absorbed. Makes about 2½ cups or 4 servings.

Mideast Salad Appetizer

Serve as an appetizer to a meal that might include roast lamb, assorted vegetables, and whole wheat rolls.

1 cup cracked wheat or bulgur
Cold water
1½ cups chopped fresh parsley
½ cup chopped fresh mint
  leaves
¾ cup chopped green onion
2 ripe tomatoes, peeled and
  chopped

½ cup lemon juice
¼ cup olive oil
1 teaspoon salt
Freshly ground pepper to taste
Romaine lettuce

Combine cracked wheat with cold water to cover and let stand 1 to 2 hours. Bring to boil; lower heat and simmer 20 to 25 minutes. Drain and press out all liquid possible.

Mix lightly with parsley, mint, green onion, tomatoes, lemon juice, olive oil, and salt and pepper. Chill. Serve on romaine lettuce leaves. Makes 6 servings.

Spoon Bread

Spoon bread is aptly named since it is soufflélike and is served and eaten with a spoon. Asparagus tips with cheese sauce and sliced tomatoes would go along nicely with spoon bread.

1 cup white or yellow cornmeal
3 cups milk
2 tablespoons butter or margarine

1 teaspoon salt
1 teaspoon baking powder
3 eggs

Combine cornmeal and milk in top of double boiler and cook over boiling water for about 30 minutes or until thickened. Stir in butter, salt, and baking powder.

Separate eggs and beat whites until stiff. Beat egg yolks until light. Fold a little of hot cornmeal into yolks and return to cornmeal. Fold in egg whites. Pour into a buttered 2-quart casserole and bake at 375°F for 30 minutes. Serve hot with butter. Makes 4 to 6 servings.

Salads
and
Salad Dressings

Numbers refer to pages where recipes appear in this book.

*indicates a recipe variation

Salads and Salad Dressings

Today's markets offer such an intriguing array of salad makings, there is no excuse for anyone to become bored with this important food. Quality, too, is excellent, with fresh, often water-misted greens awaiting our choice year-round. Several kinds of sprouts, which come in neat packages, make nutritious additions to any salad. Remember, too, how good a fine crisp coleslaw is with so many casseroles and hearty winter meals. Dress it up with carrot shreds, celery seeds, and bits of green pepper, or drained crushed pineapple with raisins—particularly good with chicken dishes.

Salad Greens

Salad greens come in such a variety that it seems one eventually chooses a few favorites and goes farther afield only when spurred by a new recipe or a major price differential. Here are some of those available:

ESCAROLE: A curly green, best used in mixed salads.

CHICORY: A slightly bitter taste—a nice addition to a green salad bowl.

ENDIVE (French or Belgian) has white straight leaves. It can be used as a base for a salad or cut crosswise into a green salad or other recipes. It is not actually a "green" but fits into that category.

BOSTON LETTUCE—known in the trade as Butterhead—is a soft-leafed lettuce that makes a good salad base or can be torn into pieces for a mixed green.

ICEBERG, actually Crisphead lettuce, is by far the most popular and widely used lettuce. The leaves are good for a base or in mixed greens; also served in wedges with dressing.

ROMAINE: A long, loose head with green leaves, romaine can be used as a base, is excellent in mixed green salads, or can stand alone as a green salad.

BIBB LETTUCE, a soft-leafed lettuce, has a tinier head than Boston. Generally available only if locally grown, bibb is delicate and can be served with a light oil-and-vinegar dressing.

SPINACH: When buying fresh spinach, save the smaller center leaves for salad. A nice color and flavor contrast.

BEET GREENS can be used in tossed salads, where they add a piquant flavor.

DANDELION LEAVES are good mixed into a green salad.

WATERCRESS: Its rather peppery flavor is a nice addition to a mixed green salad, or it can be served by itself with thin mild onion and orange slices and an oil-and-vinegar dressing. It is a delightful salad.

Other things to go into green salads include red or Spanish onions; green onions; fresh mushrooms; radishes; raw broccoli, asparagus, cauliflower, or snow peas; avocado; tomatoes; leeks; all kinds of fresh herbs; parsley; orange and grapefruit sections; chives; carrots; or cooked green beans.

To store salad greens: All salad greens should be stored in plastic bags in the hydrator section of the refrigerator. Do not wash until ready to use. Then wash, cut off any rust spots, and dry in a salad spinner or in clean towels. Some greens, such as watercress, are very perishable, so buy only when they can be used in a day or two.

To cut or tear: As a rule I cut greens, mostly because it seems to work faster for me. For iceberg lettuce use a knife, for the leafier greens the kitchen scissors. It is a matter of personal preference.

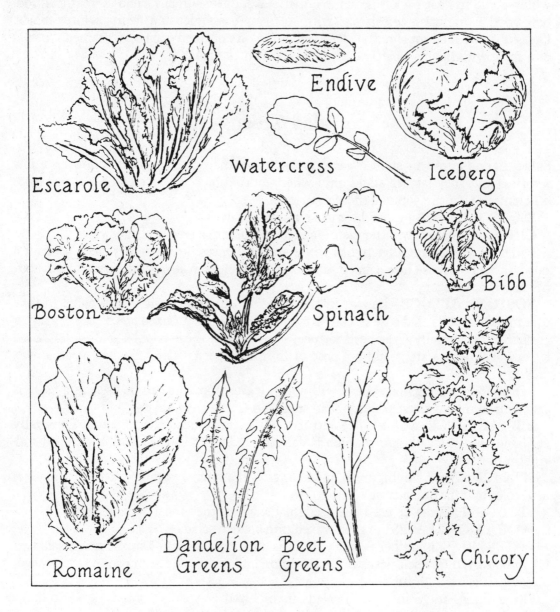

Bean Sprouts

Bean sprouts are easy and fun to grow at home.

You need a quart jar with a ring lid (actually two jars are better, because you can start the second jar before the other runs out); some cloth to cover the top—any thin, clean white cloth will do; I use pieces of a white t-shirt that gave up the ghost—water; and mung beans.

Put ⅓ cup mung beans in the jar, cover with water, and let them soak overnight. The next morning drain them and wash in a couple of waters right in the jar. Cover the top of the jar with a piece of the white cloth and screw on the ring lid. You're in business.

The theory behind the cloth cover is that you can water the beans through the cloth each day, but I find it quicker to take off the lid and fill up the jar with water and drain it through my fingers. Put the cloth and lid back on to keep the sprouts clean.

Almost at once the beans will grow. As you water them each day, shake well so they won't grow too compactly in the bottom of the jar. In the summer, you'll have bean sprouts in about three days—in the winter it may take four. I keep the jar right by the kitchen sink so I won't forget to water it. After the jar gets full, it goes in the refrigerator to stop the growing.

I eat beans and sprouts without picking off the sprouts. If you don't like the beans, you'll have to pick off the sprouts.

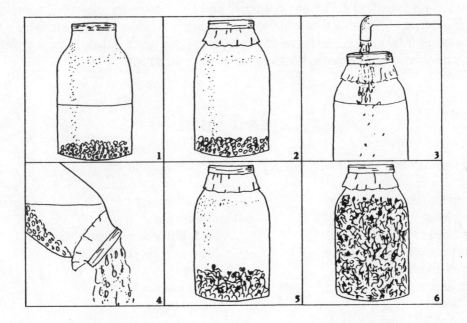

Salad Bar in a Bowl

A pretty salad to serve at a small buffet or for serving at the table as a first course. The vegetables suggested can be varied to suit your taste.

1 quart (about) cut-up mixed
   greens
1 cup cooked peas, drained
2 hard-cooked eggs, sliced
1 cup cooked garbanzo beans,
   drained
1 can (1 pound) sliced beets, drained
1 cup sliced radishes
½ cup sliced green onion

1 medium cucumber, peeled
1 small onion
1 small clove garlic
1 cup mayonnaise
1 tablespoon lemon juice
1 tablespoon sugar
1½ teaspoons Worcestershire
   sauce

Put greens in bottom of a large salad bowl, about 12 inches across; use more than 1 quart greens if a large base is needed. Put peas, eggs, beans, beets, radishes, and sliced green onions in a pattern over the greens—such as in parallel rows or any other attractive way. Cover and chill in refrigerator.

Cut cucumber and onion into chunks. Whirl in blender with garlic until finely chopped. Drain well. (The best way is to put a piece of cheesecloth in a strainer. Drain off as much juice as will come out naturally and then squeeze to remove most of the rest of the liquid.) Mix with mayonnaise, lemon juice, sugar, and Worcestershire. Chill before serving. Makes 2 cups. Serve in a separate bowl with salad. Store any leftover dressing, covered, in refrigerator. Will keep a week or 10 days.

Layered Salad

Serve this salad with rolled slices of deli ham, hard rolls, and mint iced tea.

3 cups bite-size raw spinach
   pieces
1 or 2 ripe tomatoes, sliced
3 cups romaine lettuce pieces
1 medium red onion, sliced
1 medium zucchini, thinly
   sliced
2 hard-cooked eggs, sliced

1 cup alfalfa sprouts
1 cup plain yogurt
3 ounces blue cheese, crumbled
2 tablespoons chopped fresh
   chives
1 tablespoon mayonnaise, or
   more to taste

Wash and dry greens before cutting into pieces.

Layer spinach, tomatoes, romaine, onion, zucchini, eggs, and sprouts in salad bowl in order given. Cover bowl with plastic and chill.

Combine yogurt with cheese, chives, and mayonnaise. Chill. Pour over salad and toss when ready to serve. Makes 4 to 6 servings.

Potato Salad

This is a potato salad I've been making for years. If there are any secrets to my potato salad, they might include marinating the potatoes immediately after cooking, while they are still warm; using grated onion (a personal dislike for little pieces of onion in potato salad started this habit); and sticking to a particular local commercial mayonnaise which I find enhances the flavor. (For other uses I normally make my own mayonnaise, which is quite mildly flavored.) This salad is also a nice base for adding other things, which I'll suggest at the end of the recipe.

2 medium-large potatoes	2 tablespoons vinegar
3 eggs	½ cup chopped dill pickles
Water	½ cup chopped celery
2 tablespoons grated onion	½ cup mayonnaise
½ teaspoon salt	Radishes
Freshly ground pepper to taste	Parsley
3 tablespoons oil	

Scrub potatoes and rinse. Put in a pan large enough to hold eggs as well. Cover with water and bring to a boil. Cover and let simmer 15 minutes. Remove eggs. Continue cooking potatoes another 10 to 15 minutes or until tender; do not overcook. Peel at once and dice into a bowl. There should be about 3 cups. Add onion, salt, pepper, oil, and vinegar and toss lightly. Peel eggs and tuck them in whole, with potatoes; chill both thoroughly in a covered bowl. Some time before serving, remove eggs and add pickles, celery, and mayonnaise to potatoes. Chop two of the cooked eggs back into bowl. Toss all together.

Place in a decorative bowl. Slice remaining egg and radishes and garnish bowl with egg slices, radish slices, and parsley sprigs. Makes about 5 cups.

Variations

Add chopped cucumbers to taste.

Add chilled, cooked, fresh or frozen peas or cut-up peapods to taste.

Add about 2 cups diced cooked chicken or turkey, 2 tablespoons capers, and an additional ¼ to ½ cup mayonnaise.

Tossed Dinner Salad

When time comes for getting dinner, I bring out all the plastic bags with salad items from the refrigerator and have a ball. Generally there are 2 or 3 kinds of greens and I mix them up. Then either Spanish or green onions, radishes, cucumbers, and bean sprouts. If there are any odds and ends of raw or cooked vegetables, I might put them in, and sometimes there are raw mushrooms which are added. You can see from this that it is hard to give a recipe for a tossed salad, and I think anyone who makes salads regularly has his or her own ideas about how they want to do it. But here is a formula from which to work. For dressing, I use lemon or lime juice and seasoned salt, but I include here a simple oil-and-vinegar dressing.

2 cups shredded lettuce or your
    favorite green, or a mixture
½ cup shredded raw spinach
½ cup diced celery
½ cup diced cucumber
1 or 2 green onions, cut in ½-inch
    pieces

¼ cup radish slices
3 tablespoons oil
2 tablespoons wine vinegar or
    cider vinegar
½ teaspoon salt
Freshly ground pepper to taste

Wash and dry greens before shredding. Put all vegetables in a salad bowl and toss lightly. Cover and chill in refrigerator until ready to serve. Then add oil, vinegar, salt, and pepper, sprinkling them over the vegetables, and toss lightly again. Makes 4 servings.

Note: If you want to get the salad ready in advance, it's okay. Just don't add the dressing until the last minute.

Variations

Tomato wedges or your favorite fresh herbs could be added to this basic formula. Bean sprouts add a nice texture, too.

Cucumber Salad

A wonderful summer accompaniment to cold chicken or ham.

2 tablespoons vinegar
1 cup plain yogurt
2 tablespoons grated onion
4 medium cucumbers, peeled
  and thinly sliced

2 teaspoons dried parsley flakes
  or 2 tablespoons chopped
  fresh parsley
Salt and freshly ground pepper
  to taste

Combine vinegar, yogurt, and onion in a 4- or 5-cup bowl. Slice in cucumbers. Add parsley flakes and salt and pepper to taste. Chill thoroughly. Makes 6 servings.

Brad's Prosper Salad

A coworker ensured his popularity by occasionally bringing to the office a bowlful of this concoction to share at lunchtime. I have no idea where the name "Prosper Salad" came from. This is wonderful for buffets and picnics.

2 red onions
Olive oil
2 cups scallions, cut in 1-inch
    pieces
2 cans (1 pound each) chick-peas,
    well drained

2 cans (7 ounces each) tuna,
    drained
2 tablespoons vinegar
2 tablespoons lemon juice

Cut onions in thin slices, then in pieces about 1 inch long. Put in a bowl and cover with olive oil. Let stand overnight in refrigerator. Add scallions, drained chick-peas, and tuna. Mix carefully. Sprinkle with lemon juice and vinegar; let stand at least another hour before serving. Makes 8 servings.

Baby Lima Bean Salad

The lima beans can be marinated overnight so that part of the salad is out of the way the day before. This salad is good with pork or beef or poultry.

1 package (10 ounces) frozen
    baby lima beans
2 stalks celery, finely chopped
2 tablespoons finely chopped
    onion
1/4 teaspoon salt

4 tablespoons French dressing
    (page 206)
1/3 small head crisp lettuce
1/4 cup mayonnaise
1/4 cup chopped pimiento

Cook lima beans as directed on package. Drain and cool slightly. Mix with celery, onion, salt, and French dressing. Chill well. When ready to serve, chop lettuce coarsely and mix with mayonnaise and pimiento into lima beans. Makes 4 servings.

Green Beans Vinaigrette

Green beans vinaigrette are a nice addition to a tossed vegetable salad; they fit into a buffet menu; or they can be served by themselves as a salad.

1½ pounds green beans	6 tablespoons cider vinegar or
Water	wine vinegar
2 teaspoons dry mustard	¾ cup oil
¾ teaspoon salt	2 tablespoons chopped stuffed
Freshly ground pepper to taste	olives
1 teaspoon paprika	1 teaspoon capers
1½ teaspoons sugar	Shredded lettuce

Cut off stem ends of beans and wash well. Either steam or cook in a small amount of water until beans are tender-crisp, about 15 minutes. Drain and put beans in a bowl and cool. Mix seasonings with vinegar and oil to blend. Stir in olives and capers. Pour over beans and toss well. Cover and chill in refrigerator for several days, turning beans occasionally in vinaigrette sauce. Serve as a salad on shredded lettuce (or add to tossed vegetable salad). Makes 6 servings as a salad.

Chef's Salad

A chef's salad is a popular menu item and yet if you analyze it, it is primarily a base of salad greens topped with julienned ham, chicken, and Swiss cheese. Sometimes you get sliced hard-cooked egg and tomato wedges. This recipe is a pattern on which to build your own chef's salad—it makes a good Sunday-night supper when served with assorted breads and a beverage.

1½ quarts cut-up greens	2 ripe tomatoes
8 or 10 thin Spanish or red onion	2 hard-cooked eggs
rings	Salt and freshly ground pepper
½ cucumber, thinly sliced	to taste
1 cup julienned cooked chicken	Thousand Island dressing
1 cup julienned Swiss cheese	(page 205)
1 cup julienned ham or tongue	

In a large salad bowl mix greens with onion rings and cucumber slices. Arrange on top of the greens the chicken, Swiss cheese, ham, tomatoes cut in wedges, and eggs, sliced or cut in lengthwise wedges. Serve the salad with coarse salt, the pepper mill, and Thousand Island dressing on the side. Makes 4 servings.

Note: If it is easier to make 4 individual salads, divide ingredients between 4 salad bowls.

Chicken Barley Salad

Even though I've always loved barley, the first time I saw a barley salad recipe I had to be convinced. Obviously, I was. Use this as a main dish with toasted bread. Garnish the salad with fresh tomato slices and serve a fresh fruit compote for dessert.

⅓ cup barley
½ teaspoon salt
2 cups boiling water
1 cup chopped cooked chicken
¾ cup thin celery slices
¼ cup green onion slices

½ cup plain yogurt
1 tablespoon soy sauce
Dash garlic powder
Freshly ground pepper to taste
Lettuce

Cook barley in salted water, covered, on low heat for 1 hour, stirring occasionally. Drain and cool. (The barley can be cooked the day before.) Add all remaining ingredients except lettuce and toss to blend. Chill. Serve on lettuce. Makes 4 servings.

Fresh Bean Salad

The very best three-bean salad is made with fresh green and wax beans. However, canned beans can be substituted here. Cut beans into 1-inch pieces before cooking.

2 cups green beans, cooked
  and drained
2 cups wax beans, cooked
  and drained
1 can (1 pound) kidney beans,
  drained
½ cup diced onion

½ cup diced green pepper
⅓ cup salad oil
⅔ cup vinegar
½ cup sugar
½ teaspoon salt
Freshly ground pepper to taste

Combine beans, onion, and green pepper in a bowl, mixing carefully. Mix remaining ingredients well, then pour over vegetables. Cover and refrigerate overnight. Drain off marinade before serving. Makes 6 to 8 servings.

Molded Summer Vegetable Salad

A light salad such as this goes with most any meal.

1 envelope unflavored gelatin
¼ cup cold water
1 cup boiling water
1 tablespoon lemon juice
3 tablespoons cider vinegar
½ teaspoon salt

2 tablespoons grated onion
½ cup grated raw carrot
½ cup thinly sliced celery
¼ cup diced cucumber
Salad greens
French dressing (page 206)

Soften gelatin in cold water. Dissolve in boiling water. Add lemon juice, vinegar, salt, and onion. Chill until mixture begins to thicken. Mix in carrots, celery, and cucumber, and spoon into a 3- or 4-cup mold. Chill until firm. Serve on salad greens with French dressing. Makes 4 to 6 servings.

Seven Layer Salad

It is a boon to be able to get the salad ready the day before, and this is a grand one for a picnic. Sandwiches and lemonade are good partners.

1 cup uncooked elbow
　macaroni
1 quart boiling water
1 teaspoon salt
½ head lettuce
2 cups shredded red cabbage
1 medium red onion, sliced
1 cup sliced celery

1 cup shredded cheddar cheese
1 package (10 ounces) frozen
　peas, thawed
1 cup low-calorie creamy salad
　dressing
Salt and freshly ground pepper
　to taste

Cook macaroni in boiling water with salt for 6 minutes (until al dente). Rinse with cold water. Drain and set aside. Make a bed of lettuce in the bottom of a large bowl. Layer macaroni on top. Continue with cabbage, onion, celery, cheese, and peas, using each to form one layer. Pour salad dressing over all, but do not toss. Cover and refrigerate several hours or overnight. Just before serving, toss and season to taste with salt and pepper. Makes 8 servings.

Niçoise Salad

A salad of vegetables and fish that originated in the Mediterranean, this is a meal in itself, served with crusty rolls and cheese for dessert.

½ pound green beans
½ cup oil
¼ cup red wine vinegar
1 teaspoon Dijon-style mustard
¼ teaspoon salt
Freshly ground pepper to taste
1 medium red onion, thinly sliced
1 medium tomato, cut in wedges

1 can (2 ounces) pitted ripe olives, drained
1 can (2 ounces) anchovy fillets, drained and chopped
1 can (7 ounces) tuna, drained and flaked
3 hard-cooked eggs, quartered
1 tablespoon chopped fresh basil

Wash beans and cut off stem ends. Cut into 1-inch pieces. Steam or cook in a very small amount of water until tender. Drain. Mix oil, vinegar, mustard, salt, and pepper and toss with beans. Chill. Toss all remaining ingredients with beans and dressing. Makes 4 servings.

Salmon Salad

Serve a chilled vichyssoise to start, sliced tomatoes and hard rolls with the salmon salad, and sherbet for dessert.

2 cups cold, cooked and flaked salmon
1 cup diced cucumber
1½ tablespoons grated onion
2 tablespoons lemon juice

½ cup chopped walnuts
3 tablespoons French dressing (page 206)
⅓ cup mayonnaise
Crisp salad greens

Put salmon in bowl. Add cucumber, onion, lemon juice, walnuts, French dressing, and mayonnaise and toss lightly. Chill well. Serve on salad greens. Makes 4 servings.

Marinated Beans

This is definitely a plan-ahead, but well worth it. Marvelous to have in the summer to add zip to fish or vegetable salad plates.

1 pound dried navy (pea), red
    kidney, or cannellini beans
3½ to 4 cups water
6 tablespoons oil

2 cloves garlic, peeled, whole
1 bay leaf
1 teaspoon salt

Marinade

6 tablespoons oil
6 tablespoons tarragon vinegar
    or white wine vinegar
¼ cup chopped fresh parsley
½ teaspoon crushed dried
    oregano or 1½ teaspoons
    chopped fresh oregano

½ teaspoon crushed dried basil
    or 1½ teaspoons chopped
    fresh basil
¼ teaspoon salt
Freshly ground pepper to taste

Sort and wash beans. Soak overnight in 3½ to 4 cups water. In the morning add oil, garlic, bay leaf, and 1 teaspoon salt to beans in soaking water and simmer until just tender. Do not overcook. Test first at 45 minutes. Drain, remove bay leaf and garlic, and put beans in a bowl.

Mix together the marinade ingredients and pour over beans. Refrigerate for several hours or overnight. Serve as a side dish, in salads, or over pasta. Makes 4 cups. Will keep under refrigeration for several weeks.

Red Cabbage Slaw

This is a pleasant change from the traditional coleslaw, and a colorful, tasty winter salad.

½ head red cabbage,
    finely shredded
¾ cup grated apple
¾ cup raisins

2 teaspoons horseradish
¼ teaspoon salt
¼ cup light mayonnaise
¼ cup plain yogurt

Mix cabbage, apple, and raisins in salad bowl. In a small bowl, combine the horseradish, salt, mayonnaise, and yogurt. Stir into cabbage mixture carefully. Chill. Makes 4 servings.

from Prefix, *Confidential Chat*

Honey Glazed Vegetables
(recipe on page 225)

Feta Cheese Salad

This vegetable-and-feta cheese salad is a wonderful accompaniment to barbecued steak or hamburgers and can also be served as a meal in itself on warm evenings. Serve a chilled soup first, with crusty bread or rolls.

3 large green peppers	1 large red Bermuda onion
1 large sweet red pepper	1 cup pitted black olives,
4 large tomatoes	sliced
2 medium onions	

Dressing and Garnish:

6 tablespoons good olive oil	1 tablespoon Dijon-style mustard
3 tablespoons vinegar	3 hard-cooked eggs
3 tablespoons finely chopped chives	¾ pound (or more) feta cheese, crumbled

Seed peppers and cut into thin strips. Cut each tomato into 8 wedges. Thin-slice onions and separate into rings. Drain and slice olives. Combine in large salad bowl.

To prepare dressing, beat oil and vinegar in small bowl until well blended. Add chopped chives and mustard, stirring to mix. Pour dressing over vegetables. Cut eggs into wedges and place around edge. Crumble feta cheese over top. Cover and refrigerate until serving time. Makes 6 generous servings or 8 smaller servings.

from Kindred Spirit, *Confidential Chat*

Orange Avocado Salad with Lemon Dressing

This recipe makes 6 servings.

Dressing

¼ cup lemon juice
½ teaspoon salt
⅛ teaspoon pepper

¼ teaspoon sugar
¼ teaspoon dry mustard
½ cup vegetable oil

Salad

6 cups romaine (1 medium-sized
   head)

2 cups navel orange slices
1 large ripe avocado

Beat lemon juice, salt, pepper, sugar, and mustard together in a bowl. Beat in vegetable oil in a slow, steady stream until mixture is thick and slightly creamy. Refrigerate. Shake well just before serving.

    Break romaine into bite-size pieces in large salad bowl. Place oranges in a small bowl. Chill. Just before serving, peel, pit, and slice avocado. Arrange avocado and orange slices over romaine. Drizzle lemon dressing over salad and toss gently.

from Prefix, *Confidential Chat*

Rice Salad

Try this once, and it will probably become one of your favorites.

2 cups cooked long-grain rice,
   chilled
¼ cup chopped green onion
1 small green or red pepper,
   diced
⅓ cup celery, diced

¼ cup ripe olives, drained
   and sliced
¼ cup vegetable oil
1½ teaspoons wine vinegar
½ teaspoon Dijon-style mustard
Salt and pepper to taste

In a bowl, combine rice, green onion, pepper, celery, and olives. In a small bowl, beat the oil with the vinegar and mustard. Pour over rice mixture. Toss well, seasoning to taste with salt and pepper. Chill. Makes 4 servings.

from Prefix, *Confidential Chat*

Fruits for Salad

Fruits served as salad make a very fine counterpoint to dinner. One of my favorites is made as follows:

Put a bed of greens on the salad plate—chopped or shredded, if you want them to be eaten—then fruit of most any kind: canned pineapple rings, orange or grapefruit sections, banana slices, fresh or canned pears or peaches; whatever is in season or in the cupboard. Top it with about 3 tablespoons cottage cheese and over that a good spoonful of whole cranberry sauce—canned, broken up with a fork, or your own homemade. This good and pretty salad is a hit every time.

Use fruits mixed in with greens for a pleasant flavor. Orange and onion slices are good to serve with poultry. Banana chunks rolled first in lemon juice and then in finely chopped nuts, and served with a French or cream cheese honey dressing (page 205), tempt appetites. Pears with cream or cottage cheese and a tart French dressing on a bed of chicory are always pretty and good.

Use fruits in season with a free hand. Many times I serve a generous fruit salad to double as dessert.

Molded Cranberry Orange Relish

This versatile relish can be served on a buffet table or in individual servings with lettuce and mayonnaise. It can be made year-round, which adds to its popularity.

1 package (4-serving size) orange flavor gelatin	1 orange
1 cup boiling water	1 can (16 ounces) whole cranberry sauce
½ cup orange juice	½ cup finely chopped celery

Dissolve gelatin in boiling water and add orange juice. Chill until mixture begins to thicken. Wash orange and cut into pieces. Remove seeds, if any. Chop in a processor or a blender. Add to gelatin with cranberry sauce and celery. Spoon into a 1-quart mold and chill until firm. Unmold and serve as a relish with hot or cold poultry or ham. Makes 1 quart or 8 servings.

Orange Coleslaw

A nice change from regular coleslaw. Serve as a dinner salad or with sandwiches.

1½ cups orange sections
2 cups shredded cabbage
½ cup chopped dates or raisins
⅓ cup mayonnaise

¼ teaspoon salt
1½ teaspoons sugar
¼ teaspoon celery seed

Cut orange sections in half. Mix with cabbage and dates. Combine mayonnaise with salt, sugar, and celery seed and stir into cabbage mixture until well blended. Chill. Makes 6 servings.

Summer Salad

Croissants and iced tea go with this combination of fruits.

Salad greens
3 cups grapefruit sections
2 cups melon balls (honeydew,
    watermelon, or cantaloupe)
1 cup blueberries

1 cup sliced strawberries
2 bananas, sliced
2 teaspoons lemon juice
½ cup mayonnaise
⅓ cup orange juice

Arrange salad greens on 4 luncheon-size plates. Arrange fruits on each plate to form a design or pattern. Sprinkle bananas with lemon juice. Serve with mayonnaise thinned with orange juice. Makes 4 servings.

Apple Salad

Apple salad is a good winter salad to accompany pork, ham, meat loaf, chicken—in fact about every main-dish course.

3 apples, such as Cortland,
    McIntosh, Delicious
1 tablespoon lemon juice or
    dry sherry

¾ cup chopped walnuts
⅓ cup chopped celery
½ cup mayonnaise
Lettuce

Peel 2 apples and core and dice. Core and dice other apple unpeeled. Sprinkle with lemon juice or sherry. Toss with remaining ingredients except lettuce. Serve in large lettuce-lined bowl or on individual lettuce-lined plates. Makes 4 to 6 servings.

Blender Mayonnaise

This mayonnaise may also be made in a food processor. The recipe can be doubled in the processor, but unless you are planning to use it within a week, homemade mayonnaise does not keep as well as commercial. It is so easy to make that small amounts are no problem. I whirl my oil-and-vinegar dressing in the blender to get the mayonnaise cleaned out and give a little new flavor to the French style dressing.

1 cup oil	½ teaspoon dry mustard
2 tablespoons lemon juice or	½ teaspoon salt
vinegar	1 egg

Combine ¼ cup oil, lemon juice or vinegar, mustard, salt, and egg in blender. Run 15 seconds with the lid on, then remove lid and gradually add remaining oil. When thickened, put into a jar, cover, and store in refrigerator. Makes 1½ cups.

Variations

Add 2 tablespoons each chopped fresh chives and parsley.

To ½ cup mayonnaise add 6 tablespoons plain yogurt and stir to blend. Taste and add a few drops of Tabasco, if desired.

Thousand Island Dressing: To 1 recipe blender mayonnaise add ⅓ cup chili sauce, 2 tablespoons finely chopped green pepper, 5 tablespoons chopped and well-drained pimiento, and 1 tablespoon chopped chives. Mix lightly to blend. Makes 1⅔ cups. Store, covered, in refrigerator about 10 days.

Russian Dressing: To 1 recipe blender mayonnaise add ½ cup chopped green olives, 2 tablespoons chopped sweet pickle (or same amount pickle relish), 5 tablespoons chili sauce, and 1 hard-cooked egg, chopped. Makes 1¾ cups. Store, covered, in refrigerator about 10 days.

Seasoned Blender Mayonnaise

The onions, garlic, and other seasonings in this tasty mayonnaise make it a natural to serve with cold cuts, salad greens, or tomatoes.

1 egg	1 clove garlic, chopped
2 tablespoons lemon juice	$\frac{1}{2}$ teaspoon dry mustard
$\frac{1}{2}$ teaspoon salt	1 sprig parsley, cut up
$\frac{1}{2}$ teaspoon sugar	1 cup oil
$\frac{1}{2}$ teaspoon vinegar	
2 green onions, including tops, cut up	

Put egg, lemon juice, salt, sugar, vinegar, onions, garlic, mustard, and parsley in blender and blend until smooth. Continue blending, adding oil slowly. If oil does not blend in easily toward end of addition, stop motor and push oil down into mayonnaise with spatula, blending until oil is incorporated and mixture is thick and smooth. Makes $1\frac{1}{2}$ cups. Store, covered, in the refrigerator.

Basic French Dressing

A good dressing for either vegetable or fruit salads.

$\frac{1}{3}$ cup cider vinegar or lemon juice	Freshly ground pepper to taste
1 cup oil	$\frac{1}{4}$ teaspoon paprika
$\frac{1}{2}$ teaspoon salt	1 teaspoon dry mustard
	1 clove garlic, peeled and cut in half

Combine all ingredients and shake well. Shake before each use. Store, covered, in refrigerator. Makes $1\frac{1}{2}$ cups.

Variations

Creamy Dressing: Add $\frac{1}{3}$ cup mayonnaise to above mixture and stir or shake until blended. Makes $1\frac{2}{3}$ cups.

Roquefort Dressing: Omit mustard and add 4 tablespoons Roquefort or blue cheese. Makes $1\frac{3}{4}$ cups.

Herb Dressing: Add $\frac{1}{4}$ teaspoon crushed dried rosemary or $\frac{1}{4}$ teaspoon crushed dried basil to basic dressing.

Tarragon Dressing: Omit cider vinegar (or lemon juice) and use same amount of tarragon vinegar.

Another French Dressing

This dressing, made with wine vinegar and olive oil, is good with the more flavorful greens.

2 teaspoons Dijon-style mustard
¼ teaspoon salt
Freshly ground pepper to taste

2 tablespoons fresh lemon juice
1 cup olive oil
½ cup red wine vinegar

Mix mustard with salt, pepper, and lemon juice to blend. Gradually beat in olive oil and vinegar. Makes 1½ cups.

Low-Calorie French Dressing

Use noncaloric sweetener in place of the teaspoon of sugar, if you wish to lower the calorie count by 16 calories.

1 cup water
1 tablespoon cornstarch
1 teaspoon paprika
½ teaspoon dry mustard
½ teaspoon garlic salt
¼ cup red-wine vinegar

1 tablespoon salad oil
¼ teaspoon dillweed
¼ teaspoon basil, crumbled
1 teaspoon sugar (or sweetener
   equivalent)

Combine water, cornstarch, paprika, mustard, and garlic salt in small pan. Cook, stirring, until mixture comes to boil and is clear. Cool.

Transfer to a jar and add all remaining ingredients. Cover and shake well to blend. Chill. Makes about 1½ cups.

from Prefix, *Confidential Chat*

Cream Cheese Honey Dressing

A sprightly combination for fruits.

1 package (3 ounces) cream
    cheese
½ teaspoon salt

2 tablespoons honey
½ cup orange juice
2 tablespoons lemon juice

Soften cream cheese in a small bowl and mix in salt and honey. Gradually beat in orange juice and lemon juice. Serve with fruit salad. Makes 1 cup.

Coleslaw Dressing

This has long been a favorite dressing in my family.

1 cup sour cream
1 teaspoon dry mustard
1 teaspoon salt

4 tablespoons sugar
¼ cup vinegar
1 teaspoon celery salt

Blend all ingredients well. Makes enough for 4 cups shredded cabbage.

from Mrs. Pooh, *Confidential Chat*

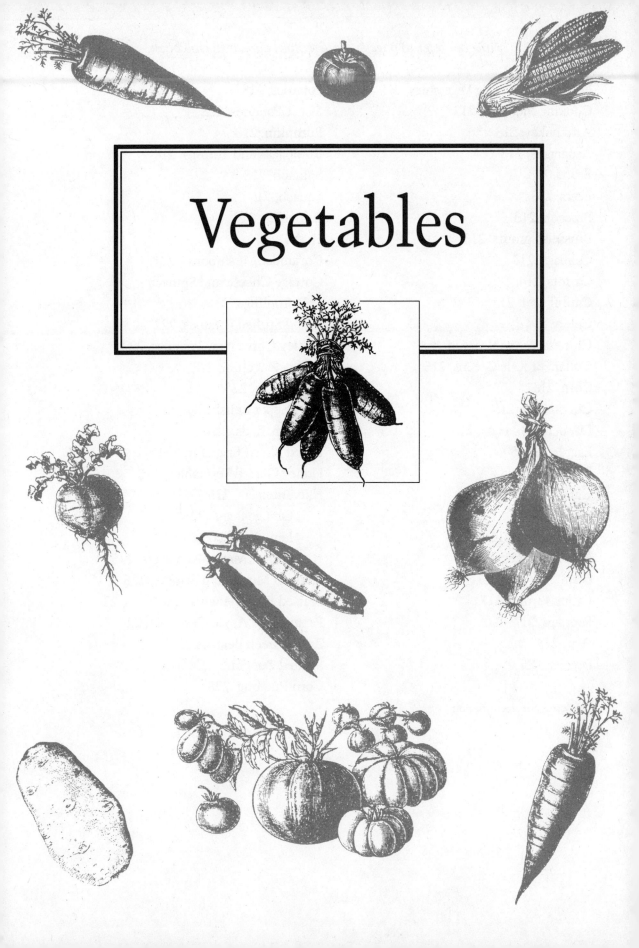

Vegetables

*indicates a recipe variation

Vegetables

We are blessed with such a variety of fresh, frozen, and canned vegetables that we often tend to take them for granted. But both vegetables and fruits add valuable nutritional benefits to our diet. They also add variety and can make a dull meal shining bright. When some dietary change (such as that caused by an ulcer) occurs, and many fruits and vegetables are eliminated from the menu, one realizes the magnitude of the loss.

Remember that vegetables add vitamins A, B_6, and C, among others—as well as iron, phosphorus, thiamine, niacin, and potassium. They also contain trace elements essential for health maintenance, an important factor, as well as providing bulk in the diet.

Buying and Storing Vegetables

When selecting vegetables from the fresh produce department, be certain they are fresh—no wilt, no brown or rust spots—and do not buy more than can be used in a reasonable time. Frozen vegetables come in such a variety, including some frozen straight from the vine, some partly cooked, some with a sauce or seasoning of some kind, and some in combination with other vegetables. Choose the pack that suits the need. Often it is less expensive to buy the large bulk sacks of frozen vegetables. The amount needed can be taken out, the remainder resealed and returned to the freezer. Whatever you buy, check that the packages are in good condition and that they are solidly frozen; and get them from the store to your own freezer in jig time.

Canned vegetables also should be chosen by need. An example would be tomatoes. If they are to be used in soup, there is no need to buy a deluxe pack such as one might want to use in scalloped tomatoes. After buying canned vegetables (and fruits), store them in a cool place, no more that 70°F or less than 32°F year-round. If you keep any size inventory, date the cans so that the first in will be used first. Canned products cannot be expected to maintain their optimum quality for more than a year.

Store fresh vegetables at home in the refrigerator hydrator. I prefer to put them in plastic bags and close with a tie. This keeps them separate and easier to find, if your hydrator is as full as mine. A week should be maximum storage, so buy accordingly.

When buying fresh vegetables, allow 3 to 4 servings per pound. Canned and frozen vegetables indicate servings on package.

Cooking Methods

The best way to cook vegetables is not more than necessary to make them tender-crisp. This can be accomplished by boiling in a small amount of water, steaming, stir-frying, baking, or microwaving. These rules apply to fresh or frozen. Canned vegetables have already been cooked done, so they only need to be reheated with the seasoning you add.

In the case of both fresh and frozen vegetables, less water and shorter cooking are better for flavor, texture, and nutritive value.

Boiling
Prepare vegetables according to preference. Put 1 inch of water in saucepan, and always use a saucepan to fit amount of vegetables to be cooked. The pan should be about ⅔ full. Bring water to a boil, lower heat, and simmer, covered, until vegetables are just tender.

Steaming
Place an inexpensive expandable steamer that fits several sizes of pans in a pan with about 1 inch of water (which should be below the level of the steamer). Put vegetables to be cooked in steamer and bring water to a boil. Cover pan, reduce heat, and steam until just tender.

Stir-Frying
To stir-fry, heat about 1 to 2 tablespoons of oil or butter in a heavy skillet or wok. Add vegetables—which should be thinly sliced, in any favorite combinations or singly—and stir and fry over medium to high heat until tender-crisp, about 2 minutes.

Baking
Potatoes, sweet potatoes, squashes, and pumpkin are good candidates for baking in their own skins, while other vegetables can be baked in a covered casserole. Slice or dice peeled vegetables, put in a casserole they fit, add butter and seasonings to taste, add 2 or 3 teaspoons liquid, cover, and bake anywhere from 350°F to 400°F for about ½ hour or until fork-tender. *Note:* Timing is difficult because of varieties that might be used and freshness.

Microwave Cooking
Check the owner's manual for directions. Most vegetables cook well and rapidly in a microwave oven.

Pressure Cooking
Almost all vegetables can be cooked in the pressure cooker, though there is hardly any need to do so except for the long cookers. Follow the manufacturer's directions.

Cooking Individual Vegetables

Artichokes

To prepare artichokes for cooking, cut off stem and 1 inch from top. With scissors, trim tips from larger leaves. Wash well. Put 4 artichokes in a saucepan into which they fit rather snugly. Add ¼ cup water, juice of 1 lemon, 2 stalks celery, 2 cloves garlic, and 3 tablespoons olive oil. Cover and simmer about 45 minutes or until leaves are tender.

To eat, pull off leaves with fingers and scrape off flesh with teeth. When you get down to the center, you will find the choke, which is not edible. Dig it out with a spoon and discard, before eating the heart.

Artichokes can be served hot with lemon butter or cold with a vinaigrette sauce or other dressing.

Asparagus

Break asparagus by holding stalk at each end and bending to break at tender spot. Wash well. Steam for about 5 minutes. Serve buttered, with hollandaise sauce, or cold in salad. Cut off woody ends and peel section remaining. Use for cream of asparagus soup or slice thinly into mixed green salad. Cook frozen asparagus as directed and serve the same as fresh.

Beans

Green or wax snap beans are the most common fresh bean. Cut off stem end and cook whole or cut into pieces. They can be boiled, steamed, microwaved, or stir-fried. Depending on maturity of beans they take from 10 to 20 minutes. Served buttered or cooked with a little chopped bacon or some chopped onion, they are a popular vegetable. Cook frozen as directed.

Beets

Beets can be purchased in bunches with their greens. Cut greens off, leaving a 3-inch length of stem on beet. Scrub beets and boil, covered with water, until tender, 25 minutes or longer depending on maturity. Peel beets, slice, and serve with butter and vinegar or as Harvard beets. Or use canned beets.

Save beet greens. Cut off stems, wash well, and cut into bite-size pieces. Cook in the water that clings to leaves for 1 to 2 minutes. Serve with vinegar.

Broccoli

Buy broccoli with good green color. Cut off and steam heads for 8 to 10 minutes. Serve buttered, with lemon juice, or with hollandaise sauce. Trim stems, cutting away woody part. Slice thinly and marinate in French dressing. Use in green salads. Follow directions on package for frozen; manufacturer's instructions for cooking in microwave ovens.

Brussels Sprouts

Brussels sprouts are like tiny cabbages. Wash well. Steam, boil, or microwave. Cook quickly and test for tenderness at 10 minutes. Serve with lemon butter, sautéed sliced almonds, or poppy seed butter.

Cabbage

There are several varieties—Savoy, with yellowish crimped leaves; red cabbage; Chinese or celery cabbage; and regular cabbage, which is generally green in spring and white in winter. With the exception of Chinese cabbage (which is used mostly in salads and stir-fry combinations), cabbages are steamed, boiled, or microwaved. Cook shredded cabbage 5 to 10 minutes; wedges no longer than 15. Use all 4 types for coleslaw or cabbage salad.

Carrots

This is one of our most popular vegetables, served cooked or raw. To cook, prepare carrots as desired (whole, sliced, or julienned). Then steam or boil about 10 minutes, or microwave according to directions. Serve with butter, lemon juice, or honey glaze. Cook frozen carrots according to directions.

Cauliflower

Cauliflower, another cabbage-related vegetable, should have flowerets removed from stems and can be steamed, boiled, microwaved, or baked. It is good with butter and lemon juice or can be served with buttered bread crumbs and grated Parmesan cheese. Stems can be trimmed, sliced, and added to vegetable salads. Cook frozen cauliflower according to directions.

Celery

While celery is thought of primarily as a raw vegetable, it is delicious when braised. Cut outside stalks into thin slices and braise in a small amount of water and butter or margarine in a covered skillet. Season with salt and pepper. Allow about 1½ stalks per serving. Celery (with some tops) is a vital flavoring ingredient in soups, stews, and pot roast.

Chinese Vegetables

Bok choy, Chinese cabbage, Chinese parsley, and snow peas are among the many varieties in this group of vegetables and can be found in many supermarkets. They are used most often in stir-fry dishes, to which they add their own individual flavors.

Bok choy can be described as having heavy celerylike stalks topped with dark green, crinkly leaves. Wash thoroughly, then cut into crosswise slices, using both stalk and leaves, and add to a stir-fry for very quick sautéeing. It is also a flavorful addition to vegetable soups.

Chinese cabbage is also known as long cabbage. Different from bok choy, it is a cylinder of tight, crinkly leaves. Its flavor is more delicate than regular cabbage, though slightly tart. The outer leaves are used for cooking, while the inner white leaves are crisp and tender and may be eaten raw or in stir-fry dishes and soups.

Chinese parsley has flat, inch-wide leaves with serrated edges. Its flavor is much more pronounced than our usual parsley and should be used judiciously so that it does not dominate a dish.

Snow peas (or Chinese pea pods) are small and flat and need only stemming for preparation (and washing, of course). Toss these sweet morsels into a stir-fry, or better yet, serve them raw in a salad or as part of a *crudité* tray.

Collard or Kale Greens

Collard and kale are very close relatives.

Wash and cut leaves in bite-size pieces. Sauté chopped bacon in skillet; add washed greens; and simmer, covered, 8 to 10 minutes. Serve with vinegar. Cook frozen greens as directed. Follow microwave directions.

Corn

Sweet corn, white or yellow, on the cob is available year-round now though locally grown corn in season is best. Remove outer husks, plunge into a large pot of boiling water, and when water returns to boil, shut off heat. Let stand in water for 2 minutes and serve. Can also be microwaved; follow directions. Corn can be cut off the cob and sautéed in butter and a few spoons of water for no more than 5 minutes. Onions can be added for seasoning, or try a tablespoon or two of chili sauce. Corn also comes frozen and canned.

Cucumbers

Slicing, pickling, and English (the long ones) cucumbers are available. While cucumbers are primarily considered a raw vegetable, they are very good sautéed. Peel cucumber and cut in ¼-inch slices crosswise. Spread slices on paper towels to dry. Then dip in flour seasoned with salt and pepper. Sauté in butter 3 to 4 minutes. Depending on size, allow ¾ to 1 cucumber per serving.

Dandelion Greens

Can be cooked or used raw in salads. Wash greens and cut up. Cook in water clinging to greens, about 1 minute. Serve with butter and vinegar.

Eggplant

Eggplants come small enough so that one might be an individual serving, particularly when stuffed; or in larger sizes up to 2 pounds. Do not peel unless the skin seems tough. There is no need to soak in salt. Slice ¾-inch-thick slices, dip successively in flour, egg, and crumbs, and fry in butter until browned on one side. Turn and brown on other side until tender when pierced with fork. Season to taste with salt and pepper.

Endive

Belgian endive can be used as a salad vegetable but is also delicious braised in butter and bouillon in a covered skillet until tender, about 10 minutes. Remove lid and allow bouillon to reduce to a very small amount. Allow about 1 head endive per person, depending on size.

Garlic

Garlic has many uses as a seasoning for meats, vegetables, fish dishes. Store away from onions and potatoes, in a covered jar. It can be chopped, squeezed through a garlic press, or used whole.

Leeks

Leeks have been popular through the centuries, principally as an ingredient for soup. But there are many other ways to serve this delicately flavored vegetable. Try boiled leeks with melted butter or various sauces, gently braised leeks, Greek style with lemon juice, vinaigrette style, even deep-fried.

As with all vegetables, choose fresh-looking, firm leeks. Cut off the root end and most of the green top, leaving the blanched lower part. Peel off the outer leaf and skin. Wash thoroughly to remove all soil; the best way to do this is to split it down the center for about 2 inches from the bottom. Fan out the leaves under running water, then turn and thoroughly wash from the top.

Cooking time will vary with the size and freshness. To boil, add leeks to about 1 inch of boiling water in a saucepan, cover the pan, and let simmer for 10 to 15 minutes, or until fork-tender.

Mushrooms

Where mushrooms were once considered an exotic food, used only by those with the expertise to recognize those that were safe to pick in the wild, we now have year-round supplies at produce counters, and fine variety as well.

There are the handsome, most often used plump whites and flavorful browns, as well as chanterelles, shiitakes, lobster mushrooms, boletes, and oyster mushrooms. The large dried Chinese mushrooms that add so much flavor to soups, stews, and Oriental dishes can be found in large supermarkets and in Oriental groceries.

Mushrooms are delicate and should be used when at their freshest. Simply brush them lightly with a paper towel or mushroom brush, then slice or chop them, discarding the very bottoms of the stems. Soak dry mushrooms in hot water before cutting into strips. Add the soaking water to the dish.

Mustard Greens

Cut up, wash, and cook in the water that clings to leaves 1 to 2 minutes. Uncooked leaves can be added to salad.

Okra

May be boiled, baked, or fried. Also used in soups and stews. Cut off stems; if pods are large, cut in half; boil 10 minutes in 1 inch water. Serve with butter and vinegar.

Onion Family

This versatile vegetable almost deserves a chapter of its own. You will find dry yellow and white cooking onions; red onions used mostly for salads; sweet Spanish onions, mild enough for salads but good for cooking; and Bermuda onions. Green onions are used primarily in salads but are also an ingredient in many cooked recipes. Leeks are large fresh bulb onions that are sold with their green tops, which may or may not be used in cooking. Shallots are another member of this family.

Dry onions should be stored in a cool dry place, preferably dark. Once cut into, what is left of an onion should be wrapped in plastic wrap and stored in the refrigerator.

Green onions and leeks should be stored in the hydrator of the refrigerator. When green onions are in good supply, they can be steamed and served like asparagus.

Frozen whole and chopped onions are used like fresh. Whole onions are also available canned.

Parsnips

Parsnips are a hardy vegetable that may be creamed, sauteed, mashed, or deep fried. Steaming brings out their nutty flavor. Choose small to medium.

Peas

Peas in the pod are available fresh. Peas also come canned and frozen. There are the regular or English peas, which should be shelled, and the Chinese pea pods or snow peas (also called sugar peas), which are cooked in the shell or can be eaten fresh in salads. Snow peas are much used in stir-fry cooking. Buy bright green pods that are fresh looking and store in the refrigerator; the same goes for snow peas. Allow about ¾ pound of English peas per serving. Snow peas can serve 4 to the pound.

Peppers

Red and green bell peppers are used in cooking and salads. To skin a pepper, char under the broiler, and under running water, scrape off the skin. If you have a gas flame, the pepper can also be put on a long-handled fork and charred over the flame. Skinned peppers are used for fried peppers: Slice, remove seeds, and sauté in olive oil with a little garlic 4 to 5 minutes. Serve as a vegetable.

Chilis, jalapeno peppers, and serranos peppers are among the hot peppers used in Mexican cooking. With the popularity of Mexican cooking, more of these little hot peppers are finding their way into the market. For very hot food, do not remove the seeds when using them.

Potatoes

Potatoes are one of our most used vegetables. They are not fattening. It is the butter, sour cream, etc. that goes into them that adds the calories. They are nutritionally a good buy, too, having fair amounts of vitamins B, C, and G (riboflavin) and a good content of iron, phosphorus, and other minerals.

Store in a cool, dry, dark area.

Potatoes can be steamed, boiled, baked, fried, or microwaved and are frozen in many forms as well as dehydrated. There are so many varieties it is not practical to list them all. The major varieties in this market area are those from Idaho (long russets, which make an excellent baking potato); round whites from Maine or other Eastern areas, good for boiled potatoes, salad, or frying; long whites from California, a good boiled potato; and round reds up from Florida, for boiling and salad.

To cook potato skins: Scrub and bake 6 russet potatoes (pierce with fork) at 400°F for about one hour. Cool and cut in half lengthwise. Scoop out potato and reserve for other use. Cut skins in 1-inch strips crosswise. Dip in flour, shake off excess. Deep fry in oil heated to 375°F for 2 minutes. Drain on paper towels. Sprinkle with seasoned salt to taste. Makes 60 potato strips.

Sweet Potatoes

Thick, chunky, medium-sized sweets tapering toward the end are the best to choose. The skin of the dry potato is usually light yellowish tan; the moist potato, brownish red or whitish tan. Yams are moister when cooked than other types. Sweet potatoes are a nutritionally excellent food. They can be boiled, baked, or fried and come canned with or without a sugar syrup. Sweet potatoes are also used in breads, pies, cookies, and cakes.

Pumpkin

The pumpkin is a member of the squash family. Cut up and remove seeds; steam until tender. Use pulp for pies, biscuits, breads, and desserts. Pumpkin also comes canned, handy for quick use.

Rutabagas and Turnips

Both are strong-flavored root vegetables and should be stored at 32°F. Both can be steamed, boiled, mashed, or used in stews. Cape Cod grows a special mild, white turnip. Regular turnips come in both yellow and white. To my taste, turnips and rutabagas should both be served with lots of freshly ground pepper and butter. They cook very well in the microwave and are also good sliced raw into salads.

Spinach

Fresh spinach is good both raw, as a salad green, and cooked. It also comes frozen or canned. It can be steamed, boiled, or microwaved. Wash the greens well to remove sand, cut out any heavy ribs, and cook 1 to 2 minutes in the water that clings to the leaves. Serve cooked spinach with butter and vinegar or chopped hard-cooked eggs. Store fresh spinach in the refrigerator.

Squash

Squash is an overall name for a great variety of different squashes.

There are the winter or hard-shell squashes such as acorn, butternut, banana, and Hubbard, which steam and bake very well. They also can be cooked in the microwave, following the manufacturer's directions. You will also find spaghetti squash, whose flesh when cooked (steamed or boiled) comes loose in ribbons like spaghetti.

Summer squashes include zucchini, yellow crookneck and yellow straight neck, and patty pan or scallops.

Butternut, Hubbard, and banana squashes are sometimes made into pies or rolls after being steamed, scraped from the shell, and mashed.

Winter squash is enhanced with brown sugar or maple syrup, butter, salt, and pepper.

The summer squashes fit into many recipes, though they are good served plain with butter and seasoning. Some of the squashes are frozen and canned.

Tomatoes

Tomatoes, botanically, are a fruit; but for cooks they come into the vegetable classification. They are widely used both fresh and cooked. There are many varieties, but the biggest differences are found between the regular salad tomatoes, the Italian plum, and the cherry. Choose tomatoes that are ripe and have no blemishes. If you cannot buy them as ripe as you wish, put in a brown paper sack with a fresh apple and close tightly. The apple releases a gas that helps ripen the tomatoes. Write the date on the sack with a pen, and remember to check each day or so. It should take about 3 days. (This method of ripening works well for peaches or pears, too.)

Sautéed cherry tomatoes with herbs are easy to prepare. For enough to serve 4, plan about 24 cherry tomatoes. Heat 2 or 3 tablespoons butter in a skillet. Add washed cherry tomatoes and sauté until tomatoes' skins just begin to break. Season with salt, freshly ground pepper, chopped fresh parsley, and dill or basil.

Herbs

Fresh herbs are one of the most lovely additions to cooking. If you have a small space of land to spare, and have not grown herbs, try growing some. Thyme is a perennial so that once you get it started it will come up each spring. Oregano can sometimes be temperamental and some years does not reappear, but is hardy in many situations. Sage, chives, winter savory, tarragon, and mint all are very faithful and come up year after year. Basil is an annual but will grow and prosper in the kitchen so you will have it all year round. Some people have luck bringing in rosemary in the fall, but if it doesn't work for you it has to be purchased each spring. Dill must be planted each year and it does grow to large plants, if space is a problem.

Just the short list of herbs above will be enough to add flavor to your cooked dishes and salads. If you have fresh herbs and the recipe calls for dried, use 3 times as much chopped fresh herbs as dried.

Here are some food-herb combinations:

BASIL: Tomatoes, eggplant, green beans, zucchini, cheese, and spaghetti dishes

WINTER SAVORY: Green or dried beans, poultry, meat salad, stuffing, scrambled eggs

TARRAGON: Green salads, mayonnaise, fish sauce, vinegar

OREGANO: Tomato dishes, cheese, eggs, vegetable and beef broths, fish

THYME: Fish, poultry, tomatoes, spaghetti dishes

DILL: Sour-cream sauces, green beans, cabbage, cucumber, potato salad, fish

ROSEMARY: Chicken, eggs, cheese, lamb, veal, tomatoes, zucchini

PARSLEY: Can be added to most any cooked dish or salad

CHIVES: A relative of the onion family; chopped, goes into meat and vegetable salads and soups; nice as a garnish

SAGE: Pork, chicken, stuffings, seafood, cheese.

Coriander Mushrooms

The lovely juice from these mushrooms should be sopped up with crusty bread, so serve in individual vegetable dishes. Good with steak.

1 pound fresh mushrooms	2 bay leaves
3 tablespoons lemon juice	½ teaspoon salt
2 teaspoons coriander seed	Freshly ground pepper to taste
6 tablespoons olive oil	

Brush mushrooms, if necessary. Cut off stem end; if large, cut mushrooms in quarters. Sprinkle with lemon juice. Crush coriander seeds with a mortar and pestle, or fold in waxed paper and crush with a rolling pin.

Heat olive oil in a heavy skillet over low heat. Add coriander and allow to heat through. Add the mushrooms and bay leaves. Season with salt and pepper. Cook and stir 1 minute and then cover pan and let cook 5 minutes longer. Let mushrooms cool to serve. Makes 4 servings.

Cottage Cheese and Spinach Dumplings

Serve buttered noodles with the dumplings. For a vegetable, peas and carrots; for dessert, a fresh fruit cup and cookies.

1½ cups very well drained chopped cooked or canned spinach (a 1-pound, 13-ounce can, or 2 10-ounce packages frozen chopped spinach)	¼ cup fine soft bread crumbs
	1 egg, beaten
	Flour
	3 cups well-flavored beef bouillon
2 tablespoons butter, melted	3 or 4 tablespoons butter, melted
1 cup dry cottage cheese	
¼ teaspoon monosodium gluta-mate (optional)	Additional grated sharp cheese (optional)
½ cup grated sharp American cheese	

Mix spinach with butter, cottage cheese, monosodium glutamate, grated American cheese, bread crumbs, and egg until well blended. Chill. Make into balls containing one tablespoon each. Roll in flour.

Heat bouillon to boiling. Drop dumplings into bouillon, and when they rise to the top remove from bouillon with a slotted spoon or fork. Keep hot. Serve with melted butter and extra grated sharp cheese, if desired. Makes 4 servings.

from B. A., *Confidential Chat*

Baked Stuffed Potatoes

Potatoes prepared this way are a boon to hostesses because they can be prepared in advance and heated at the last minute. My recipe is for four, but it can easily be multiplied.

4 large baking potatoes
Oil
3 to 4 tablespoons dairy sour
    cream or plain yogurt
4 tablespoons butter or margarine
2 tablespoons chopped chives

2 tablespoons chopped fresh
    parsley
Salt and freshly ground pepper
    to taste
Paprika

Scrub potatoes well. Pierce in several places with a fork and rub all over with oil. Bake at 400°F for 50 to 60 minutes or until tender.

Cut about 1 inch off top of each baked potato lengthwise and scrape out insides of potatoes, leaving the shell intact. Mash potatoes and beat in sour cream or yogurt, butter, chives, and parsley, beating until fluffy. Season to taste with salt and pepper. Spoon back into potato shells. Sprinkle top with paprika. Reheat in a 400°F oven for 10 to 15 minutes. Makes 4 servings.

If potatoes are prepared in advance, refrigerate, and reheat at 400°F for 20 to 30 minutes.

Parsley Chive New Potatoes

Delicious in the spring with roast chicken or fish or ground beef patties.

1½ pounds tiny new potatoes,
    unpeeled
Water
½ teaspoon salt

¼ cup butter or margarine
2 tablespoons chopped chives
2 tablespoons chopped fresh parsley
Freshly ground pepper to taste

Scrub potatoes and put in a saucepan. Put about 1 inch water in pan and add salt. Bring to boil and steam, covered, for 20 minutes or until tender. Drain and shake over heat until potatoes are dry. Add remaining ingredients and carefully stir potatoes until all are covered. Makes 4 servings.

Savory Zucchini

A quickly prepared and flavorful way to serve this readily available vegetable. A few sun-dried tomatoes, softened briefly in hot water, may be used in place of the tomato paste.

2 medium-sized zucchini	2 tablespoons tomato paste
2 tablespoons olive oil	1 tablespoon minced fresh basil
1 shallot, minced (or 1 small onion, minced)	Salt and pepper to taste
	Grated Parmesan cheese

Trim and discard ends from zucchini. Do not peel. Cut into fairly thin julienne strips, about 2 inches in length. Heat oil in heavy skillet, then add minced shallot or onion and sauté until tender and golden. Immediately add zucchini, tossing to coat with oil and shallot. Carefully stir in tomato paste. Lower heat, cover pan, and allow to steam for 2 or 3 minutes, until zucchini is just crisp-tender. Transfer to warm serving bowl; sprinkle with basil, salt, pepper, and grated Parmesan cheese. Makes 4 servings.

Ratatouille

Ratatouille is a vegetable combination that can be served hot or cold. If served cold, assorted cold cuts and cheeses, and toasted French bread, would make a good combination.

¼ cup olive oil	2 tablespoons chopped fresh basil or 2 teaspoons dried basil
2 cloves garlic, minced	
1 onion, sliced	
1 green pepper, seeded and cut in strips	1 tablespoon chopped fresh oregano or 1 teaspoon dried oregano
3 medium unpared zucchini (about 1 pound), cut crosswise into ¼-inch slices	
	1 teaspoon salt
	Freshly ground pepper to taste
1 medium eggplant (about 1 pound), pared and cubed	3 ripe tomatoes, peeled and cut in wedges

Heat oil in an 11- or 12-inch skillet. Cook garlic, onion, green pepper, and zucchini until onion is tender, stirring frequently. Add eggplant, herbs, and seasonings. Cover and cook over medium heat, stirring a few times. Add tomatoes and cook, covered, 5 minutes longer or just until tomatoes are heated. Serve hot or chill well and serve cold. Makes 4 to 6 servings.

Hot Pepper Relish

Quickly made to serve with grilled or roast meats, or good with scrambled eggs or as a filling for an omelet.

2 red sweet peppers	1 medium onion, finely chopped
2 green sweet peppers	1 garlic clove, crushed
2 tablespoons butter or margarine	½ teaspoon salt

Cut peppers in half and remove seeds and cores. Wash well and slice thinly. Heat butter in skillet and sauté onion and garlic until soft. Add peppers, sprinkle with salt, and continue cooking until just tender, 4 to 5 minutes. Serve hot. Makes 4 servings.

Crunchy Reds

Small red potatoes, cooked in their skins, are deservedly popular and versatile. Simply boil until tender, drain well, and dress with a bit of melted butter and a lot of chopped parsley. Or for a change, try the following.

12 to 14 small red potatoes	1 clove garlic, minced
½ cup vegetable oil or butter	Salt and pepper to taste

Wash potatoes, then boil just until tender. Drain well. Heat oil or butter; add garlic and sauté gently until just tender. Add potatoes and allow to brown, turning often so all sides become crisp. Sprinkle with salt and pepper. Makes 4 servings.

Baked Sliced Eggplant

A popular way to serve this vegetable, though in this version, the eggplant is baked rather than fried.

1 medium-sized eggplant	1 scallion, finely minced
Salt	1 cup dry bread crumbs
½ cup mayonnaise	½ cup grated Parmesan cheese

Peel eggplant and slice about ½ inch thick. Sprinkle with salt and let stand 20 minutes. Pat dry on paper towels. Mix mayonnaise and scallions; spread on both sides of eggplant slices. Combine bread crumbs with cheese. Coat each side of eggplant slices with this mixture, place on a lightly oiled baking sheet, and bake in a 375°F oven for 20 to 25 minutes, until golden and crisp. Makes 4 servings.

Honey Glazed Vegetables

(pictured between pages 200 and 201)

An ideal companion for a meat loaf–and–baked potato dinner.

¼ cup honey
2 tablespoons butter
½ teaspoon salt

1 pound carrots, parsnips, or
   turnips

Mix honey with butter and salt. Peel vegetable of your choice and slice or cube. Put vegetable in a buttered casserole and pour the honey mixture over. Bake at 350°F, covered, for 35 to 40 minutes, or until tender. Turn vegetables occasionally with a spoon. Makes 4 servings.

Harvard Beets

The recipe labeled "Harvard Beets" is pretty much a standard. Either cooked fresh beets or canned beets can be used.

2 tablespoons sugar
2 teaspoons cornstarch
3 tablespoons vinegar
3 tablespoons beet juice

½ teaspoon salt
Freshly ground pepper to taste
2 tablespoons butter or margarine
2 cups diced cooked beets

Mix sugar with cornstarch, vinegar, beet juice, salt, pepper, and butter in a 1-quart saucepan. Bring to a boil, then add and reheat beets. Serve hot. Makes 4 servings.

Variations

Orange Beets: Add ½ teaspoon fresh grated orange rind, and substitute ⅓ cup orange juice for vinegar and beet juice.

Lemon Beets: Substitute lemon juice for vinegar and add a dash each of cloves and cinnamon.

Ginger Marmalade Beets: Add a generous tablespoon of ginger marmalade to sauce.

Spinach Mushroom Stir-Fry

Fine flavor, good nutritive value, quick to prepare; what more could be asked for in an attractive vegetable dish?

¼ cup margarine
2 shallots, thinly sliced
1 cup mushrooms, sliced

1 pound fresh spinach, washed
and stemmed
Freshly ground pepper

Melt margarine in large skillet. Add shallots; sauté a minute or two. Add mushrooms and stir-fry for about 2 minutes. Add spinach, and over high heat, quickly stir-fry with a long-handled fork. Cook another 2 or 3 minutes, until vegetables are crisp-tender. Sprinkle with pepper. Makes 4 servings.

Braised Escarole with Pine Nuts

My first taste of braised escarole was in an Italian restaurant in New York City. It was something special then and still is.

1 medium bunch escarole
3 tablespoons olive oil
¼ cup pine nuts or slivered
almonds

1 clove garlic, chopped
(optional)
½ teaspoon salt
Freshly ground pepper to taste

Wash escarole well and cut up leaves so they will be easy to handle with a fork. Measure. There should be about 2 quarts. Heat olive oil over moderate heat in a large saucepan. Add nuts and garlic and sauté until lightly browned. Add greens and salt and pepper and cook, covered, just until wilted, about 2 minutes. Mix nuts into cooked escarole to serve. Makes 4 to 6 servings.

Parsnip and Apple Casserole

A lovely flavor combination for a fall meal.

2 cups parsnips, cooked and
    mashed
1 cup applesauce
¼ cup firmly packed brown
    sugar
1 teaspoon salt

½ teaspoon nutmeg (optional)
1 tablespoon lemon juice
4 tablespoons butter
½ cup buttered bread crumbs
Paprika

Arrange parsnips and applesauce in layers in a greased 1-quart casserole. Sprinkle with brown sugar, salt, nutmeg, lemon juice, and bits of butter. Top with buttered crumbs and sprinkle with paprika. Bake at 375°F for 25 to 30 minutes. Makes 4 to 6 servings.

from Grandma at 35, *Confidential Chat*

Zesty Green Beans

Too often this reliable and good-tasting vegetable is served in a boring and dull fashion. Even a sprinkling of pine nuts, melted butter, and pepper will make a more interesting dish. Or try the following for a somewhat more fanciful version.

¼ cup olive oil
1½ pounds green beans,
    diagonally sliced
1 small onion, minced
1 clove garlic, minced
1 small green pepper, diced

½ cup celery, diced
¼ cup dry white wine
    (or water)
Pepper to taste
1 tablespoon capers
Chopped fresh parsley

Heat oil in large skillet; add green beans, onion, garlic, green pepper, and celery. Sauté over medium heat for 5 minutes, stirring often. Add wine or water, cover, and simmer about 5 minutes, just until beans are crisp-tender. Sprinkle with pepper and capers; toss carefully to mix, then transfer to serving bowl. Sprinkle with parsley. Makes 6 servings.

Stuffed Zucchini

Many variations on this theme are possible, all yielding tasty and satisfying results. Hot boiled rice, buttered carrots, and coleslaw complete the menu.

3 medium-sized zucchini
1 tablespoon olive or
    vegetable oil
1 medium-sized onion,
    minced
1 clove garlic, minced (optional)

½ pound lean ground beef
2 tomatoes, peeled and chopped
Salt and pepper to taste
½ cup bread crumbs
½ cup grated Parmesan cheese
    or cheddar cheese

Trim and discard ends from zucchini. Cut each in half lengthwise. With a teaspoon, carefully scoop out centers, leaving shells about ½ inch thick. Reserve pulp in a bowl. Carefully place shells in a large pan of boiling water; gently parboil for 3 to 4 minutes, then drain and place shells on paper towels to drain completely of water.

Heat oil in skillet; add minced onion and garlic and cook gently until tender. Add ground beef and stir until red color is gone. Add tomatoes, salt, and pepper and allow to cook gently 3 or 4 minutes. Stir in bread crumbs, adding more crumbs if mixture is too moist. Fill each zucchini shell with mixture, then sprinkle tops with cheese. Lightly oil a baking pan; place stuffed zucchini in single layer and bake in a 350°F oven for 20 minutes. Makes 6 servings.

Variations for Zucchini Stuffing

In place of ground beef, use 1 cup chopped leftover pot roast or ½ pound sausage meat. Brown the sausage first, then drain off all excess fat. Remove from pan and then proceed with oil and chopped onion and garlic, returning sausage to pan with tomatoes.

Corn Pudding

Here is a fine version of this long-time New England favorite, particularly popular as a winter dish.

1 can (16-ounces) whole-kernel
    corn, drained
3 tablespoons flour
1 can (16-ounces) cream-style corn
2 tablespoons sugar

Pinch each salt and pepper
1 teaspoon baking powder
3 tablespoons melted butter
3 eggs
1 cup milk, scalded

Put whole-kernel corn into mixing bowl; add flour and mix well. Add cream-style corn, sugar, salt, pepper, baking powder, and melted butter. Beat eggs in separate bowl. Add scalded milk to eggs slowly and beat well again.

Pour over mixture in first bowl, mix well, then pour into casserole dish. Place casserole in pan of hot water, then bake at 375°F for 40 to 45 minutes, or until firm to the touch. Serves 6.

from Teacher of the Young, *Confidential Chat*

Barbeques

Numbers refer to pages where recipes appear in this book.

Barbecues

One of the pleasures of summer is the barbecue. Here are a few general rules and some recipes.

Barbecuing Equipment and Techniques

The camaraderie and informal fun of cooking over the coals are hard to beat. But a good barbecue meal for the family or for a party requires some planning to make it successful.

• Be sure your grill is in good shape, whether it is a small hibachi or an elaborate gas-fired barbecue.

• Collect the barbecue equipment in one place, such as in a plastic caddy easy to transport to the grill site.

• Equipment should consist of long-handled spoon, fork, spatula, and tongs; basting brush (a paint brush purchased especially for this purpose is a good baster); padded mitts; and a water-filled spray bottle to control flareups. Be sure to have sharp knives readily available.

• Spray grill rack with nonstick coating or oil it well.

• Before you start the fire, line the fire pit (except for a gas-fired one) with aluminum foil, shiny side out. This helps in cleanup and the shiny foil throws out the heat. Some grills work better if an inch or two of sand or gravel is placed in the bottom of the grill and the fire is built on that.

• Twenty to 25 briquets are enough to cook several steaks, hamburgers, or chops, and 18 briquets for 2 pounds of fish, to serve 2 to 4 people. If using the rotisserie, build fire under the rotisserie and add more fuel as needed.

• Briquets should have a gray ash and a reddish glow underneath before cooking is started. With long-handled tongs, arrange coals in an even layer.

• Start fire 30 to 40 minutes before cooking is due to begin, unless you are using briquets impregnated with fluid so they start rapidly; those coals will be ready in 15 to 20 minutes.

• To start a fire, four methods work well:

1. Use electric starter according to manufacturer's directions.

2. Arrange crushed paper and small pieces of kindling in center of grill fire box. Add a few briquets and light. When they begin to burn well, carefully add more briquets.

3. Pour liquid starter over briquets. Allow a few minutes for the fluid to soak in and then light the fire.

4. Build briquets in a pyramid or pile in a coffee can with holes punched around the bottom with a beer-can opener.

• *Never* pour liquid starter on a fire that is already going, even if not enough to suit you.

Tips on Food for Barbecuing

• Score edges of steaks, chops, or ham slices to avoid their curling.

• Trim excess fat from meat so that it won't drip and cause flareups.

• Remember that cooking time for meat will vary with the cut, thickness, shape, temperature of charcoal, position of meat on the grill, and degree of doneness desired. Test steak, chops, etc., by cutting into the center to see the extent of doneness.

• When kebabing meat, use long enough skewers so ends reach off the grill. Cook meat and vegetables on separate skewers, since they cook done in different times. Parboil vegetables like whole onions before barbecuing them.

• Plan ¼ to ½ pound boneless meat per person, ¾ to 1 pound meat with bone, depending on amount of bone.

• Toss a few herbs on the fire to give a new flavor. Sage for pork, rosemary for chicken or fish, oregano or basil for beef, tarragon for lamb, are possibilities.

• If the basting sauce has a lot of sugar in it, baste toward the end of cooking time so the food won't get too charred.

• Individual serving–sized foil packets of partly cooked vegetables, seasoned with butter and herbs, can go on the grill with the meat or before, depending on timing. The foil packets generally take about 20 minutes to finish cooking; turn once. Be certain to seal them well.

• Fish is perfectly marvelous cooked over charcoal. To make the job easier, get a hinged fish grill. The fish is securely held and can be turned easily. The fish grill fits right over the cooking rack on the barbecue.

Lemon Barbecued Chicken (recipe on page 235)
and Barbecue Spare Ribs (recipe on page 10)

Approximate Cooking Times for Some Barbecue Items			
Beef steaks (time indicated depends on degree of doneness desired)	1 to 2 inches thick	4 to 5 inches from coals	20 to 30 minutes for 1 inch 30 to 45 minutes for 2 inch
Ribs, spareribs, loins, back ribs	serving-size pieces	6 to 7 inches from low to moderate coals	1 to 1½ hours, turning frequently
Ham, fully cooked slice	¾ to 1 inch slice	5 to 6 inches from low to moderate coals	20 to 25 minutes turning frequently
Lamb chops, arm, loin, rib	1 to 1½ inches thick	5 to 6 inches from low to moderate coals	30 to 40 minutes depending on thickness
Whole fish	2 to 5 pounds dressed	4 to 5 inches from moderate coals	15 to 20 minutes per pound, or until meat flakes
Fish fillets and steaks	¾ to 1 inch thick	4 to 5 inches from moderate coals	10 to 20 minutes depending on thickness
Chicken halves and pieces		5 to 6 inches from low to moderate coals	50 minutes to 1 hour
Ground beef		3 to 4 inches from hot coals	10 to 20 minutes depending on thickness of patties and degree of doneness desired

Barbecue Glaze

This combination of ingredients gives a nice flavor and look to the meats suggested below.

½ cup ketchup
¼ cup Dijon-style mustard

½ teaspoon Tabasco sauce

Mix all ingredients well. Brush onto steaks, chicken, hamburgers, or hot dogs during latter part of cooking. Makes about ¾ cup.

Basting Sauce for Fish and Shellfish

Especially good for swordfish, flounder, salmon, and shrimp.

½ cup butter or margarine
4 tablespoons lemon juice

⅛ teaspoon Tabasco sauce

Melt butter and add lemon juice and Tabasco. Use as a baste sauce for grilled fish. Makes about ⅔ cup, enough for 2 pounds fish.

Steak Basting Sauce

A very tasty sauce to use only for basting. The ingredients can be doubled for a larger amount. However, this should be enough for one steak, with no leftover sauce to store.

2 tablespoons vinegar
1 tablespoon sugar
2 tablespoons water
2 teaspoons Dijon-style mustard
Freshly ground pepper to taste
½ teaspoon salt
Dash Tabasco sauce

½ lemon, thickly sliced
1 small onion, sliced
1 tablespoon Worcestershire
   sauce
¼ cup burgundy wine
2 tablespoons butter or
   margarine

Combine vinegar, sugar, and water with mustard, pepper, salt, Tabasco, lemon, and onion in a small skillet. Cover and simmer on low heat 15 minutes. Add Worcestershire sauce, wine, and butter and bring to a boil. Strain. Use as a basting sauce for steaks while grilling. Makes ¾ cup.

Marinade for Fish

Codfish, haddock, or swordfish would be well flavored if soaked in this marinade.

⅔ cup oil
⅓ cup tarragon vinegar
½ teaspoon salt
1 teaspoon Worcestershire
    sauce

Freshly ground pepper to taste
2 pounds fish steaks, cut 1 inch
    thick

Combine oil, vinegar, salt, Worcestershire sauce, and pepper in shallow dish. Add fish. Cover and refrigerate about 3 hours, turning occasionally.

To broil, place fish steaks on a greased hinged fish grill 4 to 5 inches from coals for about 10 minutes on each side. Makes 4 servings.

Lemon Barbecued Chicken

(pictured between pages 232 and 233)

A change for a barbecue flavor, the lemon enhances the chicken. Wrap potatoes in foil and put in with charcoal when you start the chicken.

¼ cup melted butter or
    margarine
¼ cup lemon juice
½ teaspoon garlic salt

1 teaspoon paprika
1 teaspoon Italian seasoning
4 chicken quarters

Combine butter and lemon juice with seasonings. Brush on chicken and let stand in refrigerator 1 hour.

Broil over charcoal 45 minutes to 1 hour, turning to cook both sides. Brush with butter-lemon mixture during cooking. Makes 4 servings.

Herbed Marinade

1 cup beef bouillon
½ cup red wine vinegar
½ cup oil
2 teaspoons liquid for browning
    gravy
½ teaspoon salt

½ teaspoon crushed dried
    oregano
½ teaspoon crushed dried
    thyme
Freshly ground pepper to taste
¼ teaspoon garlic powder

Combine all ingredients and use to marinate lamb, beef, or chicken. Makes 2 cups.

Marinated Lamb Cubes

By cooking lamb and vegetables separately, it is possible to control time so that neither is overcooked.

2 pounds boneless lamb cut in
    1½-inch cubes
½ cup lemon juice
½ cup olive oil
1 teaspoon dried rosemary
    leaves

1 teaspoon dried oregano
½ teaspoon salt
½ teaspoon freshly ground
    pepper
1 medium onion, sliced
1 large clove garlic, pressed

Put lamb cubes in a bowl. Mix remaining ingredients and pour over lamb. Marinate in refrigerator for 6 hours or overnight, turning lamb in marinade occasionally, or put lamb and marinade in a plastic bag that can be tightly closed.

To cook, string lamb on 4 to 6 skewers and cook 4 to 5 inches from hot coals, turning occasionally, for 15 to 20 minutes. Serve while lamb is still pink. Makes 4 to 6 servings. Serve with Vegetables for Marinated Lamb Cubes.

Vegetables for Marinated Lamb Cubes

1 or 2 green peppers, depending
    on size
12 small whole onions,
    parboiled 5 minutes

12 mushroom caps
12 cherry tomatoes
3 tablespoons melted butter

Remove seeds from peppers and cut into 1½-inch squares.

Put vegetables loosely on 2 or 3 skewers and brush with melted butter. Cook over coals 10 to 15 minutes while lamb is cooking.

Barbecued Turkey

Make a rice or macaroni salad, a bowl of crisp vegetables, and finger rolls to serve with the turkey.

2 turkey breasts (about 1½
    pounds each)
⅓ cup soy sauce

¼ cup dry white wine
3 tablespoons oil
¼ teaspoon onion powder

Wash and dry turkey. Combine soy sauce with wine, oil, and onion powder. Place turkey in a leakproof plastic bag and add sauce. Close securely. Marinate in refrigerator 3 hours or overnight, turning occasionally. Remove turkey, saving sauce. Grill about 7 inches from heat for 1 hour, turning several times. Baste with reserved sauce the last 15 minutes. Carve to serve. Makes 4 to 6 servings.

Grilled Fish Steaks with Tomato Sauce

Baked potatoes wrapped in foil in the coals (put them in 20 or 30 minutes before cooking the fish), a tossed green salad, and sourdough bread sound good with the fish.

4 salmon or swordfish steaks,
  about 1 inch thick
2 tablespoons butter or
  margarine, softened
Salt and freshly ground pepper
  to taste
3 tablespoons oil
2 tablespoons butter or margarine

1 medium onion, finely chopped
1 clove garlic, finely chopped
1 teaspoon dried dillweed
$\frac{1}{2}$ teaspoon Tabasco sauce
2 tablespoons lemon juice
$\frac{1}{2}$ teaspoon salt
1 cup chopped fresh tomatoes

Rub salmon or swordfish steaks with 2 tablespoons softened butter and add salt and pepper to taste.

Heat oil and 2 tablespoons butter together and cook onions and garlic until soft. Add dill, Tabasco, lemon juice, salt, and tomatoes. Simmer, uncovered, about 10 to 15 minutes, stirring occasionally. Makes about $1\frac{1}{3}$ cups.

Oil well a hinged fish grill, put in steaks, and cook about 5 inches above coals for 20 minutes, turning once. Serve with tomato sauce. Makes 4 servings.

Oyster Roast

Select good-sized oysters and scrub well. Grill, small lid up, about 4 inches from coals until shells open. Serve with melted butter and lemon juice. Plan number of oysters depending on people present and whether this is a first course or the meal.

If it is the meal, have plenty of buttered French bread, a platter of tomato and cucumber slices with oil and vinegar and fresh herbs, and baskets of French-fried potatoes.

Corn-on-the-Grill

Is it redundant to say that fresh corn must be fresh? Only when the corn was picked within the day will you have properly sweet, flavorful, and juicy ears. Now to gild those ears, a highly recommended cooking method.

8 fresh ears of corn   Butter

That's it for ingredients. Strip ears, removing all silk. Butter the ears lightly, then quickly dip into cold water. Wrap well in aluminum foil (or if you were careful enough, in the original husk) and place over coals. Turn occasionally with tongs during the 30 to 35 minutes roasting time. This method may also be used for oven roasting at 350°F for about 20 minutes. Makes 4 to 8 servings.

Fruits

Numbers refer to pages where recipes appear in this book.

Fruits

Buying and Storing Fruit

Fresh fruit. What wondrous food: the first, and still best, fast food that is pure pleasure to eat. What is more, fruit is good for you.

Fruits provide ample supplies of vitamins A and C as well as some of the B vitamins. Further, most fruits are low in sodium, add necessary fiber and bulk to the diet, and have almost no fat, with the exception of avocado and coconut. If fresh fruit had not been given to us in such abundance, someone would surely have had to invent it for its deliciousness and its wonderful healthfulness.

In these days of speedy transport, many fruits are available year-round. Most, however, are still best when in season locally. Just consider strawberries as an example. Sure, we can buy them in the Northeast during the dead of winter, but the time when they are truly luscious, sweet, and juicy is during our harvest time: late June and early July. Then they are truly a noble fruit to savor.

Many fruits adapt to modern methods of storage and can therefore be picked when ripe—apples come immediately to mind. Others, such as peaches, fare well even though picked early and shipped to market. Then we must finish off the ripening process at home to get the best results. Generally speaking, it is best to refrigerate fresh fruits promptly. But you can bring pears and peaches to juicy ripeness by storing them in a paper bag or fruit ripener (a plastic bowl with a dome-shaped cover, which is available in many kitchen shops) at room temperature for a few days. Bananas almost always need kitchen-temperature ripening. On the other hand, the lovely fresh pineapples shipped from Hawaii should not stand about for several days, as they do not continue to ripen after picking.

An enticing bowl of fresh fruit—apples, pears, bananas, grapes—can be at hand year-round for quick and healthful snacks. Fruits adapt to fine desserts in endless variety, from the simplest platter of melon slices and pineapple chunks to as elaborate a creation as you wish.

Cooking methods are limited only by the imagination and knowledge of the cook. Fruits can be simmered, baked, incorporated into breads, cakes, cookies, and muffins, or used to enhance poultry and meat dishes.

The following is only a partial list of fruits of the world, along with some of the varieties of each available. Many are also available in jars, cans, and frozen forms that can help bring added appeal to any meal. When purchasing canned fruits, do select those with reduced added sugar or none added at all. These usually taste better and are lower in calories than those packed in heavy syrup.

Apples
Cortland, Delicious, Granny Smith, Gravenstein, McIntosh, Baldwin, Jonathan, Stayman, Winesap—these are just some of the many varieties of apples, probably the most popular of all fruits. Apples adapt to virtually unlimited uses.

Avocados

The most familiar variety is the smooth-skinned, bright green version from Florida. The California avocado is darker in color, with a pebbly surface. When cut, both have the same smooth, buttery pulp. Avocados should be just soft to the touch when ripe and will continue to ripen at home. Placing them in a brown paper bag or fruit ripener will hasten the process. Use them in salads either sliced or cubed, or cut them in half, remove the seed, and stuff the halves with crabmeat or lobster salad for a luncheon treat. Avacado is also a very popular ingredient for many delicious dips.

Bananas

As well known and probably as popular as apples, this tropically grown fruit comes in yellow, red, and green and in various sizes as well. From babyhood through adult life, the banana is a highly recommended food, low in calories, with almost no sodium and a generous supply of vitamins and minerals.

Berries

A wondrous collection comprises this family with blueberries, blackberries, cranberries, currants, raspberries, and strawberries among the most familiar. These are the most fragile of fruits, to be used at the peak of ripeness. Berries do freeze well, however, and this is a fine way to keep a supply on hand for later use.

Cherries

There are two main categories here: sweet and sour (or tart). The sweet Bing cherries, with their lovely dark red to black hue, are enjoyed during the summer months. The Montmorency variety dominates the sour-cherry category and is very useful in many desserts, and breads, and with rich meats such as pork and duck.

Citrus

Here is another broad and wondrous family, that includes oranges, grapefruits, tangerines, lemons, and limes. The simplest way to ensure that one's daily requirement of vitamin C is met is to eat half a grapefruit or drink a glass of orange juice. Both the rind and the juice of any citrus fruit heighten flavors in other foods. A sprinkle of lemon juice on fish, meats, and salads can take the place of salt. Most citrus fruits are readily available throughout the year. Look for smooth-skinned, heavy fruit for the most juice.

Grapes

This certainly is one of the neatest of nibbling fruits. Handily arranged in bunches and with more varieties now coming to us without seeds, grapes are a fine snack food. The lovely colors of grapes add to their appeal. Mix white, red, and purple, choosing from the many varieties offered. The best-known of the whites is probably the Thompson seedless, with Niagara, Calmeria, and Lady Finger among the others. Red Tokays are now available either seedless or with seeds, and they are delicious. Other reds are the Catawba, Cardinal, and Emperor, while Ribier and Concords are the best-known purples. Grapes are vine-ripened and so need prompt refrigeration after purchase. Wash them just before serving.

Melons

This is another fine, healthful family of fruit, low in calories and high in vitamins A and C. The most familiar varieties are Casaba, Crenshaw, Persian, Honeydew, watermelon, and cantaloupe. Fortunately, many of the less-familiar melons come to market with small stickers giving their names. All make a fine breakfast fruit as well as a dessert course in the evening with cheese. Fruit compotes, salads, and soups benefit from the addition of melon.

Peaches

Peaches are such a lovely fruit when purchased from a local orchard, and too often, such a disappointment when purchased in markets. The season is a short one; in New England peaches are usually ready about the time of early apple harvesting—that is, late summer to early fall and are either clingstone or freestone. Clingstones are very good for canning, as their flesh is usually firmer. Freestones are the wonderfully juicy, sweet, and flavorful peaches that are a pleasure to bite into.

Nectarines have been crossbred with peaches to produce what could well be described as a fuzzless peach—another fine fruit that can be used just as the peach is.

Pears

Pears are generally considered to be a fall fruit, though controlled storage now allows for a longer availability. The best pears are tree ripened, but as already mentioned, the final ripening can be done at home. Poached pears make a fine, sophisticated dessert, pear cobblers and tarts are also popular. Use firmer pears for these purposes. Among the varieties most often found are the bell-shaped Bartlett (yellow with a touch of red); the long, tapered Bosc (yellow to brownish); and the large Comice (usually all green). Seckel pears (small and yellowish-brown in color) are known for their spicy flavor, which lends itself well to cooking and preserving.

Pineapples

One of the best reasons to visit Hawaii, in my opinion, is for the joy of having a freshly harvested chunk of juice-dripping pineapple offered to you. Barring that happy event, one can learn how to choose almost as fine a pineapple at market. Look for large, heavy fruit. This is one situation where biggest is definitely best, as heavy weight ensures juiciness, and large size gives the greatest yield of edible fruit. The crown should be dark green and fresh looking. Plucking a leaf from the crown is not a method of determining ripeness, nor does thumping prove anything. If the eyes are mostly yellow, and there is a pleasing fragrance, your choice is probably a good one. And while Mexico and Puerto Rico are now growing pineapples, the best still come from the Hawaiian Islands.

Plums

Plums are another mostly seasonal fruit, widely available in various forms from May through late fall. Plums also come in a variety of colors, which makes them an attractive addition to any fruit bowl. You may choose the small blue-purple Italian (prune) plum for its sweetness and for the wonderful torte it produces. Another popular variety is the greengage, often showing yellow tinges, which is sweet but with a bit of tanginess. Damson plums are usually too tart for anything but cooking and for use in jams. Winter plums are imported and therefore more expensive than summer crops, which in a good year can be very low in price.

These are our most popular and most commonly eaten fruits, but by no means are these the only fine ones available to us.

The pomegranate, an ancient and intriguing fruit that looks rather lumpy and misshapen, is savored for its tangy juice. To get at the juicy seeds, first make a cut all around the blossom and remove the top. Score the fruit with the point of the knife into about 6 wedges. Break them apart carefully and then remove the seeds. Place the seeds in a strainer and press gently with the back of a spoon to extract the juice. Discard the seeds. Grenadine syrup is made with this juice.

Kiwi fruit came originally from New Zealand, but it is now being grown on our West Coast. Kiwis are an excellent source of Vitamin C and can be eaten as is, simply cut in half and eaten with a spoon. For use in fruit compotes or salads or as a topping for cheesecake, peel off the skin with a sharp knife and cut the fruit into thin slices or wedges. The fuzzy, pale brown skin covers a bright green, almost translucent flesh that has a pleasing tanginess.

We find good supplies of the popular mangoes and papayas in our northern markets now. Both are delicious. It is easy to confuse the two until one studies the differences. The mango is about 6 inches long and oval in shape, with a smooth green skin. The flesh resembles that of a fine ripe peach, but the flavor has a bit more zest. The mango has one large stone in the center. It is best to slice the fruit in lengthwise pieces from the stone outwards until the stone is bare. Free the fruit from its skin by holding each piece at one end with a fork, and slipping the knife along the skin. Mangoes are low in calories but high in vitamins A and C.

Papayas are generally much larger than mangoes and are shaped like large pears, but with a bumpy surface. Papayas will ripen nicely at room temperature, and like all fruits, they are at their sweet, juicy best when ripe. Cut into a papaya and you will find dozens of round black seeds that are easy to scoop out with a spoon. The seeds are edible, however, and have a spicy flavor. Papayas are low in sodium and calories and are an excellent source of vitamins C and A. They make a lovely breakfast fruit and can also be stuffed with other fruits for a salad plate.

Fresh Fruit Mold

Making your own fruit-juice gelatin allows you to control the amount of sugar used, or even to add none at all if a sweetened fruit juice is used. A half cup of ginger ale may also be substituted for a half cup of juice. Add whatever combination of fresh fruits or berries you like. Do not use fresh pineapple, however, as the gelatin will not set.

1 envelope plain gelatin
⅓ to ½ cup sugar
1½ cups fruit juice

1½ to 2 cups cut-up fruit
  or berries

Mix gelatin and sugar in a heavy saucepan; gradually stir in ½ cup of the fruit juice. Stir over moderate heat until gelatin is completely dissolved. Remove from heat; stir in remaining juice. Cool, then chill until syrupy. Fold in fruit, then pour into mold and let set completely. Makes 4 servings.

Savory Spiced Peaches

A delicious and easy-to-make dessert when peaches are at their best.

2 tablespoons margarine or butter
½ cup brown sugar
⅓ cup water
1 teaspoon lemon or lime juice

¼ teaspoon nutmeg
4 large ripe peaches, peeled, halved
  and pitted
½ cup dry sherry

Melt margarine or butter in heavy saucepan; stir in brown sugar, water, juice, and nutmeg. Place over low heat and stir until sugar is dissolved. Add peach halves, cut side down. Poach gently, basting often, for 10 to 15 minutes, depending on size and ripeness of fruit. Add sherry during the last 5 minutes of cooking. Serve warm with its sauce and a pouring of light cream, if you wish. Makes 4 servings.

Baked Stuffed Apples

A wonderful old-fashioned dessert (or breakfast treat) that deserves revival. Use raisins or dates, as you prefer, for the stuffing.

6 large baking apples
⅓ cup chopped walnuts or pecans
½ cup raisins (or chopped dates)
1 cup water

¾ cup sugar
½ teaspoon cinnamon
½ teaspoon nutmeg

Core apples, then peel halfway down from top. Place in a baking dish; fill centers with mixture of nuts and raisins or dates. In a small saucepan, combine water, sugar, and spices. Bring to a boil while stirring, then simmer 8 to 10 minutes. Pour over the apples, then bake at 350°F for 40 to 45 minutes, until apples are soft. Baste apples with the syrup 3 or 4 times during baking. Makes 6 servings.

Apple Crisp

This is a quickly readied and very satisfying dessert. Serve with a pouring of light cream, a spoonful of vanilla ice cream—or plain.

6 large apples, peeled, cored,
    and sliced
1 tablespoon lemon juice
1 cup light brown sugar

1 cup flour
½ cup margarine, softened
1 teaspoon cinnamon
½ teaspoon nutmeg

Put sliced apples into baking dish; sprinkle with lemon juice. In a bowl, thoroughly combine sugar, flour, margarine, and spices. Sprinkle over apples, pressing down lightly. Bake at 350°F for 35 to 40 minutes, until apples are soft and topping is lightly crisped. Makes 4 to 6 servings.

Blueberry Streusel

A light and tasty dessert that can be dressed up with a spoonful of vanilla ice cream.

1 quart blueberries
2 tablespoons lemon juice
1 cup packed brown sugar
2 teaspoons cornstarch

⅔ cup quick-cooking oats
½ cup flour
⅓ cup margarine or butter

Put berries into an ungreased 1½-quart casserole; sprinkle with the lemon juice. Combine ½ cup of the brown sugar with the cornstarch; stir carefully into blueberries. Mix oats, flour, and remaining sugar; then cut in margarine or butter until well mixed. Sprinkle over berries. Bake at 350°F for 35 to 40 minutes, until top is golden brown. Serve warm. Makes 4 to 6 servings.

Oranges with Wine Sauce

A light dessert that can be made ahead.

4 naval oranges
6 tablespoon sugar
2/3 cup dry red wine

1½ tablespoons fresh lemon
juice

Remove thin layer of orange peel (zest) from about 1½ oranges using a potato peeler. Cut into thin slivers. There should be about 3 tablespoons. Peel oranges, removing all the white inner peel. Slice each orange crosswise into about 5 slices. Do this over a pie plate to catch all juice. Re-form oranges and hold together with one or two toothpicks. Place in a deep glass, enamel, or pottery dish that will hold oranges snugly.

Combine sugar with wine and orange zest and boil for 5 minutes. Remove from heat and stir in orange juice left from preparing oranges, and lemon juice. Pour over oranges in pan and chill several hours or overnight. When ready to serve, remove picks and serve in dessert dishes with some of the wine sauce. Makes 4 servings.

Chilled Lemon Soufflé

This is a dessert for a party. To be appreciated, it should be served at the table.

2 envelopes unflavored gelatin
½ cup sugar
4 eggs, separated
2¼ cups water
½ cup fresh lemon juice (about
2 lemons)

1 tablespoon grated lemon rind
1 cup heavy cream, whipped
Thin lemon slices

Combine gelatin and ¼ cup of the sugar in a 1-quart saucepan. Beat egg yolks with water and stir into gelatin mixture. Stir over low heat until gelatin is completely dissolved, about 5 minutes. Remove from heat and stir in lemon juice and rind. Chill in refrigerator until mixture begins to thicken, stirring occasionally.

In a large bowl, beat egg whites until soft peaks form. Gradually beat in remaining ¼ cup sugar and beat until stiff. Fold in gelatin mixture and whipped cream, blending well. Spoon into a 1½-quart soufflé dish with a 2-inch collar. Chill until firm, at least 4 hours. Remove collar to serve. Garnish with thin lemon slices. Makes 6 to 8 servings.

To make a collar on the soufflé dish: Tear off a piece of foil 4 inches longer than the circumference of the dish. Fold it in thirds lengthwise. Place it around the top of the dish and tape it or clip it so that it fits snugly.

Variation

Fold in 2 cups fresh blueberries or 2 cups sliced fresh strawberries with the whipped cream.

Rhubarb Medley Sauce

Strawberries and orange combine with rhubarb to make a wonderful spring sauce. When using rhubarb, if the stalks are large and seem tough, peel off the outside before slicing.

3 cups sliced fresh rhubarb
   (about 1 pound)
⅓ cup sugar

⅓ cup orange juice
1½ cups halved fresh
   strawberries

Cut rhubarb into ½-inch pieces. Combine with sugar and orange juice in a 1-quart saucepan. Bring to a boil and simmer 3 to 5 minutes until rhubarb is tender. Remove from heat and gently stir in strawberries. Chill. Makes 3 cups.

Frozen Strawberry Chantilly

A recipe that makes this many servings is designed for a family occasion. Note that all the ingredients can be halved if you wish to make a smaller amount; use an 8x8-inch pan for half the recipe.

½ cup butter or margarine
1 cup all-purpose flour
¼ cup firmly packed light
   brown sugar
½ cup ground walnuts
2 egg whites
⅔ cup sugar

2 tablespoons lemon juice
1 pint strawberries, washed and
   sliced
1 container (8 ounces) nondairy
   frozen whipped topping,
   thawed

With a pastry blender or 2 knives, cut butter into flour and brown sugar until well blended. Stir in nuts. Spread on a rimmed cookie sheet and bake at 325°F for 20 minutes, stirring 3 or 4 times. Cool. Reserve ⅓ cup and pat remainder in bottom of buttered 9×13-inch pan.

Beat egg whites, sugar, and lemon juice until stiff. Add sliced strawberries and beat until blended. Fold in whipped topping. Spread on top of crust and sprinkle with reserved crust. Cover tightly with foil and freeze. Let stand at room temperature about 40 minutes before serving. Cut into squares. Makes 15 servings. Can be made in advance; will keep in freezer several weeks.

Cranberry Fruit Ice

A refreshing dessert after a hearty meal.

1 pound fresh cranberries
4 cups water
2 cups sugar

½ cup orange juice
¼ cup lemon juice

Sort and wash cranberries. Cook in water until cranberries pop and are soft. Put hot cranberries through strainer, pushing as much of pulp through as possible; discard material left in sieve. Mix sugar with sieved cranberries and stir to dissolve. Add juices and pour into a 1-quart freezer tray. Freeze until firm, stirring several times. Can be transferred to a plastic container and stored, covered. Makes about 1 quart.

Poached Pears au Chocolat

Elegant pears au chocolat make a fine dessert when fresh pears are in season. Save the syrup in which the pears are cooked to reuse.

6 to 8 ripe fresh pears
1 cup sugar
2 cups water

6 lemon slices
Chocolate sauce (page 281)

Pare, halve, and core pears. Bring sugar, water, and lemon slices to a boil in a saucepan. Add half of pears and simmer, basting with syrup and turning as needed until fork tender. Remove pears to a shallow dish. Cook remaining pears in syrup until tender, remove to dish, and cover all with syrup. Chill in syrup. Drain pears and for each person serve 2 halves with warm chocolate sauce. Makes 6 to 8 servings.

Ginger Chill

A spectacularly simple dessert to use with any fruit in season.

¼ cup (about) lemon juice
4 sherbet glasses
Sugar
2 to 3 cups prepared fruit, well
    chilled

1 pint chilled ginger beer or
    ginger ale

Put lemon juice in a flat pan and dip rims of sherbet glasses in juice, then in granulated sugar. Chill.

For fruit use peach or nectarine slices, pitted black cherries, diced fresh pears, seedless green grapes, or any combination that suits you. Spoon fruit into prepared sherbet glasses. When ready to serve, cover with ginger beer or ginger ale. Makes 4 servings.

Suggestions for Fruits in Wine

Many fresh fruits combine with wine to make a fine dessert. Here are a few combinations.

Strawberries and zinfandel wine: Wash and hull berries and sweeten to taste; cover with zinfandel wine and let stand at room temperature for several hours before serving.

Peel and slice fresh peaches and cover with a chilled tawny port. Add a few seedless green grapes if you wish.

Peel and slice nectarines and cover with dry sherry. Serve well chilled. Coconut macaroons are a perfect partner.

Peel, halve, and core fresh pears. Cover with pink Chablis and a touch of lemon peel. Chill.

A fresh fruit cup with pink champagne is always a hit: Mix equal parts of diced pears, orange sections, and green grapes. Spoon into sherbet or all-purpose wine glasses. Chill well. When ready to serve fill glasses with chilled pink champagne and garnish with mint.

Sherried Bananas

An ever-popular dessert, and since bananas are a year-round fruit, good anytime.

4 medium ripe bananas	Dash salt
¼ cup butter or margarine	⅓ cup dry sherry
½ cup sugar	1 cup chilled dairy sour cream

Peel bananas and cut in half crosswise. Heat butter in skillet large enough to hold bananas, and sauté bananas over medium heat until lightly browned all over. Add sugar and salt. When sugar dissolves and bubbles, add sherry. Cook for about 5 minutes. Serve bananas and sherry sauce warm, topped with sour cream. Makes 4 servings.

Nectarines in Red Wine

The nectarines will keep for several days in the refrigerator, so if some are left over, serve another day.

6 nectarines*	¾ cup burgundy wine
Boiling water	One 2-inch stick cinnamon
Cold water	3 cloves
½ cup sugar	

Plunge nectarines into boiling water, then in cold. Slip off skins. Leave whole. Combine sugar, wine, and spices in saucepan. Add nectarines and simmer until tender, about 12 to 15 minutes. If you prefer a less spicy fruit, remove cinnamon and cloves; otherwise leave them in. Chill fruit in syrup. Serve some syrup with each nectarine. Makes 6 servings.

*Or use 6 peeled peaches or pears.

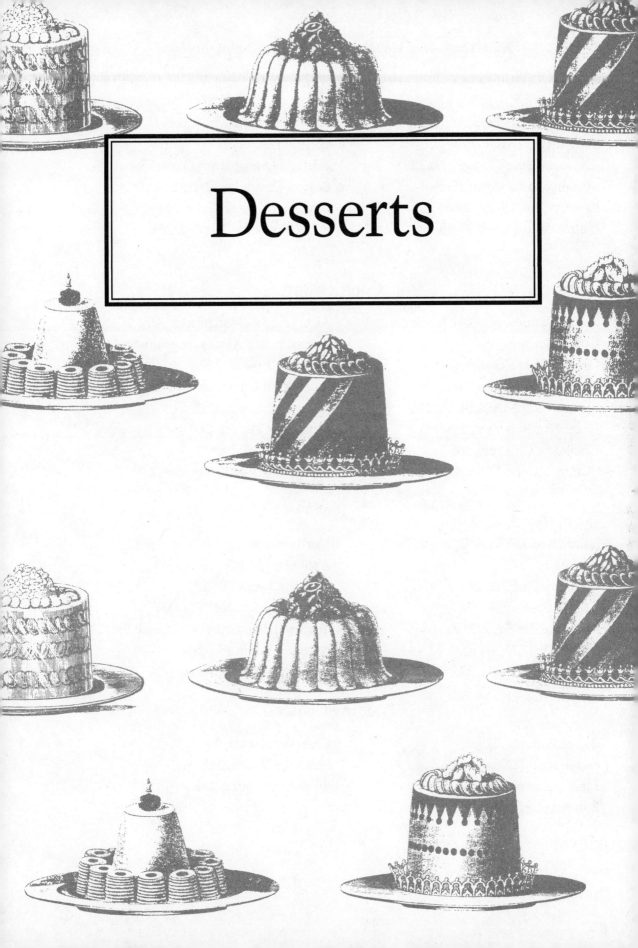

Desserts

Numbers refer to pages where recipes appear in this book.

Cakes

Cookies/Bars

Pies

Puddings/Sauces

Desserts

WHAT, NO DESSERT?!

How often has that sad cry been heard when the end of a meal came with no special sweet, no treat, for whatever reason. Perhaps time had been too short for dessert preparation; perhaps the one planning the meal felt all would benefit with fewer calories. Who knows. But whatever the reason, it once seemed that a diner felt cheated without a "real" dessert.

As we have become more aware of proper nutrition and the need for fewer calories, less sugar, fewer eggs, and less cream and butter, the course that has been most drastically affected is the dessert. Many of us have no dessert when dining at home. Dining out may bring the treat of a piece of pecan pie (my favorite) or something similar, but the days of heavy puddings and rich pies topped with large gobs of sweetened whipped cream seem gone forever.

But to take a more analytical look at the subject, there are many kinds of dessert, and certainly some have enough good merits to be included a few times a week. When there are children in the family, milk puddings have their place, as children who balk at drinking their daily quota of milk often will enjoy a light banana custard or Grape-Nuts pudding. Gelatin desserts made with fresh fruit juice and cut-up fruit also have great appeal, as well as good nutritive value.

In planning a dessert, keep the rest of the menu in mind so that the dessert does not make the meal too heavy. For instance, in warm weather, a salad meal of chilled salmon, tomatoes, cucumbers, and lettuce could very nicely have a dessert of fresh fruit cobbler. Or in the winter, a soup, chowder, or stew main course could have an elegant finish with a warm apple pie just out of the oven.

In this revision, desserts have been looked at carefully for enjoyment and for acceptance within our new diet guidelines.

Cakes

With such a proliferation of mixes for cakes, cookies, bars, you name it, available to the homemaker, a chapter on cakes may seem redundant. But there are times when a special cake is on the program, even if it is a mix with additions.

Baking Guidelines

Even with mixes, there are baking rules to make better products. When using mixes, particularly in those recipes where additions are called for, purchase exactly what the recipe calls for. There are new formulas being manufactured constantly, so it is important to watch what you buy. In a recipe, cake mix without pudding could react completely different to one with pudding in the mix. The recipe should specify the weight of a product. Then follow directions. It's fun to freelance a recipe when making stews and casseroles, but baked-goods recipes should be followed religiously. Cake and cookie recipes are actually a scientific mixture of ingredients designed to give a proper flavor and texture.

Preheating the oven is necessary when baking cakes, cookies, breads, and pies. Also, if the oven is inaccurate, this will show up most dramatically in baking. If your oven underheats, cakes will fall because they are not baked through. Cookies will bake, but will take more time. Overheating, of course, causes burning. A good mercury-type oven thermometer will help you determine whether your oven needs adjustment.

For best results in cake making, have eggs and milk at room temperature. Also, use "large" eggs, not extra large or jumbo.

Equipment

Good measuring cups are a must. It is generally recommended to have a cup for liquid measure (one with a space above the measure mark and a lip for pouring) and dry measuring cups that can be leveled off with a spatula. They come in sets of 1-, 1/2-, 1/3-, and 1/4-cup measures.

Another piece of equipment that makes baking (actually *all* cooking) easier is a **timer**. My range has a fancy timing setup which I've never learned to use, but the hand timer is easy and dependable. It is used for timing the length of mixing, when that is specified, and for all other timed processes. When I need to leave the kitchen while food is cooking or baking, I just take the timer with me.

Pans should be used that fit the specifications of the recipe. New pans may have the size stamped on the bottom. If yours do not, measure from inside the rims to get the proper sizing, and down from the top on the inside. You could write the size on the outside of the bottom with a little fingernail polish if you wish.

If you are purchasing new pans, you might consider those with teflon lining. They help food release more easily from the pan, and they are easier to wash.

Cake racks are another helpful piece of equipment. They allow cooling around the product to avoid the food steaming itself when it is placed directly on the counter.

Equipment such as mixers should suit your own style of cooking. A **hand-held electric mixer** may be adequate for some homemakers who do not do a tremendous amount of baking. And **food processors** can take over some of the work that mixers used to do.

Good-quality baking pans and cookie sheets are essential to successful baking. Thin metal warps easily and gives uneven results. Heavier pans and sheets distribute heat evenly, so do invest in the best. Such equipment will last for many years.

Most home bakers do very nicely with a square 9-inch pan, a 13×9-inch oblong, one or two loaf pans (which do double duty for loaf cakes and breads), and a tube pan. If you like layer cakes, then a pair of 8- or 9-inch round pans can be added.

Alternate Pan Chart

Three 8×1½-inch round pans are equivalent to **two 9×9×2-inch square pans**.

Two 9×1½-inch round pans are equivalent to **two 8×8×2-inch square pans** or **one 13×9×2-inch oblong pan**.

One 9×5×3-inch loaf pan is equivalent to **one 9×9×2-inch square pan**.

Chocolate Sour Cream Cake

Here is an easy-to-make and delicious cake. Cut into squares, wrap in plastic film, and it will be ready for lunch boxes or bake sales.

Cake

1 cup water
½ cup butter or margarine
2 squares (1 ounce each)
    unsweetened chocolate
2 cups ground oat flour*
1½ cups sugar

½ cup all-purpose flour
1 teaspoon baking soda
½ teaspoon salt
2 eggs
½ cup dairy sour cream

Topping

1 square (1 ounce) unsweetened
    chocolate
1 teaspoon butter or margarine

1 cup confectioners' sugar
5 teaspoons (about) hot water
¼ cup chopped nuts

For cake, combine 1 cup water, ½ cup butter, and 2 squares chocolate in a 3-quart saucepan. Bring to a boil. Remove from heat and stir in oat flour that has been mixed with sugar, all-purpose flour, soda, and salt. Mix until well blended. Add eggs and sour cream and mix well.

Pour into a greased 13×9-inch baking pan. Bake at 375°F for 30 to 35 minutes or until cake tester inserted in center comes out clean. Cool completely in pan on rack.

For topping, melt together 1 square chocolate and 1 teaspoon butter in a heavy small saucepan over low heat. Stir in sugar. Add water, 1 teaspoon at a time, until drizzling consistency is reached. Drizzle on cooled cake. Sprinkle with nuts. Makes 18 squares.

**To make 2 cups oat flour, grind 2½ cups uncooked quick or old-fashioned oatmeal, 1¼ cups at a time, in the blender or food processor until very fine, about 60 seconds.*

Mystery Cocoa Cake

The mystery ingredient gives the cake a coconutlike texture.

²/₃ cup margarine, softened
1½ cups sugar
3 eggs, beaten
1 teaspoon vanilla extract
2¼ cups all-purpose flour
½ cup unsweetened cocoa

1 teaspoon baking soda
1 teaspoon baking powder
¼ teaspoon salt
1 cup water
²/₃ cup canned sauerkraut

Cream margarine and sugar together in a large bowl. Beat in eggs and vanilla. Sift all dry ingredients together and add to bowl alternately with water.

Rinse and drain sauerkraut well. Chop, then stir into batter. Turn batter into a greased and floured 13×9-inch pan. Bake at 350°F for 30 minutes, until cake springs back when lightly pressed.

Serves 16.

from Field of Corn, *Confidential Chat*

Banana Carrot Spice Cake

To all Chat *bakers,* Cakes and Cookies *says the allspice in this recipe gives added flavor, which is true.*

2¼ cups sifted all-purpose flour
2½ teaspoons baking powder
1 teaspoon baking soda
⅛ teaspoon salt
¼ teaspoon allspice
1½ cups sugar

²/₃ cup oil
1 teaspoon vanilla extract
4 large eggs
3 medium bananas, mashed
    (about 1 cup)
1 cup finely shredded carrots

Sift together flour, baking powder, soda, salt, and allspice; set aside.

In mixer bowl, combine sugar, oil, and vanilla. Beat at medium speed until well blended. Beat in eggs one at a time, beating well after each addition.

Blend in flour mixture alternately with mashed bananas at low speed. Stir in shredded carrots, mixing thoroughly.

Turn into well-greased 13×9-inch pan. Bake at 350°F about 35 minutes, or until it tests done. Serves 20.

from Cakes and Cookies, *Confidential Chat*

Melt-in-Your-Mouth Blueberry Cake

The best *cake ever! My mother clipped this one from* Confidential Chat—*how many years ago? It never fails, is always delicious, and must continue to be handed on to new cooks.*

1½ cups all-purpose flour	2 egg yolks, well beaten
1 teaspoon baking powder	1 teaspoon vanilla
½ teaspoon salt	⅓ cup milk
½ cup vegetable shortening	2 egg whites, beaten stiff
1 cup sugar	1½ cups blueberries, lightly floured

Grease and flour a 9-inch square baking pan. Preheat oven to 350°F. Onto a sheet of waxed paper, sift together flour, baking powder, and salt. In mixing bowl, cream shortening with sugar until well mixed and fluffy; mix in egg yolks and vanilla. Stir in ⅓ of the flour mixture, then half the milk, another ⅓ flour mixture, remaining milk, finish with remaining flour and mix well each time. Fold in beaten egg whites, then blueberries. Pour batter into prepared pan; sprinkle top lightly with a tablespoon or so additional sugar. Bake 40 to 45 minutes, or until cake tester inserted in center comes out clean. Set pan on rack—it is not necessary to remove cake from pan as it may be cut and served from the pan. Makes 8 to 10 servings.

Heavenly White Fruitcake

Mission Bells states that this cake truly stands up to its name "Heavenly."

3 cups all-purpose flour, sifted	1 cup butter or margarine,
1½ teaspoons baking powder	softened
½ teaspoon salt	2 cups sugar
1½ cups filberts	5 eggs
¾ cup blanched almonds	½ cup sherry
4 cups glacé fruit, cut up	Additional sherry
2 cups white raisins	

Sift flour, baking powder, and salt together. Break pecans in pieces, leave filberts whole, cut almonds in thick slices. Mix nuts and glacé fruits with raisins and several tablespoons of flour mixture.

Start oven at 300°F (or very slow). Grease two loaf pans, 9×5×3 inches. Line bottoms with waxed paper and grease the paper.

Cream butter; add sugar gradually and cream until very smooth. Add eggs one at a time and beat well after each addition. Add flour mixture and sherry alternately, and last mix in the fruits and nuts. Put in pans, pressing batter down gently. Bake 2 hours or until cake tester inserted in center of cake comes out clean. Cool, remove from pan, and peel off paper. Wrap in foil and store in an airtight container about a month before serving. Sprinkle several times a week with a little sherry. Keeps for months in refrigerator or freezer. Makes 2 loaves.

from Mission Bells, *Confidential Chat*

Gingerbread

For Fine and Dandy, this is a dark, moist gingerbread and light in texture, says A Fireman's Wife.

1 cup sugar	1 teaspoon cinnamon
1 cup molasses	3 cups all-purpose flour
2 tablespoons shortening	2 teaspoons baking soda
2 eggs, beaten	Pinch salt
1 teaspoon cloves	1 cup boiling water
1 teaspoon ginger	

Cream sugar, molasses, and shortening together; add beaten eggs and spices, then flour with soda and salt. Lastly add water. (If an electric mixer is used, combine all ingredients except boiling water. Beat it in by hand.) Pour batter into a greased and floured 9×13-inch pan. Bake at 350°F for 30 to 35 minutes or until it tests done. Makes 12 servings.

from A Fireman's Wife, *Confidential Chat*

Nancy's Orange Rum Cake

To my thinking, this is definitely a special-occasion cake. It is work, but it is yummy good.

1 cup butter or margarine,
   softened
1 cup sugar
5 teaspoons grated fresh orange
   rind
1½ teaspoons grated fresh
   lemon rind
2 eggs
2½ cups all-purpose flour

2 teaspoons baking powder
1 teaspoon baking soda
½ teaspoon salt
4 tablespoons buttermilk
   powder*
1 cup water
1 cup finely chopped pecans
Confectioners' sugar

Rum Sauce

½ cup sugar
¼ cup water
¼ cup orange juice

3 tablespoons lemon juice
2 tablespoons rum

Cream butter in a large bowl until fluffy. Gradually add 1 cup sugar, beating until light. Stir in grated rinds. Add eggs, one at a time, beating well after each addition.

Mix flour, baking powder, soda, salt, and buttermilk powder. Add in installments alternately with 1 cup water, beginning and ending with flour mixture. Beat well after each addition. Fold in nuts. Spoon batter into a 9-inch tube pan that has been greased and floured. Bake at 350°F for 50 to 60 minutes or until cake tester inserted in center of cake comes out clean. Cool cake in pan on rack for 10 minutes. Carefully remove cake to a large cake plate.

While cake is baking, make rum sauce. Boil ½ cup sugar with ¼ cup water for 1 minute. Cool slightly and add juices and rum. Carefully spoon over warm cake on plate until all sauce is absorbed. Let cool. Before serving sprinkle with confectioners' sugar. To store, cover cake loosely. Makes one 9-inch cake.

*1 cup fresh buttermilk may be substituted for the 4 tablespoons buttermilk powder and 1 cup water; in that case, add buttermilk alternately with dry ingredients as directed in recipe.

Boston Cream Pie

When is a pie not a pie? When it is a Boston cream pie—which is actually a cake with cream filling and chocolate frosting.

Cake

1 cup all-purpose flour

1 teaspoon baking powder
¼ teaspoon salt
3 eggs
⅔ cup sugar

1 teaspoon vanilla extract

1 tablespoon lemon juice
2 tablespoons cold water
3 tablespoons butter or
    margarine, melted

Filling

⅔ cup sugar
5 tablespoons flour
¼ teaspoon salt
2 cups milk

2 eggs, lightly beaten
1 teaspoon vanilla extract
2 tablespoons butter or
    margarine

Frosting

1 cup sifted confectioners' sugar
1 tablespoon hot water

1 square (1 ounce) unsweetened
    chocolate, melted

Cake: Mix flour with baking powder and salt. Separate yolks and whites of eggs and beat whites until stiff, gradually beating in half of the sugar.

Beat egg yolks until thick and lemon colored with remaining sugar and the vanilla and lemon juice. Slowly add water. Fold in egg whites, dry ingredients, and butter, just to blend.

Line the bottom of a 9-inch round layer cake pan, 1½ inches deep, with waxed paper. Spoon cake batter into pan and bake at 350°F for 25 minutes or until top springs back when touched lightly with tip of finger. Cool in pan on rack 10 minutes. Carefully remove from pan and cool cake on rack.

Filling: Combine sugar, flour, and salt in a saucepan. Gradually stir in milk. Cook and stir over low heat until mixture boils and is thickened. Mix a few spoonfuls into eggs and return eggs to cooked filling, stirring well. Hold over low heat, stirring, about 2 minutes; do not boil. Stir in vanilla and butter. Pour into a bowl. Cover with waxed paper or plastic wrap and chill.

Frosting: Stir together sugar, hot water, and melted chocolate until blended. If necessary to make a spreadable texture, add a few more drops water.

To assemble Boston cream pie: Place cake layer on a decorative cake plate. With a sharp knife, cut crosswise into 2 layers. Spread filling on bottom layer and place other layer on top of filling. Spread top of cake with chocolate frosting. To serve, cut into wedges. Makes 6 to 8 servings.

If cake is not to be served within the hour, refrigerate until serving time.

Blueberry Cheese Cake

(pictured between pages 0 and 9)

The fact that this cheese cake is made with cottage cheese makes it less rich than some, but good nevertheless.

Crust

2 cups graham-cracker crumbs
½ cup sugar

1½ teaspoons cinnamon

Filling

4 eggs
1 cup sugar
1½ teaspoons lemon juice
⅛ teaspoon salt
1 cup light cream

3 cups cottage cheese
¼ cup all-purpose flour
2 teaspoons grated lemon rind
1 cup fresh or frozen blueberries

Mix graham-cracker crumbs with ½ cup sugar and cinnamon. Reserve ½ cup and put remainder in the bottom of a well-buttered 9-inch springform pan.

Beat eggs until fluffy. Mix in 1 cup sugar, lemon juice, salt, cream, cheese, flour, and lemon rind. Beat until smooth with an electric mixer. Fold in blueberries. Pour carefully into pan. Sprinkle with reserved crumbs. Bake at 350°F for 1 hour. Turn off heat and let cool in oven 1 hour. Chill and remove from pan. Makes one 9-inch cheese cake.

from Medico, *Confidential Chat*

Variation

Top with Fresh Blueberry Topping

Fresh Blueberry Topping

(pictured between pages 8 and 9)

3 cups fresh blueberries

½ cup currant jelly

Rinse and remove stems from fresh blueberries. Pat dry. Melt currant jelly in a small saucepan over low heat. Let cool slightly. Brush melted jelly over top of chilled cheesecake. Arrange berries on top.

Cookies/Bars

Most of the rules that apply to making cakes also apply to cookies, but there are tips that make cookie baking easier.

It is a fuel saver to have several cookie sheets. My oven will hold two on one shelf so I have four. That way the oven never waits for me. If using more than one shelf in the oven, do not place cookie sheets directly under those on the shelf above. This will block heat and result in uneven baking.

Most cookie recipes make quite a few cookies. If the quantity is more than can be used in a reasonable time, freeze part of the batter in a freezer container for future baking. Mark the container with the name of the cookies, baking temperature, and baking time. They will keep from 1 to 2 months at 0°F. Or if you wish, the cookies can be frozen after baking—I prefer freezing the batter, but it is a personal and not technical preference.

Use two iced-tea spoons to drop the batter on the cookie sheet. If baked cookies are a soft type, store with waxed paper or plastic wrap between layers.

Unless recipe specifies otherwise, remove cookies at once to a cooling rack with a broad spatula. The cookie sheet is hot and they keep on baking if not transferred.

Cocoa Oatmeal No-Bake Cookies

(pictured between pages 264 and 265)

Green Thumb Lady has had this recipe for more than 20 years and enjoyed making them when she was a child. You will too.

2 cups sugar	1 teaspoon vanilla extract
5 tablespoons unsweetened cocoa	3 cups uncooked quick oatmeal (not instant)
½ cup margarine	Hot water, if needed
½ cup milk	

In heavy 3-quart saucepan, put sugar, cocoa, margarine, and milk. Cook, stirring constantly, over medium heat until mixture comes to a boil. Continue to boil for 6 minutes, stirring constantly. Remove from heat; stir in vanilla and oatmeal. Immediately drop by tablespoonfuls onto waxed paper. Makes 36 cookies. If the mixture starts to get sugary before I finish, I add a few drops of hot water, then continue after stirring mixture back to proper consistency.

from Green Thumb Lady, *Confidential Chat*

Coffee Hermits

Always Sewing replaces molasses with cold coffee in her hermit recipe, one that her family and friends love, and it is good.

1 cup shortening	1 teaspoon baking soda
2 cups firmly packed brown	1 teaspoon salt
sugar	1 teaspoon nutmeg
2 eggs	1 teaspoon cinnamon
½ cup cold coffee	2 cups raisins
3½ cups all-purpose flour	1¼ cups broken nuts (optional)

Mix shortening, sugar, and eggs thoroughly. Stir in coffee. Stir together the flour, baking soda, salt, nutmeg, and cinnamon; blend into shortening mixture. Mix in raisins and nuts. Chill dough at least 1 hour.

Drop rounded teaspoonfuls of dough about 2 inches apart on lightly greased baking sheets. Bake at 400°F for 8 to 10 minutes or until almost no imprint remains when a hermit is touched lightly in middle. Makes 6 dozen.

If you want them shaped like store hermits, place the dough on the cookie sheets in long strips, about 1 inch wide and ¾ inch high. Put only 2 strips on a cookie sheet at one time, as they spread out when cooking. After they come out of the oven, slice into size bars desired.

from Always Sewing, *Confidential Chat*

Orange Sugar Cookies

Amaryllis sends her recipe for flavorful sugar cookies.

½ cup margarine, melted	3 cups sifted all-purpose flour
1½ cups sugar	½ teaspoon baking soda
¼ teaspoon salt	Dash nutmeg
1 egg	Colored sugars
½ cup orange juice	

Cream margarine, sugar, salt, and egg. Add orange juice, flour, baking soda, and nutmeg, then chill for an hour or so. Roll out to ¼ inch thick on a lightly floured surface. Cut cookies with a 2½-inch cookie cutter; bake at 350°F about 10 minutes. These can be sprinkled with sugar (or colored nonpareils) before baking. Makes 3 dozen.

from Amaryllis, *Confidential Chat*

Honey-Nut Cookies

A good cookie for the lunch box or for an after-school snack. Not too sweet.

⅓ cup butter or margarine, softened	1 teaspoon baking powder
½ cup honey	½ teaspoon baking soda
2 eggs	¼ teaspoon salt
½ cup dairy sour cream	½ cup chopped nuts
1 teaspoon vanilla extract	½ cup chopped dates
1¾ cups all-purpose flour	1 cup Rice Krispies cereal

In a bowl blend butter and honey with the electric mixer. Add eggs, sour cream, and vanilla and continue beating 3 to 4 minutes. Mix flour, baking powder, soda, and salt and blend into butter-honey mixture on low speed. When mixed, remove beater and fold in nuts, dates, and cereal.

Drop by teaspoonfuls on lightly greased cookie sheets. Bake at 375°F for 10 to 12 minutes or until nicely browned. Makes about 4 dozen 3-inch cookies. Store in a covered container.

Butterscotch Nut Cookies

This is a quickly mixed cookie that is crisp and chewy. It is a good keeper and has a marvelous flavor.

¾ cup margarine	¾ cup sugar
1 package (6 ounces) butterscotch morsels	1 cup all-purpose flour
1 teaspoon baking soda	2 cups uncooked quick oatmeal
2 tablespoons boiling water	½ teaspoon salt
	¼ cup chopped pecans

Melt margarine and butterscotch morsels in top of double boiler. Stir in soda and boiling water and then add all remaining ingredients. Shape into 1-inch balls and place 2 inches apart on greased baking sheets. Bake at 350°F 10 to 15 minutes.

Remove cookies to rack and cool. Makes about 5 dozen. Store tightly covered in cookie jar.

Frozen Chocolate Sundae Pie (recipe on page 279)
with Chocolate Sauce (recipe on page 281)
and Cocoa Oatmeal No-Bake Cookies (recipe on page 262)

Fudge Nut Brownies

Painted Nails has used this brownie recipe for 40 years. It's her all-time favorite way to make brownies. We like it, too.

⅓ cup shortening	1 teaspoon vanilla extract
1 cup sugar	¼ teaspoon salt
2 eggs, lightly beaten	½ cup all-purpose flour
2 squares (1 ounce each) unsweetened chocolate, melted	½ cup broken or chopped walnuts

Cream together the shortening, sugar, and beaten eggs. Add melted chocolate, then add vanilla, salt, flour, and nuts. Blend by hand until fairly smooth—batter may be slightly lumpy.

Pour into a greased 8- or 9-inch square pan. Bake at 350°F for 25 to 30 minutes. The lesser time makes them more fudgelike. Makes 16 brownies.

from Painted Nails, *Confidential Chat*

Chocolate Chippers

A cookie that always has a friend. A close relative of the famed Toll House cookies.

1 cup butter or margarine, softened	2 eggs
¾ cup sugar	2¼ cups all-purpose flour
¾ cup firmly packed brown sugar	1 teaspoon baking soda
1 teaspoon vanilla extract	1 teaspoon salt
½ teaspoon water	1 package (12 ounces) chocolate morsels

Combine in bowl and beat until creamy the butter, sugars, vanilla, water, and eggs. Add flour, soda, and salt. Stir in chocolate morsels. Drop by well-rounded teaspoonfuls onto greased cookie sheets. Bake at 375°F for 10 to 12 minutes. Makes about 5 dozen.

from Evening Star, *Confidential Chat*

Oatmeal Raisin Saucers

These are delicious cookies, but be sure to leave a good 2 inches between as they spread to become quite large. Let them stand on cookie sheet about 40 to 50 seconds before removing. Whether you get 36 or (as I did) about 50 cookies depends on how big you make them. Store cookies with waxed paper or plastic wrap between layers, so they will not stick together.

1½ cups shortening or
    margarine
1¼ cups sugar
2 eggs
2 tablespoons molasses
1¾ cups all-purpose flour
1 teaspoon baking soda

¼ teaspoon salt
1 teaspoon cinnamon
2 cups uncooked oatmeal (not
    instant)
1 cup cut-up raisins
½ cup chopped walnuts

Mix shortening, sugar, eggs, and molasses together well. Add flour, soda, salt, and cinnamon and mix well. Finally, add oats, raisins, and nuts. Drop by teaspoonfuls onto greased cookie sheets. Bake at 400°F for 8 to 10 minutes. Makes 36 cookies.

from Cakes and Cookies, *Confidential Chat*

Aunt Jennie's Monadnock Bars

Aunt Jennie's bars are good keepers and always popular.

1 cup chopped dates
½ cup boiling water
1 cup butter or margarine
½ cup sugar
½ cup firmly packed light
    brown sugar
2 eggs
1 teaspoon vanilla extract

2 cups all-purpose flour
¼ cup unsweetened cocoa
1 teaspoon baking soda
½ teaspoon salt
1 package (6 ounces) chocolate
    morsels
1 cup chopped nuts

Combine dates and boiling water and let stand until cooled. Cream butter until light. Add sugars and beat until light and fluffy. Beat in eggs and vanilla. Stir in cooled dates and water.

    Mix flour with cocoa, soda, and salt and stir into creamed mixture. Fold in chocolate bits and nuts. Spread into a greased and floured 13×9-inch baking pan. Bake at 350°F for 35 minutes or until top is firm to touch of fingertip. Cool and cut into squares. Makes 3 dozen. Store covered.

Farm Kitchen Applesauce Squares

When the Mayo Duck Farm was on the road to Nauset Beach, Orleans, these favorites were always dessert for the picnic lunch.

1 cup sugar
$\frac{1}{3}$ cup vegetable shortening
1 egg
2 cups all-purpose flour
1 teaspoon baking soda
$\frac{1}{3}$ teaspoon salt

1 teaspoon cinnamon
$\frac{1}{2}$ teaspoon ground cloves
$\frac{3}{4}$ cup applesauce
$\frac{1}{2}$ teaspoon vanilla
$\frac{1}{2}$ cup raisins

Cream sugar and shortening; beat in egg. Sift dry ingredients together, then add alternately to creamed mixture with applesauce. Stir in vanilla and raisins. Spread on greased 9×13-inch pan and bake at 375°F for 18 to 20 minutes. If desired, top with a simple icing made by stirring lemon juice into a cup of confectioners' sugar, using enough lemon juice to make a thin icing. Cut into squares. Makes 24 squares.

Walnut Chewies

These neat sweets are quickly made and quick to disappear. Be careful not to overbake.

1 egg
1 cup packed brown sugar
1 teaspoon vanilla
$\frac{1}{2}$ cup all-purpose flour

$\frac{1}{4}$ teaspoon baking soda
$\frac{1}{4}$ teaspoon salt
1 cup coarsely chopped walnuts

Grease an 8-inch square pan; preheat oven to 350°F. Stir together the egg, brown sugar, and vanilla. Stir in flour, baking soda, and salt, then mix in chopped walnuts. Spread in pan and bake 18 to 20 minutes, which will leave center still soft, as it should be. Cool completely in pan, then cut into 2-inch squares. Makes 16 squares.

Raisin-Nut Oat Cookies

There's good nourishment, as well as good taste, in these lunch-box favorites.

¼ pound (1 stick) margarine
1 cup sugar
2 eggs
1 teaspoon vanilla
1½ cups oatmeal, uncooked
1½ cups all-purpose flour
½ teaspoon baking powder

½ teaspoon baking soda
½ teaspoon salt
½ teaspoon allspice
1 teaspoon cinnamon
¼ cup milk
1 cup raisins
1 cup chopped walnuts

Cream margarine and sugar thoroughly; add eggs and vanilla, beating until light and fluffy. Stir in oatmeal. Sift together flour, baking powder and soda, salt, and spices. Add to first mixture alternately with milk. Mix until well blended. Stir in raisins and nuts. Drop by spoonfuls onto lightly greased baking sheet. If you want fat cookies, leave in mounds. If you prefer flat cookies, flatten dough a bit with back of spoon. Bake at 375°F for about 15 minutes, until golden brown. Remove to cooling rack. Makes about 4 dozen.

Chocolate Dreams

These chocolate cookies with chocolate bits added are a popular treat, particularly with youngsters.

1 cup butter or margarine,
   softened
1 cup granulated sugar
½ cup brown sugar,
   firmly packed
1 teaspoon vanilla extract
1 egg

5 tablespoons unsweetened cocoa
2 tablespoons milk
1¾ cups all-purpose flour
¼ teaspoon baking soda
1 cup chopped pecans
1 cup semisweet chocolate chips

Combine butter, sugars, vanilla, and egg in a bowl. Beat with an electric mixer until light and fluffy. Fold in cocoa and milk. Combine flour and baking soda and fold into creamed mixture. Do not beat. Add nuts and chips.

Drop by rounded teaspoonfuls on teflon-coated baking sheet. Bake at 350°F for 12 minutes, when tops should look dry. Remove to rack and cool. Makes 5 dozen.

Molasses Crispies

Always a favorite with children, these cookies are also quick and easy to make. Makes about 3 dozen cookies.

1 egg	½ teaspoon cloves
1 cup sugar	½ teaspoon ginger
¼ cup dark molasses	2 cups all-purpose flour
⅔ cup shortening	2 teaspoons baking soda
1 teaspoon cinnamon	½ teaspoon baking powder

Break egg into large bowl; add sugar, molasses, shortening, and spices; beat together well. Sift flour, baking soda, and baking powder together, then fold into the molasses mixture. Chill overnight. Roll dough between hands into 36 or 40 small balls. Dip balls into some extra sugar. Place on lightly greased cookie sheet. Press slightly with bottom of a glass. Bake at 350°F for 8 to 10 minutes. They still will be soft as they are removed from cookie sheet. Do not overbake.

from Friendly Nell, *Confidential Chat*

Chocolate Crinkles

These cookies have a chewy center, and the tops puff up and crack, making a black-and-white design. This recipe makes about 4 dozen cookies.

3 eggs, beaten	2 cups all-purpose flour
1½ cups sugar	2 teaspoons baking powder
½ cup oil	¼ cup sifted confectioners' sugar
2 teaspoons vanilla	
4 ounces unsweetened chocolate, melted and cooled	

Beat together eggs, sugar, oil, and vanilla; add chocolate, then stir in flour and baking powder. Mix well, cover, and chill for 1 to 2 hours. Roll chilled dough between hands into about 48 1-inch balls. Roll in confectioners' sugar and place 2 inches apart on ungreased baking sheet. Bake at 375°F for 10 minutes. Place on cooling racks. If you like, sprinkle with additional sugar when cooled.

from Nugs, *Confidential Chat*

Antigonish Marble Squares

These marble bars are named for the Nova Scotia town that they come from.

2 eggs
1 cup brown sugar
3/4 cup all-purpose flour
1/2 teaspoon baking powder
1/2 teaspoon salt
1 teaspoon vanilla

1 square (1 ounce) unsweetened
   chocolate, melted
1 teaspoon melted butter
Chopped nuts
1/3 cup shredded coconut

Beat eggs. Add brown sugar. Mix flour, baking powder, and salt together; add to first mixture. Stir in vanilla.

Add melted chocolate and melted butter to 1/4 of the first mixture with a few chopped nuts. Add coconut to remaining 3/4 of first mixture. Place white mixture on bottom of 8-inch square pan. Dot with chocolate mixture. Bake at 325°F for 20 to 25 minutes. Makes 16 squares.

from Niagara Falls, *Confidential Chat*

Pies

Pies continue to be an extremely popular dessert, with a freshly baked, warm apple pie still the American favorite. We no longer follow the habit of earlier generations in having pie for breakfast, but as an occasional treat, there is nothing better.

With pastry mix, frozen pie shells, and packaged graham-cracker crusts on the market, pie making can be as simple or as time consuming as you want it to be.

Equipment and Techniques

If you prepare your own pastry or use a commercial mix, there are several pieces of relatively inexpensive equipment I recommend. (1) A **pastry blender** enables you to mix the shortening and flour with ease. It can also be used to mix crumbs and butter for graham-cracker or other cookie crusts, and to make the flour-sugar-butter base for some bar recipes and the like. (2) A **pastry canvas** to put over the board on which you roll the pastry, a **stocking** for the rolling pin, and a good **ball-bearing rolling pin** are all invaluable. Sets of canvas and stocking can be purchased. I happened to have had some white canvas left over from another project and made my own, and purchased a pair of infant cotton lisle stockings (from which I cut the feet) for the rolling pin. The canvas and stocking should be washed after each use.

Pastry, after the liquid has been added, can be chilled for an hour or so before rolling out, but not much longer as it becomes too cold to roll well.

To roll pastry, flour pastry cloth and stocking. If making a 2-crust pie, divide pastry and shape each half into a flat round disc. Roll from center out with a light touch. As the pastry gets thinner and near the size of the pie plate, if the edges begin to split, pinch together in a crimped edge like the edge of a pie crust and reroll the edge. The **pastry circle** should be 1 inch larger than the pie plate all the way around. As you are rolling the pastry, add a small amount of flour to the canvas and stocking as needed, but not any more than necessary to keep the pastry from sticking.

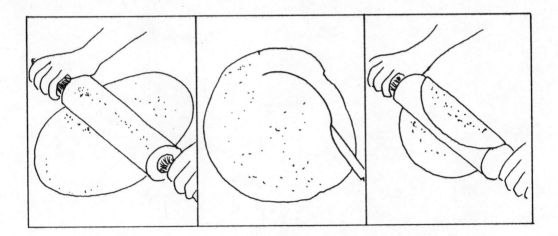

To transfer the pastry to the pie plate, put the rolling pin along one side and roll the pastry around the pin. Transfer over to the plate and unroll into the plate. Gently ease the pastry down into the pie plate. Do not stretch the pastry, as this is one of the reasons a single pie crust may shrink and buckle.

For a one-crust pie, trim the pastry, leaving an even ½-inch overhang beyond the edge of the pie plate. Turn this edge under to make a ridge that stands up from the edge of the plate. With your thumbs on the inside of the pastry and your index fingers on the outside, press the dough to make a fluted edge all around the shell. Use a fork to prick the shell all over, including the sides. Bake at 425°F for 10 to 12 minutes, until golden-brown, for a baked single pie shell.

If making a two-crust pie, roll the pastry and fit it into the pan as for a one-crust pie; this time, however, trim the edges even with the edge of the pie plate. Put in the filling, then brush the edge of the bottom pastry with a little cold water. Roll out the top crust, transfer it onto the rolling pin, and lay it over the filled pie. Trim crust, leaving about ½ inch overhang. Tuck overhang under the edge of the bottom crust, pressing gently as you go around. This will seal the edges. Crimp the edges by pressing the tines of a fork all around or by pressing (or pinching) into a fluted edge as described for a single-crust pie, by having thumbs on inside (or top) of crust and index fingers on bottom. Cut several slits in top to let steam out of pie as it bakes. Bake the pie as directed in the individual recipes.

Other pastry tricks include making a strip of aluminum foil long enough to fit around the top of a 9-inch pie plate plus several inches—it should be 4 inches in width, folded over to 2 inches. This strip can be used to cover the edge of the crust of the pie if it begins to get too brown before the rest of the pie is done. Gently ease it around the pie edge and fasten either by pinching the ends together or with a paper clip.

You will read directions for filling a single pie shell with beans or rice to keep it from shrinking and buckling while baking. This is done by cutting a circle of waxed or brown paper to fit inside the pie shell, laying the paper in, and filling with beans (the cheapest variety you can buy) or raw rice. Leave the beans in about half the baking time and then carefully remove them by grasping the waxed paper and lifting it out of the pie. The rice or beans should be stored separately from the regular stock and used only for pies. A new piece of paper should be cut each time, however, as it can become brittle from the heat and breaks easily.

Pastry Mix

This is a very easy pastry mix to prepare, particularly if you buy the 2-pound package of flour and the 1-pound can of shortening. It will save money, however, if the flour is measured from a larger package and the shortening from a 5-pound can.

8 cups (2 pounds) all-purpose flour

2 teaspoons salt

2 cups (1 pound) shortening

Put flour in a very large (4-quart) bowl. Mix in salt. Add half shortening and with a pastry blender or 2 knives cut into flour mixture until well blended. Add remaining shortening and cut into flour, lifting flour up from bottom so shortening is well mixed. This makes 8 cups of pastry mix. Store in a covered container. The mix does not need to be refrigerated.

To use for a 9-inch one-crust pie: Measure 1 cup and 2 tablespoons firmly packed pastry mix into a bowl. With a fork, lightly stir in 3 tablespoons ice water.

To use for a 9-inch two-crust pie: Measure 2¼ cups firmly packed pastry mix into a bowl. With a fork, lightly mix in ⅓ cup ice water.

This is a generous amount of pastry for a 9-inch pie. If there are scraps left over, you can cut them in cookie size, sprinkle with sugar and cinnamon, and bake 10 to 12 minutes in the 425°F oven with the pie.

If using an 8-inch pie plate, measure 1 cup pastry mix and add 2 tablespoons ice water for 1 crust; or for a 2-crust 8-inch pie, 2 cups pastry mix and 4 tablespoons ice water.

Pastry for One Pie

Anyone who reads pie recipes knows there as many pie-crust recipes as there are ways to fry chicken. Some with sugar and egg, others with milk and vinegar, or with hot water instead of ice water. Because this is a general cookbook, I'll give only one recipe for regular pastry. Once you master the technique of making a pie with this pastry, you can easily find other recipes to fly with.

2 cups all-purpose flour

½ teaspoon salt

⅔ cup shortening

⅓ cup ice water

Mix flour and salt in a bowl. Add ⅓ cup shortening and blend with a pastry blender or 2 knives. Add remaining shortening and continue blending until all shortening and flour are combined. With a fork, stir in water gradually until all pastry is moistened. Makes 1 double-crust 9-inch pie. (Make half recipe for a one-crust pie.)

Crumb Crust

Crumb crusts are very popular and easy to make. Use for fillings that are to be chilled.

1½ cups fine crumbs*
¼ cup sugar
⅓ to ½ cup melted butter or
     margarine

½ teaspoon cinnamon
     (optional)
Dash salt

Mix all ingredients thoroughly. Reserve ½ cup crumb mixture. Press remainder firmly into bottom and sides of 9-inch pie plate. The crust can be thoroughly chilled; or bake in a 325°F oven for 10 minutes. Use ½ cup crumbs to garnish top of pie.

Graham crackers, chocolate or vanilla wafers, or gingersnaps can be used for crumbs. Choose a flavor that will be compatible with filling.

Meringue Pie Shell

Make a spectacular dessert by filling the meringue shell with a pint of your favorite ice cream. Serve with a compatible fruit or chocolate sauce. Can be frozen.

3 egg whites
⅛ teaspoon salt
⅛ teaspoon cream of tartar
     (optional)

¾ cup sugar
½ teaspoon vanilla extract

Beat egg whites until frothy. Add salt (and cream of tartar, if used). Beat whites until stiff but not dry. Gradually beat in sugar and continue to beat until mixture is very stiff and glossy. Spread into a buttered 9-inch pie plate, lower in the middle and higher around the edges. Bake at 300°F for 50 minutes or until delicately browned. Turn off heat and let meringue stay in oven for several hours. A meringue shell can be made in advance and can be frozen for future use.

Squash Pie

Squash pie is a typically New England pie. Prepared squash for squash pies can be purchased canned or frozen. But if you have acorn, butternut, or other yellow winter squash in your garden, you might make your own cooked squash for pie. It takes about 2 pounds of squash to make 1 cup cooked squash. Wash well, cut into pieces, remove seeds, and steam in the vegetable steamer until tender, about 15 minutes (or cook, covered, in a saucepan with a small amount of water). Cool enough to handle and scrape squash from shell. If there seem to be "strings" in the squash, you may want to run it through a food mill. Otherwise, just mash and proceed with the pie.

1 cup cooked squash	1 cup sugar
1 teaspoon cinnamon	3 eggs
1 teaspoon nutmeg	1 cup milk
½ teaspoon ginger	1 unbaked 8- or 9-inch pie shell
½ teaspoon salt	

Mix squash with spices, salt, and sugar. Add eggs and milk and beat with a whisk to blend well. Pour into pie shell and bake on bottom shelf of a preheated 425°F oven for 45 minutes. The center of pie may still be a little soft, but it will continue to cook after it comes out of the oven and be a delicately textured pie. Cool before cutting. Makes one 8- or 9-inch pie.

Pecan Pumpkin Pie

Pour part of filling into pie shell. Place pie on oven shelf, partially pulled out; then add remaining filling and carefully push shelf into oven. This keeps filling from spilling.

1½ cups canned or steamed pumpkin*	2 eggs
	1 unbaked 9-inch pie shell
¾ cup sugar	½ cup firmly packed brown sugar
½ teaspoon salt	
1 teaspoon cinnamon	3 tablespoons butter or margarine, softened
½ teaspoon nutmeg	
¼ teaspoon ginger	½ cup finely chopped pecans
1 can (13 ounces) evaporated milk	

Mix pumpkin with sugar, salt, and spices. Beat in evaporated milk and eggs with a whisk until well blended. Pour filling into pie shell and bake on lower shelf of oven at 425°F for 40 minutes or until filling begins to become firm. Mix brown sugar, butter, and pecans. Sprinkle carefully over pie and bake 10 minutes longer. Serve pecan pumpkin pie at room temperature with whipped cream or softened vanilla ice cream. Makes one 9-inch pie.

*To steam pumpkin, remove seeds and membrane and cut pumpkin into pieces to fit into saucepan. Add about 1/2 inch water, cover, and steam pumpkin until tender, 15 to 20 minutes. Cool. Scrape pumpkin from shell and mash. Any unused pumpkin will keep in refrigerator for 10 days to 2 weeks or can be frozen and stored for months.

Marlborough Pie

This is an old New England recipe that has a fresh taste. It's not a pie to be kept over, so make it when it can all be eaten on the same day.

3 cups sliced peeled apples	½ teaspoon grated lemon rind
¼ cup butter or margarine	1½ tablespoons lemon juice
6 tablespoons sugar	1½ tablespoons sherry
1 tablespoon flour	1 unbaked 8-inch pie shell
3 eggs	4 tablespoons sugar

Steam apple slices in a steamer about 5 to 8 minutes until tender (or cook with a very little water in a saucepan).

Mash apples and mix with butter and 6 tablespoons sugar. Cool. Separate 2 of the eggs. Add to the apples the flour, 2 egg yolks and 1 whole egg, lemon rind and juice, and sherry and mix until well blended. Spoon into pie shell and bake at 425°F for 30 to 40 minutes or until firm.

Beat egg whites until foamy, then gradually add 4 tablespoons sugar, beating until stiff peaks form. Spread over pie filling. Return to oven for about 10 minutes or until lightly browned. Makes one 8-inch pie.

Apple Pie

Apple pie remains one of the favorites, particularly when served warm. A piece of warm apple pie with ice cream or a nice strong cheddar cheese is tops. Mostly I use McIntosh apples because they are generally available. I'd use Jonathan, but they are hard to find. Cortland and Newtown Pippin are also fine pie apples. In making apple pie, I've learned two tricks over the years. After the apples are peeled, cored, and quartered, slice each quarter crosswise rather than lengthwise. This gives shorter pieces and a more compact filling. Then pile the apples as high as possible so that as they cook down, there will still be a nice thick filling.

¾ to 1 cup sugar	Dash salt
1 to 2 tablespoons all-purpose flour	Pastry for a 2-crust 9-inch pie
	6 cups (or more) sliced peeled apples
¾ teaspoon cinnamon	2 tablespoons butter or margarine
½ teaspoon nutmeg	1 tablespoon lemon juice

Mix sugar, flour, spices, and salt and set aside. Prepare bottom crust as directed (page 273).

Sprinkle half the sugar mixture in the pie crust. Pile in the apple slices and top with remaining sugar. Dot with butter and sprinkle over lemon juice. Put top crust in place, seal and crimp edges, and cut several slits in top. Bake on lower shelf of oven at 425°F for 50 to 60 minutes or until crust is nicely browned and filling starts to bubble. Check apples by inserting a small paring knife through a slit to be certain they are tender. Makes one 9-inch pie.

Cherry Crumb Pie

By adding your own touch to a canned pie filling, you can make a good pie extra special.

1 can (21 ounces) cherry pie
    filling
½ teaspoon almond extract
½ cup raisins
1 unbaked 8- or 9-inch pie shell
¼ cup butter

1 cup all-purpose flour
½ cup firmly packed brown
    sugar
½ cup finely chopped walnuts
    (optional)

Gently mix pie filling, almond extract, and raisins. Pour into pie shell. Blend butter, flour, and sugar with a pastry blender or two knives. Stir in nuts. Sprinkle over pie filling to cover evenly. Bake on lower shelf of oven at 425°F for 40 minutes. Cool to serve. Makes one 9-inch pie.

Strawberry Rhubarb Pie

Strawberries and rhubarb are in season at the same time, so take advantage of this fact to combine the two.

2½ cups sliced rhubarb (about ¾
    pound)
1 cup sugar
2 tablespoons water
1 envelope unflavored gelatin
3 tablespoons water
3 eggs, separated

1 cup sliced fresh strawberries
1 tablespoon lemon juice
1 baked 9-inch pie shell
½ cup heavy cream, whipped,
    or 1 cup nondairy frozen
    whipped topping, thawed
Fresh strawberries for garnish

Scrub rhubarb and cut into ½-inch pieces. In a saucepan combine rhubarb with sugar and 2 tablespoons water and bring to a boil. Soften gelatin in 3 tablespoons water and add to rhubarb. Stir to dissolve gelatin. Beat egg yolks lightly. Add a little of the hot rhubarb mixture to the yolks and then return to rhubarb and mix well. Add strawberries and lemon juice. Beat egg whites until stiff and fold in rhubarb, blending well. Spoon into baked pie shell. Chill for 4 to 5 hours until firm.

Before serving, spread whipped cream (or nondairy whipped topping) over pie. Garnish with strawberries. Makes one 9-inch pie.

Traditional Strawberry Rhubarb Pie

A traditional version of this popular early-summer treat.

Pastry for 2-crust, 9-inch pie
1⅓ cups sugar
⅓ cup all-purpose flour
½ teaspoon vanilla

2 cups cut-up rhubarb
2 cups strawberries, halved
1 tablespoon margarine or butter

Roll out half the pastry and fit into pie pan. Mix flour and sugar together, then carefully mix in vanilla, rhubarb, and strawberries. Put into pie shell. Dot with margarine or butter. Roll out remaining pastry, cut into strips, and fit lattice fashion on top of fruit. Brush top with milk and sprinkle lightly with a teaspoon or so of sugar. Bake at 425°F for 15 minutes; reduce heat to 350°F and continue baking another 25 to 30 minutes. Cool on rack. Makes one 9-inch pie.

Orange Chiffon Pie

A pie that is not too heavy as a dessert.

1½ envelopes unflavored gelatin
½ cup sugar
1 cup hot water
3 egg yolks, beaten
1 can (6 ounces) frozen orange
    juice concentrate
3 tablespoons lemon juice or
    orange liqueur

3 egg whites
¼ cup sugar
1 9-inch crumb crust
½ cup whipped cream (or
    nondairy whipped topping)
Fresh orange sections

Mix gelatin and ½ cup sugar in top of double boiler. Add hot water. Cook and stir over boiling water until gelatin is dissolved. Add a little of the hot mixture to egg yolks. Return egg yolks to gelatin and reduce heat to cook and stir egg mixture over hot, not boiling, water until it coats a silver spoon, about 6 to 8 minutes. Remove from heat and add orange concentrate and lemon juice or liqueur. Chill until mixture begins to thicken. Beat egg whites with ¼ cup sugar until soft peaks form. Fold into thickened gelatin. Spoon into crumb shell. Chill until firm. Garnish with whipped cream and orange sections. Makes one 9-inch pie.

Frozen Chocolate Sundae Pie

(pictured between pages 264 and 265)

This is a recipe that utilizes prepared food. I've gussied it up with nuts and chocolate sauce.

1 package (4 ounces) German's
    sweet chocolate
⅓ cup milk
2 tablespoons sugar
1 package (3 ounces) cream
    cheese, softened
1 teaspoon vanilla extract

1 container (8 ounces) nondairy
    frozen whipped topping,
    thawed
½ cup finely chopped pecans
1 ready-to-use 8-inch graham-
    cracker crust
½ to ¾ cup chocolate sauce (page 281)

Melt chocolate in 2 tablespoons of the milk over low heat. Combine sugar, cream cheese, vanilla, and remaining milk, beating well. Stir in melted chocolate, mixing until blended. Fold in whipped topping and nuts. Spoon into graham-cracker crust. Freeze at least 4 hours. To serve, cut into wedges and top each wedge with chocolate sauce. Makes 6 servings. Pie may be frozen for several weeks; freeze and then wrap in freezer wrap. Will keep up to a month

Puddings/Sauces

Indian Pudding

This recipe for Indian pudding came from Boston's Durgin-Park restaurant in 1948. I have made it many times, served hot with a great scoop of vanilla ice cream. It still tastes wonderful. While many people may not make Indian pudding today, no New England cookbook should be without a recipe for it; you could do as the Pilgrims did, and bake beans at the same time.

1 cup yellow cornmeal (stone
    ground, if you can get it)
½ cup dark molasses
¼ cup sugar
¼ cup butter or margarine

¼ teaspoon salt
¼ teaspoon baking soda
2 eggs, beaten
1½ quarts hot milk
1 pint vanilla ice cream

Mix cornmeal, molasses, sugar, butter, salt, soda, and eggs thoroughly with half the hot milk. Spoon into a buttered 2-quart casserole and bake at 450°F until mixture boils, about 30 minutes. Stir in remaining milk.

Reduce heat to 300°F and bake for 5 hours, stirring occasionally. This makes 4 to 6 servings.

Durgin-Park suggested it should be baked in a well-greased stone crock.

Grape-Nuts Pudding

An old timer, Grape-Nuts pudding is still a flavorful and healthy dessert. Plan an oven dinner around the 350°F temperature, such as a baked chicken recipe and oven-baked vegetables, to take advantage of the heat.

½ cup Grape-Nuts cereal
2½ cups warm milk
2 large eggs or 3 small
⅓ to ½ cup sugar

½ teaspoon salt
1 teaspoon vanilla extract
Grated nutmeg (optional)

Soak cereal in warm milk for 10 minutes. Beat eggs with fork; add sugar to taste. Add salt, vanilla, and cereal-milk mixture. Spoon into a buttered 5-cup casserole. If desired, sprinkle top with nutmeg. Set casserole into a pan partly filled with water. Bake at 350°F for about 1 hour. Stir at least twice during the first 20 minutes of baking. Makes 4 to 6 servings. Serve warm or chilled. Store any leftover pudding in the refrigerator.

from Step Grandma, *Confidential Chat*

Fall Cranberry Pudding

Plan cranberry pudding around an oven meal such as meat loaf, baked potatoes, and oven-baked lima beans and celery.

¼ cup sugar
1 cup cranberries
¼ cup chopped pecans
1 egg
½ cup sugar

½ cup all-purpose flour
6 tablespoons butter or
     margarine, melted
Vanilla ice cream

Combine ¼ cup sugar with cranberries and pecans in a buttered 9-inch pie plate. Beat egg with ½ cup sugar. Fold in flour and butter. Pour over cranberries. Bake at 325°F for 25 to 30 minutes. Serve warm with ice cream. Makes 4 to 6 servings.

Butterscotch Sauce

This buttery sauce is good served warm over ice cream, cake, or pudding.

1½ cups firmly packed brown
    sugar
¾ cup light corn syrup

4 tablespoons butter
¾ cup evaporated milk

Combine brown sugar with corn syrup and butter and cook until a soft ball forms when a small amount of syrup is dropped in cold water. Remove from heat and stir in evaporated milk. Serve warm or cold. Store any unused portion covered in refrigerator. Makes about 2½ cups.

Variation

Stir in ½ cup cut-up pecans.

Chocolate Sauce
(pictured between pages 264 and 265)

Serve cold or hot over ice creams or puddings.

1 cup sugar
1 cup water
½ cup light corn syrup
3 squares (1 ounce each)
    unsweetened chocolate

1 teaspoon vanilla extract
1 cup light cream or undiluted
    evaporated milk

Combine sugar, water, and syrup. Bring to a boil and simmer 5 minutes, stirring occasionally. Remove from heat and stir in chocolate and vanilla, stirring until chocolate is melted and blended. Gradually stir in cream or evaporated milk. Store covered in refrigerator. Reheat over boiling water to serve hot. Makes 2½ cups.

Variations

Into 1 cup chocolate sauce, blend 1 cup marshmallow fluff. Fold in ½ cup cut-up pecans. Makes about 2 cups. Serve over chocolate ice cream for a popular dessert.
    Add ½ teaspoon cinnamon with chocolate.

Blueberry Sauce

Blueberry sauce is divine over ice cream. Try it on vanilla, butter pecan, Neapolitan, or orange or lemon sherbet.

⅔ cup sugar
Dash salt
2 tablespoons cornstarch
¼ cup water

1 tablespoon lemon juice
4 cups fresh (or dry pack frozen)
blueberries, rinsed and
drained

In a 6-cup saucepan mix together sugar, salt, cornstarch, water, and lemon juice until blended. Add blueberries and bring to a boil, stirring occasionally. Cook only until clear, 1 to 2 minutes. Chill. Use sauce as a topping for cakes or ice cream. Store unused portion, covered, in refrigerator. It will keep for up to a week. Makes about 3 cups.

Variation

Add ¼ teaspoon cinnamon with sugar

Strawberry Sauce

The pretty color and distinctive flavor of strawberry sauce go well with ice cream or puddings—or use it to make a dazzling parfait.

3 cups sliced fresh strawberries
½ cup water

1 tablespoon cornstarch
½ cup sugar

Mash 1 cup strawberries and mix with water, cornstarch, and sugar. Bring to a boil and cook and stir until mixture boils and is thickened. Cool. Fold in remaining strawberries. Chill. Store any unused portion, covered, in refrigerator. Makes about 3 cups.

Cooking
for Two

Numbers refer to pages where recipes appear in this book.

Cooking for Two

For many of us who live alone or in pairs, shopping and planning for meals can be a real challenge. Food items that come in singles (such as chops) are often expensive—and yet no one wants a diet that is restricted. This chapter offers an assortment of recipes for two; and to start off with, here are some general suggestions and hints.

Vegetables

Today most markets carry "loose" vegetables, so that you can buy the quantity you want. I use few frozen vegetables anymore, since fresh can be purchased as needed. And most raw vegetables will keep several days in the hydrator of the refrigerator, so that several kinds can be purchased at once. It is my practice never to butter vegetables until they're on the plate; then any vegetables that are cooked but not eaten can be chilled to go into a vegetable salad. Or small amounts of vegetables can be stretched with chopped celery, chopped onion, or carrots; or two leftover vegetables can be combined.

One of the greatest boons for small families is a steamer. Two servings of vegetables and a potato can be cooked at the same time. Put whatever takes longest in first and then add the others in time for them to cook.

Desserts

If you like pies and you like to make them, but if a steady diet of pie for several days in a row doesn't appeal, fruit pies can be frozen neatly. When the pie is cooled and after you have taken out at least one piece, cut the rest of the pie into servings. Wrap each piece in freezer wrap, seal, and put it back into a clean pie plate. Stick the whole thing into a plastic bag and freeze. A piece can be taken out as needed and thawed and/or heated. The pie can be stretched over several weeks that way. With a cake, likewise, use what you want when it is baked and freeze the rest to bring out as a surprise.

Fortunately, there are many other ways of solving the dessert question. Fruit can be purchased in any quantity, so fresh fruit and cheese is an ever-present answer. Or poach pears, peaches, plums, or nectarines in a light sugar syrup or a little sugar and wine. Add some lemon rind, cinnamon, orange rind, ginger, or whatever your imagination suggests, and you have a dessert that can be served warm or chilled. There is always ice cream and many commercially frozen desserts. Dessert is probably the least worry the planner of meals for two has to face.

Main Dishes

Stews always seem a problem, because if a whole recipe is prepared it seems to last forever. Make a recipe for 4; but before it is completely cooked, remove one-half and cool in refrigerator. When cooled, transfer to a freezer container, label, date, and freeze for future use. By not waiting until it reaches leftover status, the dish will be a superior product when reheated. **Spaghetti sauce** freezes well. As for **meats**, if you must buy a piece of steak (for example) larger than you wish, divide into portions, wrap, label, date, and freeze. I keep putting the emphasis on labeling, because once something gets into the freezer, it can easily get lost without a label. When ground beef is much less expensive in the larger pack, I buy it, divide it into individual portions, wrap, label, date, and freeze. Then when it is frozen I transfer the packages to a large plastic bag which I secure with a closure or a clip clothespin. It makes it easy to find the portions. **Meat loaf?** A 1-pound meat loaf isn't all that big, and half can be used for sandwiches. With a bigger meat loaf, use what is needed for one meal. Chill the remainder and slice into thin slices. Separate each slice from its neighbor with a piece of plastic wrap and pack the whole thing into a plastic freezer bag. Secure with a closure. By freezing the slices in this manner, it is possible to open and take out as many slices as are needed for sandwiches or a cold plate or to heat in gravy, and return the rest to the freezer.

Leftover cooked meat or steak? Slice thinly and combine with thin-sliced vegetables, cooked Chinese style just long enough to heat the meat. Served with rice, it makes a quick meal.

When you're dying for a **pot roast**, buy the smallest practical size. Use part of the leftover pot roast sliced for hot sandwiches and part for homemade hash. (I always cook a few extra potatoes with the pot roast to save for hash.)

For leftover roast pork, trim slices of fat and bone, dip in beaten egg and seasoned bread crumbs, air dry about 10 minutes, and brown on both sides in a small amount of oil and butter combined. Serve with cranberry or apple sauce. If I can get a small **pork shoulder**, I ask the butcher to cut off the shank end to use for bean or split pea soup. He will also cut a pork steak off the face, if asked.

Don't be backward about asking the butcher at a supermarket for a smaller amount than is on display. They do understand the problem of a single or a double household and will generally be most helpful.

Fish, eggs, and chicken are less of a problem. Here in our New England area, with so many fresh fish markets, one can buy any amount of fish. If there are bargains, **fish** freezes well to keep for future use: Freeze in serving-size portions and put them in a plastic bag to keep together.

Eggs are versatile to eat unadorned or combined with things like chicken livers, sausages, diced ham, diced fresh vegetables, or innumerable other items.

Chickens come in all sizes. I buy about 2½-pound broilers and quarter them—two quarters to eat at purchase and two to freeze. Quite small chickens can be quickly roasted to be eaten hot, with the leftovers cold.

Prepared products galore fit into cooking for two; and you can add your own touches to perk them up. Add extra cheese or diced meat to a cheese dinner. Cook up a little leftover meat or add a small can of tuna to a 14¾-ounce can of spaghetti with tomato sauce. A can of clam sauce (10½ ounces) is enough for two. If it is more convenient for you to buy canned vegetables, buy the smaller sizes. They cost a little more per ounce, but there is no waste.

Many people ask about **casseroles**. They miss some special dish that was a family favorite but that is too large to make for two.

One way is to make the casserole recipe as it has always been made, serve whatever amount you need the day it is cooked, and freeze the remainder in one or two portions (depending on the amount left) for future use. Choose the dish in which you would reheat the remainder. Line it with heavy-duty aluminum foil, leaving enough around the edge to wrap over the top, and spoon in the casserole food. Freeze uncovered, then cover the top with the extra foil. Remove from dish and seal with freezer tape, label, and date before returning to the freezer. When ready to use, remove foil, thaw in the casserole, and heat.

If you do not wish to do this, most casserole dishes stand adjustments well, if you divide the recipe. For example, if it calls for three eggs, use two small eggs in half the recipe. If the recipe calls for a 7½-ounce can of tuna, buy a smaller size. Even if it is more than half the original amount, it won't hurt the recipe. If a can of soup is called for, use half and refrigerate the remainder for a cup of soup before dinner or at lunch. If you don't have a small enough onion on hand, use half and refrigerate the remainder wrapped in plastic wrap. Instant minced onion can be used in place of fresh and it stores on the pantry shelf almost indefinitely. A substitution chart is on the jar.

Remember that a cup equals 16 tablespoons, which will help with dividing the measurements when they are as low as one-fourth or one-third in the original recipe.

The biggest thing to remember is to get a balanced diet with food from each of the four food groups and adequate protein and milk. When buying canned foods, you will see the food used in the largest quantity listed first in the ingredient list. That means if you are buying canned beef stew and the first ingredient is potatoes, the next beef, there are more potatoes than beef—and that's a bad bargain from the standpoint of protein.

And when you are struggling to remember to cook ½ pound of spaghetti instead of 2 pounds, think of all those big pots and pans you don't have to wash and the many dishes you don't have to do except at holidays.

Asparagus Soup for Two

A very good use of asparagus stalks that often go to waste.

1 cup cut-up asparagus
1 cup water
1 chicken bouillon cube
1½ cups milk

1 tablespoon flour
Salt to taste
Freshly grated nutmeg

When preparing asparagus, snap off the tip end to steam for asparagus tips. Cut the pieces that are left down to the woody part and peel. Measure 1 cup (or more) and cook with 1 cup water and bouillon cube until tender. Blend in blender until smooth. Then blend milk and flour in blender and add to asparagus. Cook and stir until mixture boils. Taste and add salt, if necessary. Serve with grated nutmeg sprinkled on top. Makes about 2½ cups or 2 servings.

Boston Style Chili

A bowl of chili can be a meal in itself. Served with pilot crackers, fruit, and cookies, it is an easy meal for two. Any left over will keep for several days in the refrigerator or can be frozen for 1 to 2 months. Have you ever served heated leftover chili over hot frankfurters? Cumin (listed below) is one of the ingredients in chili powder, and the extra cumin called for here enhances the flavor; but if you don't have any, don't worry. The chili will still be good. The combination of beans plus beef allows cutting down on the beef used and still makes a nutritious dish.

¼ pound ground beef
1 clove garlic, chopped
   (optional)
1 medium to large onion,
   chopped
1 can (15 ounces) kidney beans
1 can (15 or 16 ounces) tomatoes

1 tablespoon chili powder
½ teaspoon ground cumin
½ teaspoon salt
Freshly ground pepper to taste
1 teaspoon Worcestershire
   sauce

Combine beef, garlic, and onion in a heavy 1-quart saucepan and stir-fry until meat is lightly browned and onions tender. Add all remaining ingredients. Bring to a boil, reduce heat, and simmer, covered, 1 to 2 hours, stirring occasionally. Taste for seasoning and add more chili powder, if desired. Makes about 5 cups or 2 servings.

Celebration Steak

The mushroom sauce can be prepared in advance and the steaks peppered ahead of time so that there is only the last-minute cooking. Big fat baked potatoes with sour cream, tossed greens with tomato wedges, and poached pears for dessert complete this festive meal.

2 tablespoons butter
½ cup chopped mushrooms
½ cup dry sherry
1 cup water
2 beef bouillon cubes
2 sirloin or round steaks, 1 inch
    thick (½ pound each)

1 tablespoon peppercorns or ¾
    tablespoons cracked pepper
½ teaspoon salt
1 tablespoon butter
1 clove garlic, finely chopped
¼ cup red wine

Heat 2 tablespoons butter in a small saucepan and sauté mushrooms for 3 minutes. Add sherry and cook until reduced to half. Stir in water and bouillon cubes. Cook over low heat about 15 minutes, covered. Makes about 1 cup. Reserve.

Trim all fat from steaks. Crush whole peppercorns between 2 sheets of waxed paper with a wooden mallet until coarsely cracked (or use cracked pepper). Season steak with salt and press pepper into both sides of steak.

Heat 1 tablespoon butter in a 10-inch skillet and cook steaks over medium heat 5 minutes on one side and 3 minutes on other (for medium rare). Remove steaks to platter and keep warm.

Add garlic to skillet and let cook 2 minutes. Add red wine and cook until reduced to half. Add reserved mushroom sauce and bring to a boil. Serve with steaks. Makes 2 servings.

Homemade Hash

Hash can be prepared, then refrigerated for several hours or overnight before cooking. (In fact the flavors blend when allowed to stand.) For a quick meal, add a canned mixed vegetable, sliced tomatoes, and ice cream for dessert.

2½ cups chopped cold cooked
    beef
1¾ cups chopped cold cooked
    potatoes
1 teaspoon Worcestershire sauce
½ teaspoon salt

Freshly ground pepper to taste
1 cup chopped onion
½ cup leftover gravy, pan juices,
    or water
3 to 4 tablespoons margarine or
    vegetable oil

Combine meat, potatoes, seasonings, onion, and gravy and mix lightly. Heat margarine in skillet and cook hash, covered, over medium heat 20 minutes. Uncover and cook 10 minutes longer, stirring up from bottom of skillet. Makes 2 to 3 servings.

Favorite Spaghetti

For those of you who might not be as experienced in seasoning a spaghetti sauce as Second Year (who contributed this recipe), I'd suggest a good flip of pepper, a pinch of basil, and a pinch of oregano.

4 ounces spaghetti	1 small onion, chopped
2 quarts boiling water	3 or 4 small ripe tomatoes
1 teaspoon salt	Seasoning to taste
3 slices bacon, diced	

Cook spaghetti in boiling water with salt about 10 minutes. Drain. While spaghetti is cooking, fry bacon until done, but not crisp. Add onions and dry until lightly browned. Dip tomatoes in boiling water and peel. Chop and add to bacon and onion. Cover and simmer 10 minutes. Season to taste. Add sauce to hot spaghetti. Makes 2 to 3 servings.

from Second Year, *Confidential Chat*

Beef with Noodles

Serve with steamed green beans and a lettuce wedge with Russian dressing, and for dessert a mixed fruit cup.

1 tablespoon oil	¾ cup dry white wine
½ pound beef for stew	1 teaspoon steak sauce
2 medium onions, sliced	½ teaspoon salt
1 garlic clove, chopped (optional)	Freshly ground pepper to taste
1 tablespoon flour	4 ounces noodles, cooked
1 jar (2½ ounces) sliced mushrooms	

Heat cooking oil and brown beef, onions, and garlic. Stir in flour, mushrooms and their liquid, wine, and seasonings. Bring to a boil, reduce heat, and simmer covered about an hour or until meat is tender, stirring occasionally. Cook noodles as directed on package. Serve beef with noodles. Makes 2 servings.

Quick Spaghetti Sauce

Serve a tossed salad and Italian bread with this quick spaghetti and you'll eat as well as if you'd been slaving for hours. It's a great trick for when you get home late and there's little time to cook.

4 links sweet or hot Italian
    sausage
1 large onion, coarsely chopped

1 can (8 ounces) tomato sauce
½ can water
Cooked spaghetti for two

Remove skins from sausages and crumble into skillet. Add onions and cook and stir over moderate heat until onion and meat are lightly browned. Add tomato sauce and water and simmer, covered, for about 45 minutes or an hour. Serve over hot cooked spaghetti. Makes 2 servings.

Stuffed Green Peppers

This is a "meal in a skillet" and needs only bread and a hearty salad.

2 large green peppers
1 medium onion, chopped
1 stalk celery, chopped
1 teaspoon Worcestershire
    sauce
¼ cup uncooked rice

1 cup diced leftover meat
½ cup leftover gravy
Salt and freshly ground pepper
    to taste
1 can (16 ounces) stewed
    tomatoes

Cut peppers in half lengthwise and remove stem ends and seeds. Wash well. Place in a 3-inch-deep skillet, hollow side up. Mix onion, celery, Worcestershire, rice, meat, gravy, and salt and pepper, and spoon into pepper shells. Spoon tomatoes over and around filled peppers. Bring to a boil, reduce heat, cover, and simmer about 30 to 40 minutes. Check, and, if necessary, add a little water toward end of cooking time. Makes 2 servings.

Beans and Pork Chops for Two

Acorn squash and apples baked at the same time would complete this thrifty oven meal.

1 can (1 pound) New England
    style baked beans
1 small onion, chopped
1 tablespoon molasses

1 tablespoon chili sauce or ketchup
1 teaspoon prepared brown mustard
2 pork chops

Combine beans with onion, molasses, chili sauce, and mustard. Spoon into a buttered flat 1-quart casserole. Trim fat from pork chops and fry fat slowly in skillet until crisp. Brown pork chops quickly on both sides in fat. Place chops on beans. Cover and bake at 300°F for 1 hour. Makes 2 servings.

Braised Pork Steaks

A rangetop dish for two and a flavorful way to prepare pork. Serve buttered carrots, celery slaw, and orange sherbet to complete the menu.

2 fresh pork steaks (about 1
    pound in all)
2 tablespoons flour
¼ teaspoon salt
Freshly ground pepper to taste
2 tablespoons oil
1 clove garlic, chopped
2 medium onions, sliced

2 medium mushrooms,
    chopped
¾ cup dry white wine
1 chicken bouillon cube
Chopped fresh dill to taste
    (optional)
2 boiling potatoes, halved, or 4
    small potatoes

Remove fat from pork steaks and pound around bone area with meat mallet. Mix flour with salt and pepper and rub into steaks. Heat oil in skillet and brown steaks on both sides. Add garlic, onions, and mushrooms and continue cooking 5 minutes. Reduce heat; add wine, bouillon cube, and dill. Cover and simmer over low heat for 45 minutes. Add potatoes and continue cooking until potatoes are tender, about 25 minutes. Makes 2 servings.

Creamed Finnan Haddie

Finnan Haddie is smoked haddock, although sometimes codfish is used. It has a marvelous flavor. Some people like to serve it for breakfast, in which case, serve it with toast instead of mashed potatoes.

1 pound finnan haddie	Salt and freshly ground pepper
3 tablespoons butter or margarine	to taste
2 tablespoons flour	Mashed or boiled potatoes for 2
1½ cups milk	Chopped fresh parsley or paprika

Cut off a tiny piece of the finnan haddie and taste to see how salty it is. If it is very salty, soak for several hours in cold water. Drain and cut into serving-size pieces. Place in a large skillet. Cover with water and bring to a simmer. Cook below boiling point for 5 to 8 minutes or until fish flakes easily. Remove from water with spatula and keep hot. Pour water from skillet. Add butter and flour and cook together, about 2 minutes. Stir in milk and bring to a boil, stirring. Taste and add salt and pepper if needed. When thickened, serve with finnan haddie and potatoes. If desired, sprinkle with chopped fresh parsley or paprika. Makes 2 to 3 servings.

Lamb Patties with Yogurt Sauce

Serve with kasha (buckwheat groats), sliced tomatoes and cucumbers, and pita bread.

½ pound ground lamb	½ teaspoon salt
1 medium onion, grated	½ cup plain yogurt
1 clove garlic, finely chopped	1 teaspoon lemon juice
1 egg, beaten	¼ cup chopped fresh parsley
½ teaspoon dried thyme	

Mix ground lamb with onion, garlic, egg, thyme, and salt. Shape into 2 oblong patties and chill for 30 minutes. While lamb is chilling, combine yogurt, lemon juice, and parsley.

Broil lamb patties 4 inches from source of heat about 3 minutes on each side (for medium). Serve with yogurt sauce. Makes 2 servings.

Chicken Livers for One

The chicken livers can be purchased especially, or saved from chicken. They freeze well. This recipe is designed to be easily multiplied up for 2, 3, or 4.

2 tablespoons butter or margarine
1 clove garlic, chopped
2 fresh mushrooms, diced
¼ pound chicken livers
1 tablespoon flour

½ cup dry red wine
Salt and freshly ground pepper
   to taste
¾ cup hot cooked rice

Heat butter in a small skillet. Add garlic and mushrooms and sauté about 3 minutes. Cut chicken livers into 2 or 3 pieces, depending on size, and sauté quickly, stirring. Sprinkle flour over livers, add wine, and bring to a boil. Cook 1 minute, season to taste, and serve at once over hot cooked rice. Makes 1 serving.

Turkey Patties

Ground turkey is readily available in most supermarkets, and it is a good source of protein with less fat than ground beef. If it comes in a larger size package than you can use at one meal, it freezes well.

1 slice bread
1 egg
2 tablespoons chopped fresh
   parsley
½ teaspoon salt

Freshly ground pepper to taste
½ teaspoon poultry seasoning
½ pound ground turkey
2 bacon slices (optional)

Blend bread, egg, parsley, salt, pepper, and poultry seasoning. Mix with ground turkey and shape into 2 patties. Put a bacon slice around each patty and secure with toothpick. Broil about 8 minutes on each side, 3 inches from heat source. They are about 1½ inches thick, and you want them well done. Makes 2 servings.

Skillet Chicken and Rice

An electric skillet is handy for this dish. For top-of-the-stove cooking, use a skillet with a tight-fitting cover. The whole meal is in the pan; add cranberry sauce to the menu if you like, or a fruit salad.

2 chicken legs	Salt and pepper to taste
2 chicken thighs	¾ cup uncooked rice
1 tablespoon oil	1½ to 2 cups chicken stock
1 small onion, diced	2 carrots, cut in quarters

Rinse chicken and dry thoroughly on paper towels. Heat oil in skillet; add chicken, and over medium heat, brown on all sides. Sprinkle with onion, salt, and pepper. Push chicken to one side of pan, add rice, and stir for 3 or 4 minutes, until rice is golden. Carefully add 1 cup of chicken stock to rice, stirring well with wooden spoon. Cover and lower heat to simmering point. Check to see when more liquid is needed, as rice will absorb stock. Stir rice as you add more liquid. Allow rice to cook about 15 minutes, then place carrot pieces around chicken. Cover and continue simmering until rice and carrots are tender, about 25 minutes in all. Makes 2 servings.

Veal Emince

Cut the veal in tiny pieces. Serve the finished dish with steamed rice, a green vegetable, and a watercress-and-onion salad. It's a very good way to use one of the less-expensive cuts of veal. This recipe can be doubled to serve 4.

½ pound boneless veal for stew	1 cup dry white wine
2 tablespoons butter or margarine	½ cup tomato sauce
1 cup chopped fresh mushrooms	¼ teaspoon dried rosemary
1 tablespoon chopped onion	½ teaspoon salt
1 tablespoon flour	

Cut the pieces of veal into small bits, removing and discarding any cartilage. Heat butter in skillet and brown veal, mushrooms, and onions over moderately high heat. Sprinkle flour over and stir. Add all remaining ingredients. Cover and cook over low heat, stirring occasionally, for about 45 minutes. Makes 2 servings.

Scalloped Potatoes for Two

These easy scalloped potatoes can go into the oven with a baked main dish.

3 medium potatoes
Salt, freshly ground pepper,
   and nutmeg to taste

½ cup plain dry bread crumbs
1½ tablespoons butter or margarine
¾ cup milk

Peel and thinly slice potatoes into a buttered 7-inch pie plate. Sprinkle with salt, pepper, and nutmeg to taste and with bread crumbs. Dot with butter. Pour milk over all and bake at 400°F for about 35 to 45 minutes or until potatoes are tender. Makes 2 servings.

Fruit with Sour Cream

A dessert that can be easily prepared and yet seems elegant to eat.

¾ cup dairy sour cream
¼ cup soft brown sugar

1 cup prepared fresh fruit

Mix sour cream with brown sugar. Fold in fruit and serve in your prettiest glass dessert dishes. Makes 2 servings.

   Use fruit such as fresh strawberries, seedless green grapes, fresh pineapple, bananas, peaches, nectarines.

1 & 7, Corn Relish (recipe on page 308). 2 & 14, Cranberry Pineapple Jelly (recipe on page 302). 3, 6, 11, & 12 Cranberry Orange Marmalade (recipe on page 306). 4, Year Round Relish (recipe on page 309). 5 & 8 Brandied Dates (recipe on page 308). 9 & 13, Pear Chutney (recipe on page 307). 10, Wine Jelly (recipe on page 303).

Vegetable Medleys

Combinations of vegetables are far more interesting and tasty than the same ones served alone. Try a quick sauté, in 1 teaspoon of olive or vegetable oil, of thin strips of zucchini with minced onion and a small skinned and cut-up tomato. Cook 4 or 5 minutes, just to crisp-tender point for the zucchini, season with pepper and a dash of salt, and serve.

To crisp-tender cooked green beans, well drained, add a small minced onion and a cut-up peeled tomato. Sprinkle with pepper, salt if desired, and a bit of minced basil, then cover and simmer 2 or 3 minutes.

Cook 6 Brussels sprouts in water to cover for 10 minutes; drain well. In a skillet, cook a tablespoon of chopped onion in 2 teaspoons margarine until onion is just tender. Add the sprouts, cover, and simmer another 5 minutes. Season to taste.

An easy top-of-the-stove scallop:

1 teaspoon oil	1 tablespoon flour
2 carrots, thinly sliced	Salt and pepper
1 stalk celery, thinly sliced	3 tablespoons milk
1 small onion, thinly sliced	

Put the oil in the bottom of a heavy saucepan. Layer the vegetables in the pan, sprinkling each layer with flour and salt and pepper to taste. Pour on milk, cover, and cook over very low heat until all vegetables are tender, about 8 to 10 minutes. Makes 2 servings.

Beef Stroganoff

A quickly prepared dish that turns a small amount of steak into a delicious meal for two.

½ pound tenderloin or sirloin steak	2 tablespoons minced shallot or onion
2 tablespoons flour	1 small clove garlic, minced (optional)
¼ teaspoon pepper	1 teaspoon tomato paste
1 tablespoon oil	1 teaspoon tomato paste
1 tablespoon butter or margarine	½ cup beef stock or bouillon
4 mushrooms, stemmed and	½ cup sour cream
thinly sliced	Hot cooked noodles (4 ounces, uncooked)

Cut steak into thin strips, about ¼ inch wide and 2 inches long. Combine flour and pepper on a sheet of waxed paper; toss strips in mixture until coated well. Heat oil and butter or margarine in a heavy skillet. Add steak and quickly brown on all sides, stirring with a wooden spoon to brown evenly. Add mushroom slices, shallot or onion, and garlic, again stirring quickly. Sprinkle with any remaining flour mixture, carefully stirring to mix. Combine tomato paste and beef stock; stir into pan. Stir in sour cream and heat gently for just a minute or two. Do not allow to boil, as sour cream will curdle. Serve over hot noodles. Makes 2 servings.

Baked Stuffed Fillets

Just a bit of leftover lobster or crabmeat, or a small amount of scallops, makes a fanciful dish out of popular fillet of sole. Serve a green vegetable as accompaniment and coleslaw for crisp contrast.

4 pieces fillet of sole
    (about 1 pound, total)
1 tablespoon butter or margarine
1 teaspoon minced shallot or onion
¼ pound scallops, crabmeat, or
    lobster

Pepper to taste
2 tablespoons dry white wine
2 tablespoons dry bread crumbs
Paprika

Wash and dry fillets; place 2 in a lightly greased baking dish. In a skillet, melt butter or margarine; add shallot or onion and cook until just tender, but do not brown. Add whatever shellfish you are using and stir for 3 or 4 minutes. Add wine, then stir in bread crumbs. Divide mixture and spoon over the two fillets in dish, then top with remaining fillets. Put a tablespoonful of wine in the dish, dot tops of fish with a little butter, and sprinkle with paprika. Bake at 350°F for about 12 to 15 minutes (depending on thickness of fillets). Fish should be milky white and flake easily when done. Makes 2 servings.

Chicken Marsala

This will provide generous servings for 2, with no doubt enough left over for next day's lunch. Serve with hot rice or noodles and a green vegetable.

2 medium-sized whole chicken
    breasts, skinned, boneless
½ cup flour
4 tablespoons butter, divided
5 ounces Marsala wine (not cooking
    wine)

5 ounces fresh mushrooms, sliced
⅛ cup chicken stock
2 ounces julienned ham
2 tablespoons finely chopped
    parsley

Cut chicken breasts in half. Detach the small fillet under each half so there are 4 large and 4 small pieces. Cut each large piece in half crosswise, making 12 pieces in all. Coat chicken with flour; shake off excess.

Melt 2 tablespoons of the butter in large skillet over medium heat. Add chicken pieces and sauté about 4 minutes per side, until golden brown. Drain excess butter from skillet. Add wine and let reduce by ⅓. Add sliced mushrooms, stock, ham, and remaining butter; stir, then remove chicken to serving plates. Continue to cook sauce for 1 minute more, until it is slightly thickened. Pour over chicken. Garnish with parsley. Makes 2 servings.

Made with Love, *Confidential Chat*

Preserving

— *and* —

Pickling

Numbers refer to pages where recipes appear in this book.

Preserving and Pickling

This section is devoted to a few interesting recipes that you might like to make. It's no primer on the preserving of food. If you want to get deeply involved in it, the books put out by the companies who make the jars you need for canning are very good and relatively inexpensive. Your local United States Government Extension Service has many bulletins on home canning, pickling, and preserving. Any charge on the government material is minimal.

Here are explanations for some of the terms that turn up in pickling and preserving and a few general directions.

Equipment and Techniques

Some equipment that makes food preservation easier includes:
- A wide-mouth funnel which is used when food is being ladled or poured into the canning jars.
- A candy thermometer for checking the temperature when making jams or jellies.
- Some good tongs for picking up jars, etc.
- A waterbath canner.
- A wire basket to make it easier to blanch fruit for peeling.
- A household scale.

Before you start, examine jars for cracks or chips on the rims. If any are found, discard those jars for canning. Always use jars that are specifically manufactured for canning.

Always wash jars with soapy water and rinse well. Put jars and screw bands in clean hot water until ready to fill. Put jar lids in boiling water and hold for a few minutes until they go on the filled jar. If you use jars with a one-piece lid and rubber band, follow manufacturer's directions. If you wash jars in the dishwasher, leave them in the dishwasher until ready to use.

You will read directions for processing pickles, jams, and jellies in a boiling waterbath. Under this method, you first place the jar lid on the filled jar, put on the screw band, and tighten it as tightly as possible by hand. Stand the jars upright on a rack in a pan of boiling water that comes at least 1 inch above the top of the jar. Bring the water back to the boil and boil hard for 5 or 10 minutes or whatever time the directions indicate. (It varies with the product and size of jar used.)

There are special large kettles for waterbath canning, with racks for holding the jars. If you do not have one of these, use a pan deep enough so the jars can be covered 1 inch above the jar top, and improvise a rack to hold jars off the bottom from wooden slats or wire. The boiling water must circulate around the bottom, as well as the sides and top of jar, to be effective.

The purpose of the boiling waterbath is to sterilize the food and jars. In order to sterilize the preserved material completely, it is recommended that all pickles, jams, and jellies be processed in a waterbath.

After processing is completed, remove jars from waterbath and place on a rack or folded cloth. Allow space between the jars for circulation of air. Do not set jars in a draft, and do not cover them. Do not tighten screw bands. When jars are completely cold, test for seal by tapping lid with a spoon. A clear ringing sound means the jar is sealed. Remove screw bands.

Before storing, wash jars of food with warm soapy water, rinse, and dry. Label with name of product and date. Store in a dark, cool place.

Pepper Jelly

Sloan Street serves pepper jelly on crackers with cream cheese or as a condiment with roast beef or lamb. Another good way to try it is on roast beef and sharp cheddar cheese sandwiches. Both are good uses for this delicious jelly.

1 cup seeded, chopped green peppers	1½ cups cider vinegar
⅓ cup canned jalapeno peppers, seeded and rinsed	6 cups sugar
	1 bottle (6 ounces) liquid pectin
	5 drops green food coloring

Place both green and jalapeno peppers (rinsed well before handling) in blender container with 1 cup of the vinegar. Blend until smooth. Pour into a heavy 4- or 5-quart pan. Rinse blender with remaining ½ cup vinegar; add that to pan. Stir in sugar. Over medium-high heat, bring to a rolling boil that you cannot stir down. Remove pan from heat; allow to stand 5 minutes. Skim and discard any foam from top.

Stir in pectin and green food coloring. Pour jelly immediately into hot, clean 6-ounce jars with screw tops, filling each jar to within ⅛ inch of top. Wipe rims and put on lids. Put on screw bands and tighten as tightly as possible by hand. Process in boiling waterbath 5 minutes. Makes six 6-ounce glasses.

from Sloan Street, Knightsbridge, *Confidential Chat*

Cranberry Pineapple Jelly

(pictured between pages 296 and 297)

The nice thing about this pretty and tasty jelly is that it can be made any time of year. Try it on toasted English muffins.

3 cups bottled cranberry juice cocktail	⅓ cup lemon juice
1 cup canned unsweetened pineapple juice	1 package (1¾ ounces) powdered fruit pectin
	5 cups sugar

In a large saucepan combine cranberry, pineapple, and lemon juices with pectin. Bring to a boil. At once stir in sugar and bring to a full rolling boil and boil hard 1 minute, stirring constantly. Remove from heat; skim foam, if any. Pour into hot, clean 6-ounce jars with screw tops, filling each jar to within ⅛ inch of top. Wipe rims and put on lids. Put on screw bands and tighten as tightly as possible by hand. Process in boiling waterbath 5 minutes. Makes six or seven 6-ounce jelly jars.

Wine Jelly

(pictured between pages 296 and 297)

A wine jelly can accompany the main course; or serve it with cream cheese for dessert.

 2 cups wine *   ¼ bottle liquid fruit pectin
 3 cups sugar

Combine wine and sugar in the top of double boiler. Mix well. Place over rapidly boiling water and heat and stir about 3 minutes, or until all sugar is dissolved. Remove wine mixture from water and stir pectin in at once. Pour quickly into hot, clean 6-ounce jars with screw tops, filling each jar to within ⅛ inch of top. Wipe rims and put on lids. Put on screw bands and tighten as tightly as possible by hand. Process in boiling waterbath 5 minutes. Makes about five 6-ounce glasses.

*Use any wine that pleases you such as Chablis, zinfandel, Sauternes, rosé, dry sherry, or tawny port.

Beach Plum Jelly

Beach plum trees (or shrubs) are native to the sandy, windswept coast of Cape Cod and other Northeast coastal areas. In May the low beach plum trees, which lean with the wind, are like a drift of snow with their covering of white blossoms. People who do not have beach plum trees on their own property mark them well so that in late August or early September when the plums begin to mature, they can, hopefully with the consent of the owner, pick enough to make some cherished jelly. They should be picked when three-fourths of the plums are reddish blue and one-fourth are more nearly red. Beach plums are about an inch in diameter.

 4 cups beach plum juice   3 cups sugar
    (recipe below)

Combine juice and sugar in a large saucepan. Cook and stir until mixture reaches the jelly stage, 220 to 222°F, or sheets from spoon. (This is another jelly test: Dip a metal spoon in the jelly and hold it over the saucepan tipped so that the jelly can run off back into the pan. When several drops which form on the side of the spoon run together to form one drop, that is called "sheeting.") Ladle jelly into hot, clean jars with screw tops, filing jars to within ⅛ inch of top. Wipe rims and put on lids. Put on screw bands and tighten as tightly as possible by hand. Process in boiling waterbath 5 minutes. Makes five 6-ounce glasses.

Beach Plum Juice

3¹⁄₃ pounds (about) beach plums   1¹⁄₂ cups water

Wash plums in running water. Lift clean fruit from water to avoid dirt that might collect in bottom of pan. Place washed fruit in a saucepan and crush slightly. Add water and bring to a boil slowly and simmer until most of the juice has come out of the plums. The juice wil jell better if about a quarter of the plums are underripe.

Drain through a jelly bag or cheesecloth lined strainer. If bag is squeezed to remove maximum juice, then re-strain juice through a cheesecloth (for a clear jelly) and do not squeeze this time.

Rhubarb Jam

The strawberry-flavored gelatin gives this rhubarb jam a beautiful color, and the combination of flavors is very pleasant.

5 cups rhubarb, cut in ¹⁄₂-inch   1 cup drained, crushed canned pineapple*
    pieces (about 3 pounds)   1 package (3 ounces) strawberry gelatin
4 cups sugar

Combine rhubarb, sugar, and pineapple and let stand at least half an hour. Bring to a boil and let boil 12 minutes, stirring so it will not stick. Remove from heat and stir in gelatin. Ladle into hot, clean jars and cover with lids. Cool, then store in freezer. Makes five ¹⁄₂-pint jars.

*1 cup fresh or frozen unsweetened strawberries may be used in place of canned pineapple.

from the Recipe Lover, *Confidential Chat*

Green Tomato Marmalade

When green tomatoes start piling up in the fall, let this marmalade recipe come to the rescue.

5 lemons	2 pounds sugar
1 cup water	½ teaspoon salt
4 pounds green tomatoes, cubed or sliced	

Peel lemons (being sure not to cut away any white part), cut peels into thin slices, and boil for 5 minutes in 1 cup water. Discard water and taste peel. If it still tastes bitter, repeat cooking in a fresh cup of water. Slice lemon pulp and remove seeds.

Combine tomatoes, sugar, salt, lemon pulp, and drained peel. Heat slowly and stir until the sugar is dissolved. Continue stirring and boil slowly for about 1 hour or until mixture is somewhat thick and fruit clear. Stir occasionally, but toward the last, stir more often so mixture does not stick to the bottom of pan and burn. Pour into hot, clean pint jars with screw tops, filling to within ⅛ inch of top. Wipe rims and put on lids. Put on screw bands and tighten as tightly as possible by hand. Process in boiling waterbath 10 minutes. Makes 3 pints.

from My Husband's Wife, *Confidential Chat*

Blueberry Jam

This lightly spiced blueberry jam is always a treat.

4 cups blueberries*	3 cups sugar
1 tablespoon lemon juice	½ teaspoon cinnamon
½ cup water	⅛ teaspoon ground cloves

Sort and wash blueberries. Mix with all remaining ingredients in a large saucepan. Bring to a boil and boil rapidly, stirring constantly, until mixture reaches 220°F or until thickened, about 15 minutes. If you do not have a thermometer, put a small amount of boiled mixture on a plate and put it in the freezer for a few minutes. When it stays round, and does not run all over the plate, the jam should be done. Remove from heat and skim, if necessary. Ladle into hot, clean 8-ounce jars to within ⅛ inch of top. Wipe rims and put on lids. Put on screw bands and tighten as tightly as possible by hand. Process in boiling waterbath 5 minutes. Makes about four 8-ounce jars.

Blueberries frozen without added sugar or syrup may be used.

Strawberry Preserves

The bright color and summery flavor of strawberry preserves is always welcome on toast, hot muffins, biscuits, or whatever it suits you to make as a go-with.

1 quart strawberries
1/4 cup lemon juice

3 1/2 cups sugar

Wash and drain berries well. Remove hulls. Combine with lemon juice in a saucepan and boil 3 minutes. Add sugar and boil 6 minutes. Stir often. Ladle into hot, clean 1/2-pint jars with screw tops, filling jars to within 1/8 inch of top. Wipe rims and put on lids. Put on screw bands and tighten as tightly as possible by hand. Process in boiling waterbath 5 minutes. Makes about three 1/2-pint jars.

Cranberry Orange Marmalade

(pictured between pages 296 and 297)

A nice treat for yourself or for giving at the holidays.

2 oranges
1 lemon
2 1/2 cups water
3 cups fresh cranberries

1 package (1 3/4 ounces)
   powdered fruit pectin
6 1/2 cups sugar

Remove peel from oranges and lemon. Scrape out white membrane and cut peel into thin strips. Add peel to 2 1/2 cups water in large saucepan and cook, covered, over low heat 20 minutes. Section oranges and lemon, discard membranes, and cut fruit into small pieces. Add with cranberries to peel and simmer 10 minutes, stirring constantly. Stir in pectin and bring to a boil. Stir in sugar. Bring to a full rolling boil. Boil hard 1 minute, stirring constantly. Remove from heat and skim foam, if any. Let stand 15 minutes, stirring now and then. Ladle into hot, clean pint jars to within 1/8 inch of top. Wipe rims and put on lids. Put on screw bands and tighten as tightly as possible by hand. Process in boiling waterbath 5 minutes. Makes 4 pints.

Mango Chutney

The mango originated in India but is today cultivated extensively in southern Florida and in Mexico. When the peel turns yellowish and the fruit yields slightly to gentle palm pressure, the mangos are ready to use. To peel, score peel lengthwise into segments and pull back.

1 cup vinegar
3¼ cups sugar
6 cups green mango slices
    (about 6 to 7 peeled mangos)
¼ cup finely chopped fresh
    gingerroot

1 small clove garlic, minced
2 fresh chili peppers, seeds
    removed, finely chopped
1½ cups raisins
½ cup sliced onion
½ teaspoon salt

Boil vinegar and sugar 5 minutes. Add mangos and all other ingredients. Cook ½ hour or until thickened, stirring often. Pack into hot, clean pint jars with screw tops, filling each jar to within ⅛ inch of the top. Wipe rims and put on lids. Put on screw bands and tighten as tightly as possible by hand. Process in boiling waterbath for 5 minutes. Makes 4 pints.

Pear Chutney

(pictured between pages 296 and 297)

Mangoes are the original chutney fruit, but if they are not available, other fruits such as apples or pears make a fine chutney. Chutney is generally served with a curry dish but is good with any meat.

1 lemon
1 clove garlic, chopped
5 cups chopped peeled fresh
    pears*
2¼ cups firmly packed brown
    sugar
1½ cups chopped pitted fresh
    California dates

¾ cup chopped candied ginger
1½ teaspoons salt
½ teaspoon Tabasco sauce
½ cup chopped onion
2 cups cider vinegar

Chop and remove seeds from lemon. Combine with all remaining ingredients in a large saucepan and cook slowly about 45 minutes until mixture thickens. Stir often. Ladle into hot, clean pint jars with screw tops, filling jars to within ⅛ inch of top. Wipe rims and put on lids. Put on screw bands and tighten as tightly as possible by hand. Process in boiling waterbath 10 minutes. Makes about 3 pints.

*About 1 dozen pears, depending on size.

Brandied Dates

(pictured between pages 296 and 297)

Delicious to eat as is or scrumptious over ice cream.

½ cup white vinegar
1¼ cups water
2¼ cups sugar
2 pounds (5¼ cups firmly
    packed) pitted fresh
    California dates

½ cup lemon juice
1½ cups (about) brandy

Mix together in a medium saucepan the vinegar, 1 cup of the water, and ¼ cup of the sugar. Bring to a boil, stirring to dissolve sugar. Boil 5 minutes. Add dates, cover, and cook gently 5 minutes. Drain off and discard liquid. Put dates in a bowl. In the same saucepan, mix together the remaining ¼ cup water, 2 cups sugar, and lemon juice. Bring to a boil, stirring to dissolve sugar. Boil 5 minutes. Add dates, cover, and cook very gently 10 minutes. Pack dates in hot, clean ½-pint jars with screw tops, filling each jar to within ¼ inch of the top. Pour equal amounts of syrup in which the dates were cooked into jars. Fill jars with brandy to within ⅛ inch of top, covering dates completely. Wipe rims and put on lids. Put on screw bands and tighten as tightly as possible by hand. Process in boiling waterbath 5 minutes. Makes six ½-pint jars.

Corn Relish

(pictured between pages 296 and 297)

This corn relish may be made with either fresh or frozen corn, which makes it another recipe for cooler weather. It is another favorite New England recipe.

6 cups fresh or frozen corn
    kernels*
1 cup chopped green pepper
⅔ cup wine vinegar
⅔ cup water
½ cup sugar

2 teaspoons salt
½ teaspoon freshly ground
    pepper
½ cup chopped pimiento
½ teaspoon turmeric

If frozen corn is used, thaw. Combine with all remaining ingredients. Bring to a boil and cook 10 minutes. Pack into hot, clean ½-pint jars with screw tops, filling jars to within ½ inch of top. Wipe rims and put on lids. Put on screw bands and tighten as tightly as possible by hand. Process in boiling waterbath 10 minutes. Makes about five ½-pint jars.

*Depending on size of ears, about a dozen ears will make 6 cups when corn is cut off the cob.

Year Round Relish
(pictured between pages 296 and 297)

A trip to the freezer will make this relish a breeze. Serve it with roasted meats or cold cuts.

1½ cups frozen cauliflower
1½ cups frozen lima beans
1½ cups frozen cut green beans
½ cup chopped green pepper
½ cup chopped onion
¼ cup sugar

1 tablespoon mustard seed
1½ cups white vinegar
½ cup water
1 jar (4 ounces) pimiento,
    drained and cut into strips

Thaw vegetables. Mix with all remaining ingredients. Bring to a boil and cook 5 minutes. Pack into hot, clean 8-ounce jars with screw tops, filling jars to within ½ inch of top. Wipe rims and put on lids. Put on screw bands and tighten as tightly as possible by hand. Process in boiling waterbath 10 minutes. Makes about five 8-ounce jars.

Pickled Carrot Sticks

Pickled carrot sticks are good served with meals, but also remember to bring them out for an appetizer. They will be popular served as is or with a cheese dip.

2 quarts carrot sticks (2 to 3
    pounds)
3 cups vinegar
1 cup water
1½ cups sugar

1 tablespoon mustard seed
3 red chili peppers, fresh or
    canned
1½ tablespoons mixed pickling
    spice

Peel and cut carrots into sticks about 4 inches long. Pack pencil style into hot, clean pint jars with screw tops. Combine vinegar with all remaining ingredients and cook together 5 minutes. Remove red peppers and pour hot syrup over carrots in jars, filling to within ¼ inch of top. Wipe rims and put on lids. Put on screw bands and tighten as tightly as possible by hand. Process in boiling waterbath 5 minutes. Makes 4 pints.

Quick Dill Pickles

Besides just for eating, dill pickles are used in many recipes, so that making your own is smart.

¾ cup sugar
½ cup salt
1 quart cider vinegar
1 quart water
3 tablespoons mixed pickling spice

30 to 40 medium pickling
    cucumbers, without wax
7 cloves garlic, peeled
    (optional)
Green or dry whole dill heads

Combine sugar, salt, vinegar, water, and spice in a saucepan. Bring to a boil and simmer 15 minutes.

Wash cucumbers well in several waters. Rinse and lift from water so no dirt will cling to cucumbers. Cut in half lengthwise and pack upright in hot, clean pint jars with screw tops. Put a clove of garlic (if desired) and a head of dill into each jar. Strain spices from vinegar mixture and bring back to a boil. Pour over cucumbers in jars, leaving ¼-inch space at top. Wipe rims and put on lids. Put on screw bands and tighten as tightly as possible by hand. Process in boiling waterbath 15 minutes. Makes 7 pints.

Patience Pickles

These pickles are aptly named for they do take a fair share of time to reach the final stage of processing.

12 medium pickling cucumbers,
    without wax
Boiling water to cover
8 cups sugar

2 tablespoons mixed pickling
    spice
5 teaspoons salt
4 cups cider vinegar

Wash cucumbers well in several waters. Rinse and lift from water so no dirt will cling to cucumbers. Cover with boiling water and let stand overnight. Drain. Repeat 3 times.

On the fifth day, drain the cucumbers and slice crosswise in ¼-inch-thick slices. Combine sugar with spice, salt, and vinegar and bring to a boil. Pour over cucumbers. Let stand two days, then bring to a boil and pack into hot clean pint jars with screw tops, filling jars to within ¼ inch of top. Wipe rims and put on lids. Put on screw bands and tighten as tightly as possible by hand. Process in boiling waterbath 15 minutes. Makes 5 to 6 pints.

Candy

Numbers refer to pages where recipes appear in this book.

Candy

From time immemorial people have liked to eat sweets—our word "candy" comes from the Arabic word *quand*—and candy making is one of the fun things about growing up. When you get into making candy, you have a sense of accomplishment along with something really dreamy to eat.

Equipment and Techniques

If you have a **candy thermometer**, use it when cooking up a batch of candy. If not, the chart below will help you to keep from over- or undercooking it.

To make the cold water test, use a measuring cup; each time you make the test, rinse it out and fill with fresh cold water up to the ½-cup mark. Drop in ½ teaspoon of the boiling candy and proceed with the test as indicated in the chart.

Temperature Fahrenheit	Cold Water Test
230–232 degrees	**Very Soft Ball:** Can be collected into a soft ball but not picked up.
234–240 degrees	**Soft Ball:** Can be picked up when formed into a ball.
242–248 degrees	**Firm Ball:** Tends to form into a ball without shaping with fingers. Maintains form when removed from water.
260–270 degrees	**Hard Ball:** Hard ball that cannot be pierced. Makes noise when dropped to bottom of cup.
275–300 degrees	**Medium Crack or Brittle:** Syrup brittle under water but becomes pliable when removed.
310 degrees	**Hard Crack or Very Brittle:** Makes crackling sound when hits water. Threads formed from tip of spoon break with a snap.

A **heavy saucepan** is an aid in making candy as it helps keep the candy from sticking or burning. A sturdy spoon for use in beating (and a strong arm) is also helpful. Whether you use a wooden spoon or a metal spoon is a personal preference.

Get the required pan buttered before you start beating the candy, as the last-minute beating is often crucial in getting the candy into the pan.

Top Secret Fudge

Twenty Minute Gal says, "this is quite expensive to make, but it makes almost 4 pounds, and is good for church fairs, etc. Very easy to make, too," with which I agree.

4½ cups sugar
Pinch salt
2 tablespoons butter
1 can (14 ounces) evaporated milk
1 package (12 ounces) chocolate morsels

3 packages (4 ounces each) German's sweet chocolate
1 pint marshmallow fluff
1 cup chopped walnuts or pecans
2 teaspoons vanilla extract

Combine sugar, salt, butter, and evaporated milk in a saucepan.

In a large bowl put chocolate bits; sweet chocolate, broken up; and marshmallow fluff.

Bring sugar mixture to boil and cook over moderate heat for 6 minutes, stirring constantly. Pour at once over chocolate in bowl and stir until chocolate is melted and ingredients are blended. Stir in nuts and vanilla. Pour into two buttered 8×8×2-inch pans. Cool before cutting. Makes 4 pounds.

from Twenty Minute Gal, *Confidential Chat*

White Fudge

A candy made without chocolate may appeal to many. Save cherries from Christmas baking.

2 cups sugar
½ cup dairy sour cream
⅓ cup light corn syrup
2 tablespoons butter or margarine
¼ teaspoon salt

2 teaspoons vanilla extract or rum or brandy flavoring
¼ cup quartered candied cherries
½ cup chopped walnuts

Combine sugar with sour cream, corn syrup, butter, and salt in a heavy 6-cup saucepan. Bring to a boil slowly, stirring until sugar is dissolved. Boil without stirring over medium heat to 236°F on the candy thermometer or until ½ teaspoon of the boiling candy dropped into ½ cup of very cold water forms a soft ball when it is removed to the palm of the hand.

Remove from heat and let stand 15 minutes. Do not stir. Add flavoring and beat until mixture starts to lose its gloss (about 8 minutes). Quickly stir in cherries and walnuts and at once spoon into a buttered 8×8×2-inch pan. Cool. Makes about 1½ pounds.

No-Cook Fudge

A reliable and easy way to turn out a lovely batch of fudge. Use walnuts or pecans or no nuts, as you prefer.

6 ounces cream cheese, at
    room temperature
4 cups sifted confectioners'
    sugar
2 tablespoons light cream

1 package (6 ounces) semisweet
    chocolate bits
½ teaspoon vanilla
1 cup chopped nuts

In a large bowl, beat cream cheese until smooth. Gradually blend in sugar and cream; beat well. Melt chocolate bits over hot water; add to first mixture, along with vanilla. Beat until smooth, then stir in nuts. Put into a well-buttered 9-inch square pan, cover, and refrigerate overnight. Cut in squares. Store in refrigerator in an air-tight tin. Makes about 1¾ pounds (or less, if nuts are omitted).

Quick Chocolate Fudge

A recipe for fudge to whip up in a hurry.

4 tablespoons butter or margarine
3 squares (1 ounce each)
    unsweetened chocolate
½ cup light corn syrup
1 tablespoon water

1 teaspoon vanilla extract
1 pound confectioners' sugar
½ cup chopped nuts or 1 cup
    miniature marshmallows

In a 2-quart saucepan melt butter and chocolate over low heat. Stir in corn syrup, water, and vanilla. Remove from heat. Add confectioners' sugar and nuts or marshmallows. Stir until mixture is well blended and smooth. Spoon into a buttered 8×8×2-inch pan. Cool. Cut into squares. Makes 1¾ pounds.

Double Boiler Fudge

An easy-to-make fudge that is foolproof.

1 can (14 ounces) sweetened
    condensed milk
1 tablespoon butter
1 package (12 ounces) chocolate
    morsels

½ cup chopped walnuts
    (optional)
1 teaspoon vanilla extract

Put milk in upper part of double boiler over hot water. Add butter and let it melt, then add chocolate bits. Stir until chocolate is all melted. Add ½ cup chopped walnuts, if desired. Finally add vanilla extract.

    Pour into a buttered 9-inch-square pan and cover with foil. Let harden in refrigerator. This will be softer than most fudge, and it melts in your mouth. Makes about 1¾ pounds.

from Little Greek Girl, *Confidential Chat*

Quick Nut Penuche

This candy has the nice warm flavor of brown sugar usually associated with penuche but does away with some of the work.

½ cup butter or margarine
1 cup firmly packed light brown
    sugar
¼ cup milk

1 teaspoon vanilla extract
2 cups (about) sifted
    confectioners' sugar
1 cup chopped nuts

Melt butter in saucepan. Add brown sugar. Cook over low heat for 2 minutes, stirring constantly. Add milk and stir until mixture boils. Remove from heat and cool. Add vanilla. Gradually add confectioners' sugar until mixture is the consistency of fudge. Mix in nuts. Spread in a buttered 8x8-inch pan. Let set until firm. Cut into squares. Makes about 1½ pounds.

Sugared Pecans

This is a nice confection to have at the holidays for teas or just for nibbling.

1 cup sugar
⅓ cup water
2 teaspoons cinnamon

2 cups pecans
½ teaspoon vanilla extract

Combine sugar with water and cinnamon. Bring to a boil and cook 3 minutes. Add pecans and cook 2 minutes longer. Remove from heat. Add vanilla and stir with a wooden spoon until syrup sugars. Pour onto a lightly buttered plate and separate nuts. When cool, store covered. Makes about 2½ cups.

Caramel Peanut Popcorn

One of those treats you can't keep your hands off! Good for Halloween treats.

4 quarts freshly popped corn
2 cups lightly salted peanuts
1 cup firmly packed light or
     dark brown sugar
½ cup butter or margarine

½ cup light or dark corn syrup
½ teaspoon salt
½ teaspoon vanilla extract
½ teaspoon baking soda

Spread popcorn and peanuts in a large shallow roasting pan. In a heavy 6-cup saucepan stir together sugar, butter, corn syrup, and salt. Cook over medium heat, stirring constantly, until mixture boils. Continue cooking, without stirring, 5 minutes. Remove from heat and stir in vanilla and baking soda. Pour over popcorn and peanuts. Stir to coat well. Bake at 250°F uncovered for 1 hour, stirring occasionally. Break apart when cooled and store in tightly covered container. Makes 1¼ pounds.

Homemade Popsicles

Popsicles—like popovers—are another food that is hard to put into a particular category. But since they are beloved of children of all ages, and recipes for those that can be made at home seemed appropriate, we put these in to the candy chapter.

Fruit Flavor Popsicles

Choose compatible flavors of gelatin and drink mix to combine for these fruities.

1 package (3 ounces) fruit flavor gelatin	¼ cup sugar
1 envelope unsweetened powdered drink mix	2 cups hot water
	2 cups cold water

Combine gelatin and drink mix with sugar and hot water and stir until dissolved. Add cold water. Pour into popsicle molds and freeze. Makes about 16 popsicles.

Or freeze in ice-cube trays, inserting a popsicle stick in each "cube" when they are not quite frozen. Makes 2 full trays. When frozen, remove from trays and store in freezer container or plastic bags.

from Mrs. W. C. of M, *Confidential Chat*

Chocolate Pops

These chocolate pops are a good way to get some extra milk into anyone who doesn't like milk.

1 cup presweetened instant cocoa mix	2 cups dry milk powder or granules
	2½ cups cold water

Combine cocoa mix, dry milk, and cold water and stir until dry ingredients are dissolved. Pour into popsicle molds. Freeze until firm. Makes about 1 dozen.

from Rod Svenska Stuga, *Confidential Chat*

Index